C000186313

Going
FREELANCE

Going

THIRD · EDITION ·

FREELANCE

GODFREY GOLZEN

KOGAN
PAGE

First published in 1985 by Grafton Books, a division of the
Collins Publishing Group.
Second edition 1989, published by Kogan Page.
Third edition 1991.

Apart from any fair dealing for the purposes of research or private study, or
criticism or review, as permitted under the Copyright, Designs and Patents
Act, 1988, this publication may only be reproduced, stored or transmitted, in
any form or by any means, with the prior permission in writing of the
publishers, or in the case of reprographic reproduction in accordance with the
terms of licences issued by the Copyright Licensing Agency. Enquiries
concerning reproduction outside those terms should be sent to the publishers
at the undermentioned address:

Kogan Page Limited
120 Pentonville Road
London N1 9JN

© Godfrey Golzen 1985, 1989, 1991

British Library Cataloguing in Publication Data

A CIP record for this book is available from the
British Library.

ISBN 0-7494-0405-1

Typeset by DP Photosetting, Aylesbury, Bucks
Printed and bound in Great Britain by
Biddles Limited, Guildford

Contents

Part 1
The Business of Freelancing

Introduction

The term 'the flexible firm' may lack the elegant simplicity of 'small is beautiful', but it is one which an increasing number of observers of the employment patterns of the future feel that we will be hearing more of. What it means, according to a survey published by the influential Institute of Manpower Studies, is that the old rigidities of the labour market are gradually dissolving in favour of 'an emerging model of ... segmentation into a core workforce, which will conduct the organisation's key, firm-specific activities, surrounded by a cluster of peripheral groups'. The advantage of this is that, 'a range of alternative contractual and working time arrangements permits firms to secure precisely the number and type of such secondary workers as they might require at any time.'

John Atkinson, the author of the Institute's report, went on to define this pattern in terms that point clearly in the direction of freelance work. He sees the 'core group' as consisting of full-time career employees who possess skills and experience that cannot readily be bought in. But, 'where jobs are not at all firm-specific because, for example, they are very specialized (eg systems analysis) or very mundane (office cleaning) the firm is increasingly likely to resource them outside, through the use of subcontracting, self-employed jobbers, temporary help, agencies, etc.' He cited the growth of privatised subcontractors in the public sector as being 'perhaps the most well-known aspect of this trend to the use of outsourcing'.

In the private sector that same trend has begun to emerge under what Atkinson calls, 'uncertainty about market growth, technological changes in both products and production methods and reductions in working time'.

Such changes, it is generally thought, reflect a longer-term shift in the general pattern of work, brought about by the advance of information technology. Information technology has created a climate of change in organisations and markets which has destabilised the comparative economic and technological certainties that, up to the 1980s, enabled management to plan staff number needs on the assumption that they would develop in a predictable way. At the same time, many people, especially those with particular skills, have developed a taste for the independence that may initially have been forced on them by circumstances. Having once got through the uncertainty barrier, they have discovered that it is a relief to be free of office politics, office hours, commuting and all that is implied in the 9–5 routine – and that there is great satisfaction in being rewarded directly for what you do. That view is confirmed by Department of Employment statistics, which indicate that about half the women and a quarter of men in work are employed in the flexible workforce.

Telecommuting and teleworking

The vision of the future put forward in the Institute of Manpower Studies' report, and also by the management guru Professor Charles Handy in his books *The Future of Work* (Blackwell) and *The Age of Unreason* (Hutchinson), has been accelerated by the rapid spread of personal computers and facsimile transmission of documents (fax). This is in the process of creating a new kind of worker who in many cases will be a freelance – the teleworker or telecommuter.

A report put out by the influential Henley Centre for Forecasting predicts that by the mid-1990s about half the workforce could be doing at least some telecommuting – working from home and communicating with the office by fax and personal computers linked in to databases. Forecasts about the future often have to be taken with a large pinch of salt – remember the 'paperless office' which was supposed to be the shape of things to come in the 1970s – but there are strong socio-economic as well as technical factors supporting this one. The soaring prices of office space and housing in the south east, the ever-increasing horrors and cost of commuting, contrasted with the falling costs of hardware and the constantly growing user-friendliness of information technology software all put the Henley forecast into the realms of probability.

But working at a distance from one's employer also loosens one's ties with the organisation itself. How long will it be before the teleworkers draw the logical conclusion from their position and go freelance? If you can link up with one organisation you can link up with several; and if you have a particular area of expertise that is in great demand, why not sell it on the open market? Future work is generally forecast to consist of the application of expert knowledge, rather than carrying out routine tasks which will increasingly be undertaken by the computers themselves. The teleworkers sitting at home will be evaluating the information that comes up on their VDU screens or figuring out new tasks for computers to do.

This poses a whole new set of challenges for management – indeed knowing how to manage freelances may well become a key management task in the 1990s. It will involve such issues as what to do about the confidentiality of the information on which freelances will be working by clarifying the nature of intellectual copyright, of creating appropriate reward systems and of devising a new basis of loyalty between parties whose relationship, in Mrs Thatcher's words, is 'semi-detached'. For their part, freelance workers will have to come to grips with some of the matters discussed in this book; managing working relationships that are very different from those of employees in daily contact with fellow-workers and bosses; for instance, making sure they get a clear brief when they undertake an assignment, keeping proper records and getting paid an appropriate rate for the job and on time. They will also have to make sure that the skills on which their livelihood depends are kept up to date, by setting aside time and money for training and self-development.

The definition of freelancing

Though not many freelances earn more than employees, they find that the tax advantages of self-employed status mean that their take-home pay is higher than that of employees earning a similar gross amount. At above normal levels of skill they can sometimes earn a good deal more, which is why many media personalities opt to freelance as soon as their reputation is established. In the slightly more mundane field of management, Germany and the Netherlands offer a portent for the future. There the trend is for senior managers to operate as quasi-freelances, at least on a serial basis. They hire themselves out to one employer for a fixed term of contract, negotiating a salary that is independent of – and, of course, higher than – the corporate salary structure. They then make their own arrangements over benefits such as pensions. Although Mr Ian McGregor, the ex-chairman of the National Coal Board, was leased out by his employers Lazard Frères to the UK Government, it is possible that this could be a forerunner to a similar way of hiring out one's managerial expertise in a purely independent way.

At a lower rung in the labour market, something similar is already established practice in the building trades in the UK and elsewhere. Good building workers are hard to find in the more prosperous parts of the country, so they are increasingly hiring themselves out as subcontractors to undertake specific tasks for a number of employers. Indeed, they in turn subcontract parts of jobs they are unable to do – for instance, when they run into problems connected with plumbing or electrical work.

The activities of these building workers, who were among the first large group of employees to see that their skills had a market value higher than that which was recognised in the orthodox salary/wage structure, attracted the attention of the tax authorities in the late 1970s. It turned out that they could not only earn more money operating in this way – they could also change their income tax status from Schedule E, the PAYE version which covers employees, to the much more advantageous Schedule D. Under this, expenses incurred in deriving earned income are tax deductible; for instance, an employed building worker could not deduct the cost of his journey to the site from his tax liability – but he could if he was self-employed. The tax authorities then laid down that to qualify as Schedule D taxpayers these workers would have to hire out their services to more than one employer: you could not, in other words, simply go to your firm, elect to be treated as a subcontractor rather than as an employee and ask the Inland Revenue to assess your earnings on the basis of Schedule D. In defining a legitimate working relationship to qualify for Schedule D assessment in this context as being one where you offer your services to more than one employer, the tax authorities defined what a freelance is: in essence, someone with a skill for hire to whoever flags them down.

The professions as freelances
That takes us beyond the definition in the *Chambers Dictionary* – 'an unattached journalist, politician, etc'. That dismissive view has hidden the fact that in reality freelances already play a significant and prestigious role in the economy. The professions, for instance, are freelances of a kind. Principals in professional practices are generally classed as self-employed, though they are not conducting business in the way that it is generally understood. For instance, until recently they were – and some still are – prohibited by codes of professional conduct from certain common business practices, like advertising. But in working for, or acting on behalf of, clients who pay for their services, they act in essence as freelances; but we will not be dealing with the more specialised subject of the professions in this book.

Performing artists generally operate as freelances and so do many professional sportsmen and women. Indeed, in the performance field there is a tendency to opt for freelance status as soon as these people reach a level of skill that establishes them as individual personalities, therefore enabling them to negotiate their own fees. This is even true of 'unattached journalists', among whom many of the biggest earners have contracts to write or broadcast for certain media. There has also always been a tendency in that unstable occupation to make a virtue of necessity: in other words to work as a freelance rather than to go on the dole – very often by continuing to write for their previous paper on this basis.

The employers' attitude to freelancing

Using freelances has many attractions for employers, as the Institute of Manpower Studies has pointed out. They, too, have found virtues in the necessities imposed by economic instability. 'The capacity of the labour markets to adjust to changes in the structure of consumer demand and changes in technology is widely recognised as a key element in the achievement of economic growth,' says the Institute. They point out that employers have not publicised the changes they have been making to introduce the 'flexible firm'. One reason for this, no doubt, is that paying outworkers to carry out tasks that were previously done by staff who have been made redundant would not be popular from an industrial relations point of view. The fact that an activity can be economically viable for an outside individual when it is uneconomic within a firm that has to carry high overheads and cope with an uncertain flow of work is hard to demonstrate and sometimes to prove to those who are unwilling to depart from traditional patterns of employment. It is even harder to explain when the freelance is – apparently – earning a higher rate than persons carrying out similar or equivalent jobs within the firm, even though freelances have to carry more risk, spend a great deal of time in the unpaid activity of looking for work, and make their own arrangements for benefits like paid holidays that employees take as a matter of course.

Not all employers pay a higher rate for freelances, though they should do, for these very reasons. Even then, they will find that employing freelances works out cheaper than having people on the payroll. The reason for that is not only, in John Atkinson's words, 'the greater commitment of the self-employed to getting the job done', but primarily that the true cost of an employee is at least twice his or her wage or salary, when overheads, benefits and employer's NI contributions are taken into account. There are, however, other and even greater advantages in using freelances, which are spelled out in the Institute of Manpower Studies report. Chiefly, they are:

- *Functional flexibility* – people can be brought in (or, it must be admitted, dropped off) in accordance with functional demands. For instance, outside consultants might be called in to deal over a period of time with a functional area like export sales, rather than merely in the traditional consultancy role of ad hoc trouble-shooting.
- *Numerical flexibility* – freelance workers can be taken on to deal with peaks in demand, without any risk of having them standing idle on the payroll when there is a decline. A long-established example of this is seen in films and television, where a company

is often set up to produce an individual project, hiring actors and technicians only for the duration of that assignment.

- *Financial flexibility* – the employer can pay the rate for the job – which may be over the odds in relation to his normal remuneration structure, without causing an upheaval among the workforce. That, of course, calls for discretion among the freelances concerned about what they are being paid. Though such payments pass through the firm's gossip grapevine – employers are fairly naïve in their belief that wages and salaries are kept confidential – freelance payments are much harder to attribute to exact functions or even hours.

- Finally, and though it is not a category included by the Institute of Manpower Studies, there is also the question of *quality flexibility*. An employer stuck with a poorly performing employee can sack that person, though in practice this is often only done as a last resort and after he or she has inflicted a good deal of damage on the employer by not doing the job properly. In the case of freelances it is much easier not to use that person again. It is not usually a question of painfully confronting someone whom you might see every day and with whom you might be on friendly terms in other respects.

Employing freelances

Though employing freelances offers clear advantages to employers in these terms, it is not an easy way out of the disciplines of working relationships. Rather, it requires different ones, the most important of which is in formulating the brief. That calls for a real understanding of what the job is about. 'The externalization of activities,' says the Institute of Manpower Studies report, 'should be determined according to the necessary attributes of the job in question, rather than contingent attributes.'

Unfortunately, grasping what these attributes are and communicating them to a third party is one of the more difficult arts of management, which is why freelances are often not used to full effect. For instance, in book publishing there has been a great move towards reducing staff by putting out desk editing, which means, among other things, querying inconsistencies, omissions and obvious errors in the author's manuscript. One publisher who decided to externalise this activity kept on a single desk editor to whom freelances returned the scripts on which they had worked with long annotations on points to be cleared up with the author. That meant, of course, that the internal desk editor then had to read much of the text in order to put the queries in context, thus reducing the value of the exercise. The essential attribute of the process, in other words, was communication between publisher and author; the actual business of sorting out the script was a contingency, however vital in itself. The problem was solved by paying the freelances for the additional time and trouble involved in taking the job to its logical conclusion, which was to prepare clean copy for the printer. The task of the internal editor was to find reliable freelances and to act as a court of appeal when major textual problems arose.

The same principle of establishing 'necessary attributes' can be applied to management consultancy or design or catering or to any of the freelance occupations described in this book. Putting together a clear brief is absolutely vital, both from the point of view of the freelance and of his or her client. Furthermore, it has to be framed in a way that will not call for constant reference back and forth between client and freelance. Working with someone who only comes into the office to pick up an assignment is an entirely different proposition from having them on call within the same building or even the same organisation. There may be regular meetings to review progress – indeed, the frequency and necessity of such meetings is an essential part of the brief – but apart from that the role of the freelance is that of an independent subcontractor, not that of an employee who happens to work on the outside. Many freelances, and the clients who commission them, fail to grasp the implications of this important distinction.

Working as a freelance

It is, of course, just as much the responsibility of the freelance to ensure that a clear brief is obtained as it is of the client to give it. Indeed, even more so. The watchword of every freelance ought to be that of one UK airline: 'we never forget you have a choice.' If a job comes unstuck because you were not given a clear brief, the client will tend to blame you, irrespective of the merits of the case, and turn to someone else next time.

Learning to communicate your wishes and intentions to someone you have not worked with before is not easy, though. It is at least as difficult as delegating, which very few people are good at. It involves, on both sides, a certain amount of knowledge of how the other party's mind works. For this reason, many freelances get their first assignments from people they have previously worked with as colleagues or employees. This is a good way of learning to tackle the very different working relationships that freelancing involves. In this way both parties receive an insight into such matters as formulating the brief and the problems of allowing, financially and in other ways, for time that is not visibly expended on the assignment itself, but essential to completing it.

To take an extreme example of a matter that an inexperienced client may find hard to grasp, a photographer will have to spend hours setting up a shot, though looking through a viewfinder and pressing the button only takes a fraction of a second. After that, the development of the result will again take hours in the darkroom, though the finished picture can be assessed at a glance. The same principle applies to most freelance activities. For this reason, it is important, certainly when dealing with clients you do not know, to provide an estimate or quote that roughly itemises the tasks that the assignment is likely to involve. A picture researcher, for instance, may have to spend a lot of time and fare money hunting an image for which the source is not immediately obvious.

A former employer or colleague may understand that doing a particular job involves much more than the product of its visible result, though it is best to take nothing for granted – an informal discussion of the brief is always a good idea. There are, however, other reasons why the best way of starting out on your career as a freelance is to get work from people you already know. In the first place it is the easiest way of priming the financial pump during the initial weeks or months when you have to scout around for work, not always fruitfully. One of the important points to remember before you launch is that you will not be engaged on paid work all the time, but that even when you are established at least a day a week will be spent marketing your services. At the outset it is usually more than that, so, if you can rely on even one regular source of work to start with, that means you can spend time getting round to see potential clients without worrying whether you will have enough income to cover ordinary running expenses.

Second, having even one client to start off with helps you overcome the biggest barrier that any new enterprise faces: credibility. It shows that someone thinks you can do a good job. It can also provide you with samples of work that you are doing, and if you are going on to freelance from a regular paid job you should collect as much documentary evidence of your achievements as possible before you leave: reports you have written, designs you have produced, letters from satisfied clients or whatever is appropriate to your line of work.

The third advantage of starting with some known sources of work – or even one – is that it keeps you in contact with other people. Working for yourself is a lonely business and, if you live alone anyway, it can mean that you are virtually deprived of human company. Some people can stand that better than others, but unless you are a confirmed loner, even the absence of the mental stimulus that comes from working alongside and exchanging ideas with other people can affect the quality of what you do. Most freelances recommend that if you can get a regular assignment one day a week or fortnight that keeps you in touch with other people, it is worth taking even if the fee is on the low side.

Fees

Because of the growth in freelancing a number of formal or informal organisations have grown up – where they exist, they are mentioned in the selected survey of freelance occupations in Part 2 – which are trying to establish recommended fee scales. These are not mandatory and, indeed, some are thought to be unrealistic by clients – few publishers, for instance, will pay the NUJ's minimum rates for freelance editors. But they provide a benchmark and it is worth joining whatever associations may exist to exchange ideas and information about fee rates. Generally, if there is some solidarity by competent freelances about how much to charge, clients will at least approximate towards that figure – particularly since, quite often, they have no idea themselves what the going rates should be. If evidence can be produced for your claim, for instance, in the form of recommended fees by a particular body, not necessarily one that is formally constituted, it can greatly help you in your negotiations.

In any case such rates, where they exist, are not purely arbitrary. They are based partly on market forces of supply and demand and partly on the realisation of what it takes to cover your costs and earn a viable living. Even when there are no recommended fees these are the principles you ought to observe in fixing your charges. More detailed guidance on this is given in Chapter 5, but the question that immediately arises is whether your proposed activity has built into it a sufficiently strong and consistent demand to support you.

It probably will not do so initially in the style to which you are accustomed. Nearly all freelances report a sharp drop in income until a body of work builds up; but it should certainly have that potential. If it does not you should think again. Maybe there are ways in which your activity could be modified or the market for it extended. Either a broader or a more specialised service – for instance, guaranteeing a faster turn-round than competitors – can put you in a different price bracket.

The other and more welcome side of the coin could be that you could charge more than you think. A specialist management consultant reports that she began by charging £150 a day. She found that there was no objection to that figure and that £200, £300 and even £350 were accepted without a murmur. It was only when she went over £400 that she encountered some price resistance, so she decided that around £400 a day was about right. In unknown areas of activity it may be simply a question of testing the law of supply and demand by some fairly rough and ready method such as this.

Getting work

This kind of market research and exploration of possibilities is best done from a position of strength – either when you are in paid employment or established as a freelance. At the beginning the temptation – or indeed the necessity – may be to take whatever jobs come your way at whatever money is offered. There are two reasons why this is dangerous.

The first is that whatever rate you start out by setting for a client becomes the base against which future charges are measured. If you begin by quoting a rate of £15 an hour, it will be very difficult to persuade him or her to pay you £25 an hour for the next job if you discover that this is the going rate, or that £15 does not give you an adequate margin of profit. The same is true of expenses. If you did not charge travelling time on the first occasion you did a particular job, it will be hard to introduce it subsequently. Deciding on what your costs are likely to be, in other words, is an essential factor in planning the direction in which your search for assignments is going to go. That may, on occasion, prompt you to take on a job at less than your usual fee, providing the income is enough to pay your running expenses and the duration is not so long as to take you away from more lucrative work – except, as we have stated, where a regular one day a week or fortnight contract is on offer.

The other danger is to take on jobs that you are not really qualified to do. Stretching your talents is one thing. Rushing in where angels fear to tread is best left to the proverbial fools because the real disaster for freelances is doing a job badly. When that happens within an organisation, the employee will be told not to repeat his or her mistake and nothing will happen unless they persist in it. A freelance, however, will not usually be given a second chance. The client will go elsewhere. This rule, of course, applies not only to the performance of the task itself, but to such factors as reliability, punctuality and care in setting out and sticking to the brief. More positively, though, the best advertisement a freelance can have is a satisfied client, not only because you can use him as a reference, but because he will tend to spread the word about you.

The business of freelancing

In stating that considerations like reliability play as important a part with clients as what you actually do – no use being a cordon bleu cook if you cannot produce a meal on time – it follows that you need to be organised and businesslike in the way you go about things

The majority of the principles and methods that apply to running a business also apply to working as a freelance.

That is a discovery that has in recent years been made by many professional people whose activities, as we have seen, resemble those of freelances. Until fairly recently many members of the professions – architects, for instance – distanced themselves from ordinary business in order to preserve a Victorian distinction between 'trade' and the professions. To reinforce that, they operated mandatory fee scales and adopted other practices that kept the concept of competition at bay, which also meant that they tended to neglect related business methods like costing and cash-flow forecasting. Legislation, reflecting changes in public opinion, has removed many of the self-protecting features of professional life and put the professions into the marketplace in which other types of freelances operate. In that marketplace, proper estimates have to be given, the basis of charges agreed beforehand, a time budget established, and invoices must correspond to what was previously agreed in all these respects. The fact that you are no longer operating as a corporate employee does not absolve you from the responsibility of running your freelance show on businesslike lines. Quite the reverse.

The freelance and income tax
This principle does not only apply to the relationship between you and your client. It is also necessary to keep at bay that perpetual spectre at the freelance feast – the tax inspector.

There are, as we shall show in Chapter 6, considerable tax advantages in self-employment because all expenses directly concerned with your business are chargeable against income. For instance, as an employed person you are not allowed to deduct fares to your place of work from your taxable income – illogically so, because unless you went to work you would have no income to declare. As a self-employed person, this anomaly is corrected. Every time you travel to see a client, the fare and incidental expenses like a reasonable amount of subsistence can be claimed. But in order to do so, you will have to keep a record, backed up by receipts and vouchers where possible, of what you spend. You do not need to keep ledgers or books of accounts for this purpose. But you do need to be businesslike about keeping track of such costs – not only to provide a basis for your charges to clients and as a historical record on which to base estimates in the future – but for the immediate purposes of cutting down your tax bill.

The organisation of this book
Working successfully as a freelance means more than being

competent at what you do. It involves understanding some basic business concepts. Steering by the seat of your pants is fine for short journeys, but it will not take you through a long one. There is nothing very complicated about the basics of running a small business – which is what you will be doing – as the first part of this book will show.

The second part shows some of these principles in operation. It does not cover all the numerous and growing number of freelance options, but it deals with the main ones and in doing so should at any rate give the reader a kit of parts to apply to whatever he or she is thinking of doing.

1
Have You Got What It Takes?

Having said that freelancing is a business like any other, there is an important difference between it and most other forms of self-employment: it generally requires little start-up capital and in many cases none at all. Only people like photographers, repairers and freelance 'makers' need to invest in equipment to carry on their business. Those providing a pure service, like consultancy or translating, can start off with virtually nothing except the tools of their trade: reference books, a typewriter or word processor, stationery and an answerphone. Most freelance occupations, furthermore, can be followed from home. Overheads and start-up costs, which arise irrespective of income and are the bane – often the death – of new small businesses, are minimal for freelances.

Nevertheless, there are certain costs which have to be taken into account. Some of your present outlays like telephone, postage and travel may go up quite appreciably because their use needs to be increased to make your availability known. Domestic bills for heating and lighting are likely to increase in winter because you are at home more often. And however frugal you may be about your costs in other ways, you still have to eat and pay the rent or mortgage. You may even, in a modest way, have to entertain clients in the course of business.

The question of financial resources cannot therefore be left out of the reckoning. At one end of the scale you may be free to pick and choose your assignments because for one reason or another you are not dependent on your freelance income. At the other end, your choice of what you take on may be limited because you have no other potential source of earnings: freelancing in that case might be the only alternative to going on the dole. Somewhere between the two are the majority who are balancing the options between going freelance and remaining as employees.

In this third category are those who will have to calculate their resources most carefully. Can you earn enough from freelancing to make it worthwhile – or even to survive the first year or so while you build up clients and income? The answer depends on three factors: your own credibility in your chosen field, the marketability of the skills you have to offer and your own temperament when it comes to dealing with the uncertainties and pressures of working as a freelance.

To some extent you will have to look at these aspects whatever lies behind your decision to go freelance. You lose your entitlements to unemployment benefit if you are self-employed in the UK and you will have to make National Insurance contributions, so you will have to make sure that your potential freelance income will in the foreseeable future exceed what you would get on the dole.

Credibility

Freelancing, by definition, involves offering your skills to a variety of clients. You are claiming some specialist expertise, be it management consultancy, journalism, graphic design or in some area which is generally considered to be a blue-collar one, like vehicle repair. But whatever it is, in order to make that claim, you must either have done the job before, or be trained in it in some convincingly applied way. It is possible to become a freelance designer, for instance, on the basis of having done a degree course because such courses are generally practically oriented; or to become a translator, having taken a language degree. Your credentials would be less impressive if you tried to set up as a management consultant, having had no experience other than a business studies qualification, or if you tried to become a journalist on the basis of an English degree. The first thing you will have to do as a freelance, therefore, is to see that your level of expertise is appropriate to the area where you want to apply it as a freelance.

In many cases, freelances are ex-employees and they generally begin by working for their ex-employers. A common situation, for instance, is that a firm closes down a functional area like in-house PR or building maintenance or catering for directors and asks the people who were doing it before to take it on as freelances. This means that the freelances can offer the same service to a variety of clients without incurring the overheads that become attached to corporate activities. Quite often a function that is uneconomic for a firm to sustain, either for that reason or because it is not fully used, becomes very profitable to freelances. Beginning your freelance career by working for existing contacts is the ideal way to start. As a freelance each approach to a new client is rather like applying for another job and, as with a job application, establishing your credibility by showing that you can do what the job entails is an essential first step.

One way to do that is to demonstrate that you are already busy and a list of existing clients – particularly if they are well-known ones – validates that claim. Some freelances do this informally. For instance, a cameraman said recently, 'I never admit I'm not particularly busy. The way I put it is that I've got a spare week or so between assignments and I mention a couple of things coming up, even if they're not definite at that time. Nobody's going to check up. I'm well enough known in my field for what I say about my work schedule to be credible. But if I went in and said, "I'm a bit short of work at the moment – anything doing?" they'd assume I was going off a bit and wouldn't offer me anything.' In other branches of freelancing formal evidence of work done needs to be produced. Some kind of brochure with the names of your clients and what you did for them is a good investment as soon as you get a few names under your belt.

There is another good reason why starting by freelancing for people who already know you is a good idea. As we have already mentioned in the Introduction, working as a freelance is in many ways different from being an employee. When you are in the next office or at least in the same building as the person or department to whom you are reporting, it is easy to check back and clarify aspects of the job as you go along. As a freelance you are on your own and in many cases the client is paying you to get on with the job without bothering him or her. If you have been engaged as a freelance copywriter, for instance, the person who commissioned you does not want to have to deal with last-minute queries about where the copy is appearing so that you can get the writing angle correct or whether he or she wants a reply coupon to go with the ad. These are the sort of questions that should have been raised at the briefing session. The client wants a finished article that can be handed over to the printer or designer on the due date – in the same way as a manager wants a consultant's report or a group of directors want lunch on the table, not a last-minute discussion about the menu.

If you have worked for an organisation before you probably know their likes and dislikes about the way work is presented, but in the case of a first-time assignment all this is uncharted territory. Picking up this different way of working has to be learned and the best way of doing so is with people who already know you and vice versa. You will at least be tolerant of each other's mistakes and not ask for the temperamentally and functionally impossible. For instance, if the person you are reporting to is careless about checking subordinates' work, that places an extra burden on you to be correspondingly careful.

Marketability

How ready your existing contacts are to put freelance assignments your way is an invaluable clue as to how marketable your skills are. To some extent you should know from your own experience what the demand is for freelances in your chosen sphere: for instance, if you are a technical illustrator, whether there are enough technical publishers who employ outsiders rather than in-house staff and, if so, what the rates of pay are. If the demand is strong or rising, how successful you are likely to be depends on your own skill and speed.

The question of your own ability is one that has to be faced in considering your chances. Freelancing is not an easy option for those who cannot hold down a job on grounds of competence – though it may sometimes be right for those who, while possessing other qualities, find it difficult to handle working relationships on a day-to-day basis. You have to be good at what you do to freelance successfully because the client will turn to someone else if you are not. The client will extend a much greater degree of tolerance to people on his or her payroll.

If the reaction to your attempts to set up as a freelance is muted, you will have to think carefully about the reasons before proceeding. Assuming that these have nothing to do with your competence, consider the following:

- There may be too many people offering a similar service. A field of activity that seems to be wide open will not necessarily remain so because you will not be the only person who has seen its potential. Private messenger services, for instance, have boomed in recent years and local ones have gone nationwide. To break into that market now as a freelance you would have to offer either very competitive rates or think of some way of adding a useful value to your services.
- Your proposed charges are too high. Some skilled freelance areas are rather badly paid – picture restoration, for instance, is not particularly well rewarded for the combination of manual skills, knowledge of paint, materials and art history that it calls for. The answer in such cases is to add value to what you are offering. With picture restoration that might be framing and gilding. A freelance typist might justify higher charges with a quicker than usual turn-round; and so forth.
- You may be in the wrong neighbourhood. Setting up as a tour guide will not bring you enough business unless there are attractions in the area that bring tourists in large numbers. Location is said to be vital to the success of a business and, though as a freelance you are not tied to a particular site, the socio-economic mix remains an important factor.
- The market may be too diffuse geographically. A highly specialised form of consultancy would have to be available nationally to bring an adequate return. But can you afford to canvass clients on that basis, and if you live in the south will a

client in Aberdeen pay your fare and expenses in addition to your fee?

- Your presentation may be faulty. Does it overcome the credibility gap? Can you demonstrate that you have the experience and the resources to tackle the kind of work you are looking for?
- The kind of activity you are proposing is not one that is commonly put out to freelances. Although freelancing is on the increase, there are still tasks that are done mainly in-house. Newspapers, for instance, tend to reserve the more interesting, glamorous or perk-laden assignments for their own people or to put them out to 'big names' who will pull in readers. They are not much attracted to freelance travel, food or sports writers who do not fit into these categories. In management consultancy the problem may be of a different dimension. For instance, nervousness about confidentiality is often a problem: a client may feel he ought to be talking to a large recognised firm who are used to handling sensitive assignments.
- Lack of resources. Clients think of a freelance as a one-person set-up which cannot handle more complex assignments. You may have to demonstrate that you yourself can call on other freelances to deal with problems that you are personally less experienced in handling.
- It may be a 'rubbish-bin' job. When a temp comes into an office, he or she notoriously gets all the jobs no employee would want to do. In some freelance occupations this is a risk; for instance, a person with a word processor may be stuck with holding and cleaning mailing lists – still a deadly job, in spite of new technology.

These are all questions you will have to ask yourself in advance and prepare to deal with, but even if the wind seems fair for the first few months and you have some good clients, or at any rate potential ones, lined up, there are further important considerations. How are you intending to keep going thereafter? You need to be reasonably sure of a continuity of work, rather than just a temporary peak in demand that is causing an equally temporary demand for freelancing. Certainly, one of the things you will need to take into account is that however good you are, and however extensive your contact network is, you will have to spend a good deal of time marketing yourself. In many cases as much as 40 per cent of it will be spent looking for work, often unproductively; and, of course, nobody pays you when you are not working directly for them. As an employee you are earning when you are not working, at weekends and on holiday. You are also earning when you are working at half speed having lunched not wisely, but too well, or when you are simply sitting and thinking. As a freelance you are only paid for what you do.

Temperament

Freelancing is an uncertain way of making a living. For a great many freelances it is a life of feast or famine in which there is either too much to do or not enough. Very few freelances ever turn work away, however busy they are. The fear is that, though they may not need the money now, they may do so at some point in the future and that a client turned away is a client lost for good.

Experienced freelances suggest that there are occasions, however, when jobs should be turned away:

- When you are offered something you are not really competent to do. It is better to leave a job alone than to do it badly. For instance, a translator is not usually competent to act as an interpreter, except at a fairly simple level of discussion.
- When it is below the level at which you like to operate. That may be necessary at times to pay the bills, but should be avoided otherwise. It is bad for morale and, worse, may get you typecast in low-level assignments.
- When it is a dead-end distraction that takes you away from the main lines you have decided to pursue. If a furniture restorer becomes involved in restoring architectural timber, for example, it may mean that his or her regular business is clogged up for weeks. Unless there was a continuing prospect of profitable work in this field and the restorer enjoyed doing it, he or she would be ill advised to become involved in something that would lead to the loss of regular customers but not lead to anything else.
- When the money is not good enough and you already have enough work to do. A customer who pays poorly is unlikely to turn into one who pays well, however good you are. He or she will take the first rate he or she offered you as the datum point.
- When the client already owes you money that is overdue or has been difficult over money or other matters in the past. The principle of never throwing good money after bad holds true in most cases.

When you turn work away for whatever reason, however, even from an existing debtor, it should be done politely. If you give a reason – and the truth is generally best in these circumstances – it will not put the client off trying you again. On the contrary, the more discriminating you are about what you take on, the more keen the client is likely to be to use you on another occasion. With a good client, it also helps if you suggest another freelance who can do the job. Bread thrown on the water in this way can be reciprocated on another occasion, though it is best not to be too naïvely trusting over such matters.

The one thing you must never do is to let clients down. At worst you should warn them in good time if you find you are unable to complete to schedule. The point is that your contribution is often part of a jig-saw on the completion of which other people's livelihood may depend – sometimes even the job of the person who entrusted you with the commission.

This underlines the point of not over-committing yourself by taking on more jobs than you can do reliably and well. Inevitably, therefore, freelancing often involves working under pressure and you have to ask yourself whether you have the temperament and indeed physical endurance that can stand up to that kind of situation. The other aspect is that working in this way can affect your social life: dates may have to be cancelled, weekends given up.

This is all the more difficult because freelancing is already a lonely life in itself. In giving up the 9–5 routine of working in an office, studio or factory, you are also giving up the companionship of your colleagues. These relationships are hard to sustain, however good your intentions, once you leave. If you already live on your own and have chosen a form of freelancing that does not bring you into contact with other people except in the course of going out to get work, you could be in the position of almost cutting yourself off from human contact. That is bad from the point of view of mental stimulus as well as morale, and is another good reason why it is a good idea to try to get at least one regular assignment once a week or fortnight.

It might be thought that freelancing is the ideal way of life for a loner but, although it has that attraction, you still have to stay in touch with potential clients. You have to be able to market yourself hard and convincingly and the sort of temperament that can best do that is a gregarious and articulate one.

If you have faced this and the other issues summarised in this chapter and feel confident about your ability to respond positively to them, freelancing will hold no terrors for you. Whether it is a road to fame and fortune will depend somewhat on your skill, but also on how well you observe the business principles that are outlined in the following chapters.

2
Setting Up in Business

Freelancing covers a wide range of business relationships. At one end of the spectrum they are fairly close to regular employment: for instance, in the case of a journalist who contributes a regular column to a newspaper for a contracted period, but who nevertheless has other writing irons in the fire; or that of an outworker who cuts patterns for a fashion retailer as a regular but non-exclusive arrangement. At the other, they may more closely resemble casual labour, however genteel its form. The same journalist, instead of being guaranteed work by one or more media, may simply offer material on spec to whoever will pay for it.

There are other spheres of freelancing that are close to more orthodox notions of small business, except that it is an activity carried on from home or at the client's premises rather than from premises taken especially for that purpose. Examples of these forms of freelancing are organising conferences or vehicle repair. The forms in which work comes in vary as well. It may be routed through an agency or the freelance may be the prime mover in the process. In other words, there is no strict definition of what a freelance is, except that it is someone who has no full-time commitment to any one employer, client or source of work.

Bearing that in mind, a freelance has to operate as a form of business entity that, from a legal and tax point of view, is different from that of the wage-earning employee. As soon as you have established your freelance status, you should inform your tax office, your bank manager and your local DSS office. In some cases you will also need to notify your planning officer and/or your landlord, but in the first place you will have to decide whether you are going to start as a limited company, a sole trader or a partnership. That decision has far-reaching implications for your tax position and in some cases your relationship with your clients.

Forming a private limited company

The myth that setting up a limited company is a magical talisman that will ward off the tax inspector while giving you instant credibility with clients and the bank dies hard. All a limited company does is to create what is, in law, an entity that is distinct from the shareholder who own it. This means that if the company goes bankrupt, creditors' claims are limited to the assets of the company. These will include any *issued* capital – that is, money put into it by the shareholders. Their personal assets cannot be touched.

The fact that you have decided to establish yourself as a limited company will not unduly impress the bank or any other experienced lender, should you wish to borrow money, unless the issued share capital is substantial or if you are prepared to offer personal guarantees to override the company's limited liability status. By the same token, the fact that a client is a limited company is by no means a guarantee of soundness. In some cases, it may be quite the reverse, simply because liability for debts is limited in the way that has been described. Authorised or nominal share capital, by the way, is quite meaningless in this context. It is merely the amount of capital the company is authorised to issue, and it is quite possible to have a company with £2 worth of issued share capital and £10,000 worth of authorised capital. A client who tries to blind you with the latter figure while having only a moderate amount of issued share capital should be treated with great circumspection.

Forming a private limited company is quite cheap. The registration fee is only £50. It is, however, a matter in which you need legal advice. The procedures are routine to a trained professional, though complex to a lay person. The whole exercise will cost you about £300, including professional fees. The common method is to buy a readymade 'off-the-shelf' company from a registration agent. The existing shareholders, who are usually the agent's nominees, resign in favour of those appointed by the new owners.

A company acquired in these circumstances will often have an odd or unsuitable name, though that is quite easy to change, subject only to certain fairly obvious provisions about using odd or misleading names or those that closely resemble an established name in the same field. You will also have to check that the Memorandum – a document which sets out the main objects for which the company is formed – does not contain anything that runs counter to what you intend to do.

Your legal adviser will guide you on these points and also on the obligations you assume by forming a company. Chiefly these are:

- To maintain a formal structure. A company has to have at least one director and a company secretary – who need not be a shareholder.
- To file annual audited accounts with the Registrar of Companies.
- To hold formal company meetings at regular intervals.
- To show the address of its registered offices as well as its

registered number and country of registration on letterheads and order forms.
- To show the name of the company in a reasonably conspicuous way outside the business premises.

If directors' names are shown on stationery, then the first names as well as surnames of *all* directors must be given in full.

The paperwork implications of forming a company at the outset are considerable. Is it worth it? At the scale at which most freelances are operating the answer has to be negative unless you are in the position of incurring substantial, unavoidable and uninsurable liabilities on behalf of clients. A graphic designer, for instance, might be ordering printing, or a conference organiser be in the position of making bookings in his own name on behalf of a client. Such situations should be avoided where possible. If they cannot be, then opting for limited liability might make sense; but not otherwise. Apart from the extra bureaucracy involved and the fact that the income from a company will be assessed on Schedule E, not the more advantageous Schedule D, its status has been eroded by legislation.

- Shareholders in companies cannot take advantage of the income tax concession whereby losses in the first four years of starting a business can be used to recover tax paid on income from other sources in the preceding three years.
- The extent of limited liability is narrowed in cases where companies have gone into liquidation. Although the intention is to prevent improper use of limited liability, it is inevitable that some shareholders whose companies have gone under through no fault of their own will be affected. It is already the case that shareholders are personally liable for certain statutory payments such as National Insurance in a way that overrides limited liability.

The one case where it might be advantageous to go for corporate status as a freelance is where you are a subcontractor operating for one client. As we have seen, the Inland Revenue take the view that this is not a true freelance relationship and in such cases they would require the client to deduct tax from your remuneration on a PAYE basis. You could avoid this trap by forming a company. Your earnings from the company would be taxed under PAYE, but you should be able to organise a modest level of perks and expenses 'on the company' that would escape tax.

Setting up as a sole trader

In the majority of cases freelances start by operating as a sole trader

– you can always form a limited company later if your professional advisers think the pattern of your business warrants it. Being a sole trader simply means that you are in business for yourself and the Inland Revenue will treat you as a self-employed person even if you eventually employ other people to help you. Your statutory paperwork obligations are more or less confined to the records that you will have to keep anyway to support your tax return. On the other hand, you will be personally liable for all debts you incur, though early losses, as we have just indicated, can be set off against preceding income for tax purposes.

The question of tax will be dealt with in more detail in Chapter 6, but there is one aspect that freelances will need to be careful about at the very beginning. You should, of course, notify your local tax inspector that you are setting up in business on your own account, and if you were previously employed you should send him your P45. He will want to make sure that your change of status is genuine. As we have seen, the borderline between independence and at least some degree of *de facto* employment can be blurred and the tax implications of this are wide ranging. You will therefore have to satisfy the Inland Revenue that your arrangements with clients are contracts *for* service, not *of* service. The main criteria for establishing this are as follows:

- You have no contract, written or implied, with any one client from whom you derive all or a substantial part of your work.
- You do not rely on using the client's premises and equipment or tools to carry out the work you are doing for him or her. That does not mean that you cannot use the client's photocopier or telephone on occasion. But if, for instance, you were a telephone sales person you would find it difficult to establish your freelance status if you operated from clients' offices, using their telephone. This would be true even if they did not pay you a wage or fee but only a commission on sales.
- You do not have to work in hours laid down by the client.

You will have to exercise a certain amount of common-sense about how much to tell the tax inspector. Tax inspectors have an enormous amount of work on their plates and will not have the time in most cases to hunt down anyone who deviates from the rules, the interpretation of which is, in any case, largely a matter for their individual judgement. They are unlikely to object if a freelance designer gets a studio assignment for a month where he or she does have to turn up at specified hours or use the tools of the trade available there. On the other hand, if the client in this situation deducts PAYE instead of treating you as self-employed, it is highly unlikely that you would get the tax back by an appeal to the inspector.

Partnerships

Freelances are solo performers almost by definition, but just as forming a limited company can be the next stage forward if your venture is successful, so can establishing a partnership. The implications of a partnership, from a legal and tax point of view, are in many respects very similar to those of a sole trader. The partners are personally liable for debts, but the crucial feature is that these debts accrue to the partnership as a whole, not merely to the particular partner who incurred them. Thus, if one partner bought a Concorde ticket to New York without consulting the others, they would have to chip in for the bill even if they passionately felt that a Superapex economy flight would have been more appropriate. Furthermore, if one partner defaults on his or her financial obligations arising from the partnership, creditors are at liberty to recover the money from the others. The liability of each partner is unlimited, in proportion to the way in which they split the profits between them.

It follows that taking a person into partnership is not a step that should be taken lightly. You should get a solicitor to draw up a partnership deed that spells out how the profits are to be divided, how decisions are taken and what course of action should be followed if, for instance, one of the partners wants to withdraw. Even where the partnership is a husband and wife one, this is advisable. The fragile bond of marriage is dissolved as often as it is cemented by the experience of working together with your nearest and dearest.

Other statutory preliminaries

Apart from notifying your local tax office about your change in status, you will also need to contact your local DSS office to arrange payment of your Class 2 National Insurance contribution. Class 1 contributions are based on a percentage of salary and made by employer and employee. Class 2 contributions are flat rate – the amount is increased more or less in line with inflation at each Budget – and can be paid either by direct debit or by buying N stamps at a post office and sticking them in yourself. If you earn only a certain minimal amount – again the figure is increased each year – you can apply for exemption from Class 2 contributions. This is not granted automatically, no matter how low your income. A specific application has to be made.

Though the self-employed enjoy some advantages through being taxed on Schedule D, which we will deal with in Chapter 6, these are balanced by the fact that they get a poor deal from National Insurance.

- You cannot get unemployment benefit if work dries up – though you can get sickness benefit.
- You are not eligible for industrial injuries benefit.
- You do not qualify for the earnings-related State Pension Scheme.
- You have to pay, in addition to your Class 2 contribution, the so-called Class 4 contribution. This is an earnings-related percentage, though these earnings are subject to a maximum and a minimum. Currently, a contribution of 6.3 per cent on earnings above £5450 and below £18,200 is payable. The net earnings correspond to the sum on which you are assessed for Schedule D tax – ie your total receipts, less allowable expenses. Self-employed people are allowed to offset 50 per cent of their Class 4 contributions against their income tax liability.

In some cases it is possible to get exemption from Class 4 contributions. People who are employed through agencies, for instance, may already be paying Class 1 contributions even though they are otherwise regarded as self-employed for tax purposes. In that case they would not be asked to pay Class 4 in addition.

Class 4 contributions are collected along with your income tax assessment. In effect, they are simply a levy on the self-employed since no benefit arises from making them.

Planning permission

Theoretically, you ought to get permission from the planning department of your local authority if you are going to carry on a business at your place of residence. You will certainly have to notify the planning officer if you are going to use it as the premises of a limited company because by law you have to display a sign to that effect. Your application should state what you intend to do, on what scale and at which hours.

It is unlikely that the planning officer will put up any objections to your proposal unless it is one that could disturb the neighbours or affect the character of the street; for instance, if you were intending to give evening lessons in trumpet playing or repair vehicles in your front yard.

Apart from such amenity factors, the planning officials are looking for actions that would constitute a 'change of use', as would be the case if you were going to use your house primarily as a workshop. They might either withhold permission altogether, on amenity grounds, or re-assess any property taxes or rates on a commercial basis.

For some activities you will have to get permission from other local authority officials as well. Freelance caterers intending to prepare food from home would need to secure clearance from the environmental health officer.

Apart from statutory obligations there are also some private contractual considerations to take into account:

- Restraining covenants in your lease, where you are not the freeholder.
- The terms of your household and contents insurance policy. This will usually extend only to domestic use and you must notify insurers of any extensions to that. Normally, they will agree without calling for extra premiums, unless what you are proposing to do entails additional hazards from fire or corrosion.

Registering for VAT

The subject of VAT is dealt with in more detail in Chapter 6, but if you expect your turnover to be more than £35,000 a year you will have to register for VAT. The operative word is *turnover* (your total invoiced sales) – not profit – and it is quite possible for some kinds of freelances to achieve that figure, for instance, those who are ordering materials for work done on behalf of a client. There may also be circumstances where it pays you to opt for voluntary registration, despite the extra paperwork involved; for instance, if you are having to buy in materials or incurring other expenses that carry VAT and if your customers are VAT registered. In that case, they can recover the VAT you charge to them, just as you yourself will be able to recover VAT charged to you once you are VAT registered. Circumstances differ from case to case and you should ask your accountant's advice on your situation.

3
Outside Advisers

Although some tax inspectors are well disposed towards self-employed people, others are not. Thus, one freelance describes how she has thrown herself on the tax inspector's mercy to the extent that he regularly advises her on how to present her financial records and organise her affairs in such a way as to minimise her tax liability. Her experience is balanced by others who complain about having to haggle with bloody-minded zealots over points of interpretation over what constitutes legitimate business expenses. It is not generally realised that a good deal of discretion is left to tax inspectors as to allowable items within the general framework outlined in Chapter 6. One of the most useful roles of an accountant in this situation is that of an intermediary between the tax inspector and the individual making the return. If the accountant has a general record of good relations with the tax people and of claiming allowances in a truthful and reasonable way, the chances are that the tax inspector will accept returns made through that accountant – even if not every claim is supported by vouchers. Tax inspectors are an overworked breed and even the most conscientious cannot examine every invoice – though that is no reason not to keep as many as you can.

Accountants and solicitors

Employing an accountant is not cheap, so on the principle that expenses ought to be minimised until justified by income, should you employ one from the outset? The answer is affirmative, for several reasons other than the ones stated:

- An accountant will check your annual assessment, making sure that all claims for allowances have been covered.
- An accountant will make appeals against over-assessments on your behalf.
- An accountant will advise you on what books and records you will need to keep to control your progress. There are no universal rules for all freelances – the requirements will vary from case to case. For instance, some people will need to record and prove expenditure incurred on behalf of clients in

relation to particular assignments. Others will require only a more general record of expenditure for their own purposes.

- An accountant will advise you on which expenses are deductible and how to present them accordingly. He or she should also be able to suggest ways of making tax-beneficial pension arrangements. As a self-employed person under 50 you can get tax relief at top rate on up to 17.5 per cent of your annual income on any pension premiums you pay. Higher rates apply if you are over 50 – up to a maximum of 27.5 per cent if you are over 61.

- An accountant will be invaluable in helping you make your case to the bank should you need money to expand your freelance activities. He or she will also be able to advise you on when and whether to form a company and explain what your obligations are in that case.

The accountant's professional fees are themselves tax deductible, but nevertheless the money to pay them has to be earned and there are ways of minimising these costs. Quite simply, the more of the routine work you do yourself, the easier it will be for the accountant to put together the information needed for your tax return and this will be reflected in the bill you get. Consequently, you should find out how he or she would like income and expenditure to be itemised and analysed in the books. To enable him or her to give you an intelligent answer, you will obviously have to give a picture of the scale and nature of your freelance activity and what you expect the significant cost/income factors to be. Ideally, if you have already begun your freelance career, you should bring along to the initial meeting:

- Bank statements;
- Cheque stubs;
- Any records of receipts and outgoings you have already been keeping;
- Invoices sent or received.

If you already have an accountant with whom you are satisfied, you should obviously stick with him or her. However, accountants, like solicitors, come in varying degrees of competence and experience, which are only loosely related to professional qualifications. If your accountant has never saved you a penny in tax or shown you how you could do so, the chances are that you have someone who is either merely a glorified book-keeper and form-filler or so important and busy that your petty affairs are handed over to an articled clerk. Neither of these types of accountant is of any use to you, and could be a positive menace once your affairs become more complex. A small- to medium-sized firm, preferably within easy reach and with at least a couple of partners, is ideal for the average freelance – all the more so if it has been personally recommended.

A further point to bear in mind is that your accountant should also have some experience in representing to the tax inspector the kind of problems that arise in your chosen occupation. There are, for instance, accountants with a special knowledge of the business of performing artists, writers, designers and so forth, and who have a shrewd idea of what the tax people will regard as deductible expenses.

This rule also applies to choosing a solicitor, though in most cases freelances will not need one at the outset, unless they are forming a partnership or a limited company. However, if you are engaged in any activity where contractual or other legal issues play an important role – for instance, if you are asked to sign a contract for service – a solicitor's advice could be valuable.

One thing neither an accountant nor a solicitor can do is to tell you whether your proposed activity is a good idea or not. Professional advice, moreover, should only be resorted to if you really need it. It is expensive and the fact that you have not asked for a written recommendation does not mean that you will not be charged for telephone time. Most professional offices log incoming calls and attach fees to them if the enquiry involves giving advice.

Bank managers

One of the attractions of freelancing is that in many cases the initial cash requirements are minimal. Nevertheless, the bank manager is high on the list of outside advisers you ought to consult. Here again the size and location of the unit is an important factor, and if your account is with a big high street branch it might be worthwhile switching to a local one, if only for convenience – though, of course, you can always make an arrangement to put transactions through your nearest branch. However, as is the case with other professional advisers, a small local office is more likely to have time to attend to the problems of a small business than one in a central urban location with many big accounts among its customers.

If you are going to need a loan, the bank manager will ask for a lot of information about your proposed business. He will look for a 'business plan', of which the essential elements are:

- An outline of what you intend to do.
- Why you think there is a need for it.
- What your qualifications and those of people associated with you are.

- What you can reasonably expect your costs and revenue to be, at least over the first year.
- Potential risks and pitfalls – and how you would overcome them.
- How much money you need for what purposes.

This would have to be accompanied by a cash-flow projection (see Chapter 4). If your freelance activity is one that requires finance – for instance, you may need to buy equipment to get started – then you would be well advised to get help from an accountant to prepare your approach to the bank, though several of the big four have produced helpful free pamphlets on how to do this.

Even if you are in the happy position of being able to fund what you are doing from your own resources, a talk with the bank manager is usually helpful – particularly if you are abandoning paid employment with a regular monthly cheque for the uncertainties of a freelance existence. This will change the pattern of your account and may make it necessary to secure an overdraft facility. Few things are more damaging to the all-important matter of establishing your credibility as a freelance than a bounced cheque.

Insurance

The Americans are a litigious lot and it is probably due to the propensity there to sue professional advisers if recommendations turn out badly that this custom is beginning to spread to the UK. Such cases seldom get into the papers because they are generally settled out of court by the insurers. They do, however, underline the growing importance for those engaged in freelance services exposed to suits for professional negligence to take out professional indemnity insurance.

In most cases the premiums are fairly modest, though it depends on what the claims record is for the occupation concerned. Architects, who like most professionals are in effect freelances, have to pay out substantial four figure sums each year, but premiums are much lower for accountants whose exposure to claims has until recently been smaller. Similarly, in freelance consultancy, a specialist in security matters paying a high premium reflects the risk of claims, justified or otherwise, for professional negligence in this sphere. It is easy to be over-cautious about spending money on insurance but the cost of contesting a claim is usually formidable, win or lose.

There are some kinds of insurance that are essential for freelances. As already indicated, you have to tell your insurers if you are proposing to carry out work from home, since this situation will not normally be covered in your domestic policies. You will also need to take out a policy for public liability in case you cause injury to a member of the public in the course of business. If you work with a partner, or come to employ people, you will need third-party public liability. There are also policies under which you can insure against losing your driving licence or being sued under various Consumer Protection Acts. A Combined Traders Insurance Policy will cover most of these risks, though you will need a separate policy to cover your car if you are going to use it in the course of business.

Insurance companies vary surprisingly in the premiums they charge and to some extent in the cover they are prepared to offer for them. The best plan is not to go direct to any one company – not even the one you are currently insured with – but to work through a broker. Brokers do get a commission from the insurance companies for whom they write business, but they are not employed by them and their advice is reasonably impartial.

Government advice

The policy of encouraging self-employment to which both the Labour and Conservative parties are pledged – albeit with varying degrees of enthusiasm – has led to the creation of a number of sources of free or heavily subsidised advice which is available to individual freelances as much as to small firms. The most universally useful of these is reckoned to be the Local Enterprise Agencies of which some 300 are now in operation, mainly in urban areas. In rural areas, their equivalents are the various offices of the Rural Development Commission, formerly CoSIRA. These offices are staffed partly by local authority employees, partly by professional managers seconded by large firms or by the banks.

They can tell you what sources of financial help are available and how to approach them – and often about suitable properties if you are unable to work from home. They will generally be prepared to comment on your business plan in the light of their knowledge of local conditions. The more active offices operate as a sort of marriage bureau between people offering services and products and potential clients. Some now publish registers of such information. They also run courses on various aspects of management. A list is published in the BBC's *Small Business Guide*, along with much other useful data on the various kinds of organisation, both local and national, from whom advice can be obtained.

The other widespread service is the government's Small Firms Service. By ringing 0800 222 999 you will be given the address of the office nearest to you. Though their advice and the free booklets they issue are geared to small firms rather than to individual freelance enterprises, they should be able to tell you whether you are eligible for any particular form of government financial assistance: notably the Enterprise Allowance Scheme, which is dealt with in more detail in the next chapter.

4
Raising Money

Most kinds of freelancing take the form of offering a service. Even where it involves making something, it is generally by way of acting as subcontractor for a customer, so that financial risks and outlays are minimised. One of the attractions of freelancing is that it takes very little money, but there are two basic financial considerations:

- You may need some working capital to meet essential personal and business outgoings until the money starts to come in. For instance, there are likely to be some outlays on publicising your activity, even if they are only fares and telephone calls to potential clients. Legal advice, extra insurance and so forth also have to be paid for.
- You will need to acquire the essential tools of the trade that you do not already have. In most cases you will need an answerphone, a typewriter or word processor, some decent stationery, a filing cabinet and, quite often, a car or a van. In some occupations you may also need to think about renting some kind of workspace.

The most common source of borrowing for such purposes are the banks. For short-term, working capital needs, it is likely to take the form of an overdraft facility. Longer-term requirements to buy equipment are generally financed by a bank loan.

- An *overdraft* is a facility to borrow up to a certain pre-arranged amount at a rate of interest 2 or 3 per cent above base lending rate. You are only charged interest on the amount borrowed – not the extent of the facility – so when you make a repayment the interest element drops.

  There are two disadvantages to overdrafts. First, the bank manager can withdraw the facility and oblige you to repay what you have borrowed – though this seldom happens except where the borrower habitually defaults on the interest payment. Second, the amount of interest is related to bank rate, which can vary widely. It has been as high as 17 per cent, making overdrafts very expensive.
- A *bank loan* is a fixed sum of money, repayable with interest

over a pre-arranged period of time, usually anything from 1 to 10 years. There is usually a minimum amount that can be borrowed below which the administration is not worthwhile. Repayments of the capital sum are integrated with the interest element, which makes it easier for both parties to organise.

Bank loan interest is also related to base rate at the time you obtained the loan, but the banks do now adjust it if the rate changes during its term, in the same way as mortgage interest charges are adjusted from time to time. Apart from that, a loan is a somewhat inflexible instrument from the point of view of the borrower – you cannot normally repay it before the agreed period, though the interest charge is relatively very high as you come towards the end of that period. By the same token, that makes loans a good deal for the banks and they are quite keen to lend money on anything that looks like a sound business proposition – though, admittedly, their judgement of what that constitutes is notoriously conservative. However, a good deal of discretion is left to individual managers about lending policy. The fact that you are refused by one bank manager should not discourage you from approaching another bank or even another branch of the same bank.

When loan facilities are granted, the bank will quite often suggest a combination of the two types – an overdraft to provide working capital and a loan to fund longer-term requirements.

Leasing
Alternatively, the bank may suggest a leasing arrangement for any major item of equipment you require; the banks have tie-ups or direct relationships with leasing companies. Unlike the terms on bank loans and overdrafts, there are quite considerable differences in those on leases, so it will pay you to shop around.

At the end of the leasing period, the leased item will still be the property of the lessor, though he or she may give you the opportunity to buy it at a favourable price. That is one of the points that you should look for in the leasing agreement. The other is what happens if you want to terminate the lease before it runs its course, as can occur if something better comes on the market – or if, for one reason or another, your freelance activity ceases. In that case, you may be liable to pay all outstanding amounts for the full period of the lease. Whether the leasing company accepts responsibility for maintenance and who pays for that is another important point to consider. It cannot be stressed too strongly that the fine print of the leasing agreement needs to be read carefully – do not be tempted by initial 'payment holidays' and similar sales gimmicks; and where an expensive item is concerned, consult a solicitor.

Hire purchase

In the case of hire purchase, the item becomes your property at the end of the agreed period. Here too, though, there are considerable differences in the terms put forward by companies offering HP. One of the essential items to look at is the APR (annual percentage rate). The point is that the sum you borrow under HP is reduced by repayments of the capital, but the HP company or its agent quotes a rate of interest based on the original amount. Thus, if you buy a piece of equipment on HP for £100 over a five-year period at 14 per cent you are still paying £140 interest in the last year, even though the amount borrowed has been enormously reduced by all the repayments you have made. The APR gives the true rate of interest, which is sometimes twice the one you have been quoted. This advice applies equally to purchases through your local gas or electricity showrooms.

Presenting your case to the bank

One of the reasons why people turn to dubious finance arrangements is because they have been refused a loan by a bank. Banks, as stated earlier, do have a reputation for caution in lending money, but this is often because borrowers do not make a very good case for themselves. Bank managers' performance is judged by the quality of their lending and they have to be reasonably sure that if they allow people to borrow money they will get it back, with interest; hence, the importance of the business plan referred to in the previous chapter. They will not be expert in the subject of your freelance activity, so they will need to be given enough information to enable them to make up their mind whether it has a reasonable chance of success. Most of the banks, by the way, now produce booklets that tell business borrowers how to present their case and what the bank manager needs to know.

Apart from the business plan, the other important item in this exercise is the cash-flow forecast. All this formidably technical-sounding term means is a forecast month by month, for about the first year, of expected income and outgoings. It is easy to be optimistic about the former and to overlook things in the latter, but the result of that could be embarrassing. The overdraft facility that the bank gives you is based mostly on the cash-flow forecast, and if you consistently under-perform on income and over-perform on expenditure, they may ultimately advise you to take your overdraft elsewhere.

Outgoings vary with the kind of activity you are engaged in, but here are some items that will be common to most:

Own drawings	Telephone
Travel	Share of heat, light, power
Postage	Share of rent/rates
HP/loan charges	Subscriptions to journals/papers
VAT	Advertising
Professional advice	Stationery
Membership of relevant associations	Materials

Inevitably, some months will show a deficit, but the bank manager will not be concerned about that, provided he sees an underlying gradual trend towards a surplus.

Though banks are not the only source of finance, similar criteria are applied in the comparatively rare instances where a freelance activity qualifies for government aid. This could be an option worth investigating if you are working in one of the favoured high technology specialisations, or if you are opening an office in a development area. The National Westminster Bank produces a useful guide to such schemes – *Official Sources of Finance and Aid for Industry in the UK*. It is also worth discussing with the nearest Local Enterprise Agency whether you qualify for a local authority grant – some authorities make small grants for such purposes as market research if you have a credible track record.

The most readily available form of government assistance is the Enterprise Allowance Scheme which is currently granting £200 million a year. You have to have been out of work and claiming unemployment benefit for 8 weeks to qualify for it, and to have £1000 of your own money to invest in your idea. This latter proviso, though, is not interpreted too strictly – if you can persuade a relative or even the bank to lend you £1000 an official blind eye seems to be turned – and the range of activities that qualify under the scheme is wide. Virtually any competently presented idea for self-employment that has any chance of success will qualify you to receive the allowance of £40 a week for 52 weeks. See your nearest Jobcentre or Local Enterprise Agency for details of how to apply. But you must do so before you actually start as a freelance.

Using your own money

You can forget about merchant banks and finance houses as sources of funds. Even though they often figure in rags to riches stories, they are not interested in the kind of small business venture that even the most sophisticated freelance operation represents. If you fail to get a bank loan, you should ask yourself a few hard questions about why they don't like your idea – and there is no reason why you should not put them point blank to your bank manager as well, because he or she might point out some basic faults you had not thought of. If you remain convinced that there is no satisfactory reason for refusal other than the innate conservatism of the bank, you might consider what you yourself have in the way of resources. They could be greater than you think. Here are some assets that either could or will have a value:

- Market value of your house;
- Shares;
- Surrender value of life insurance policies;
- Antiques or other collectibles.

To this you obviously add building society and bank deposits and deduct liabilities such as outstanding mortgage and HP commitments and other outstanding bills. Used household or hobby equipment has a poor cash value as a look round any junk shop will tell you, and selling your car is not usually a good idea. However, deducting liabilities from assets will give you an indication of how much cash you can put together, though it also raises the question of how much you are willing to risk to pursue your idea.

Unless you are convinced that it will work it is not usually worth putting your house in hock by raising a second mortgage, particularly since interest rates on these are very high. A better plan would be to sell your house, buy a cheaper one and use the profit – free of capital gains tax if it is your principal residence – to finance your scheme. But you need to be reasonably sure that the return you can expect eventually to get from your activity by financing it yourself will be more than you would obtain merely by putting it on deposit with a bank or other financial institution.

Private loans

Putting your money where your mouth is can be persuasive in getting others to back you – in the case of a small-scale freelance activity, usually members of your own family. Since money is, alas, one of the things even nearest and dearest frequently fall out over, you ought to agree in writing the repayment terms and the rate of interest, if any. You must also make it clear, tactfully, to the lender that making a loan gives him or her no say in the way you conduct your business or your life in general.

Is borrowing really necessary?

Before you crawl to the bank, pass the hat round to relatives or sell an heirloom, consider whether you need to borrow money at all. Can you get by with hiring or borrowing apparently essential equipment until you are really sure that it will pay its way? One freelance said she never bought anything unless she had had to borrow it at least three times. And what about the second-hand market? A lot of perfectly good equipment can be picked up cheaply because its owners have traded up to something bigger, faster or better – or given up.

It is also worth remembering that a lot of working finance can be raised simply by taking full advantage of any credit period you are allowed, while at the same time sending out your own invoices as soon as you can – and making sure you get paid promptly. One freelance consultant gives a 5 per cent discount on bills settled within a week. The cost of such an inducement is much less than that of borrowing money. Finally, there is the option of increasing your revenue by charging more. That is the subject of the next chapter.

5
Establishing the Right Price

Knowing how much to charge is one of life's great mysteries for most freelances – especially if they provide a service like consultancy, rather than a tangible product. In the latter case there are at least the clear-cut costs of the materials to be recovered, and that has to be reflected in the price. There are, however, many activities that fall between these two poles in that they involve some material costs, but these are a relatively small element in the product – as one might loosely call it – that emerges in the end. Repairing things, for instance, involves buying materials that in some occupations can be expensive. But they are a relatively insignificant item compared to the time devoted to doing the repairs, not to mention the years of training that are required to do the job at all. That is also true of the numerous kinds of freelance work that are purely skill or knowledge based – illustrating, writing or research, for instance – and which have virtually no identifiable material ingredient other than paper and typewriter ribbons.

Most forms of freelancing have either a largely or a purely labour ingredient, and the tendency both by freelances themselves and by those who employ them is to undervalue it. However, your labour, its skill ingredient and the time it takes to acquire it, is itself a product, as Karl Marx pointed out. It is certainly one of the things you should take into account in establishing your prices, along with your other costs:

- Rent, rates and utilities related to your premises, or a share of them if you work from home;
- Insurance;
- Telephone, postage and stationery;
- Advertising;
- Travel;
- Repayment and interest on loans;
- Depreciation of equipment (ie its declining value and the cost of replacing it);
- Hire purchase or leasing charges;
- Subscription and fees to professional bodies and essential literature.

These are what are called fixed costs, in that you incur them largely irrespective of the amount of work you get. Employers tend to have large fixed costs, especially in staff and premises, and where freelances and self-employed people in general score is that they can keep these costs fairly low – provided, of course, that they follow the precept of not buying things unless they are sure that they will pay their way in terms of the extra business they will bring in.

The other kind of costs are variable ones. They relate almost entirely to actual jobs, and if you are not very busy they will be at an accordingly low level; though there are some costs that are borderline between the two – for instance, telephone, travel and postage costs might rise when work is slack because you need to put more effort into trying to get it.

In the case of some freelance jobs, the client will pay for some or all of your variable costs – a freelance caterer, for instance, will generally get the client to pay for the food that has to be bought and a journalist will usually be reimbursed for expenses where a commission involves travel or long-distance telephone calls. What you charge should in the first instance be enough to cover all your fixed and variable costs.

But what about your own labour, which is often the same as or a very substantial part of your profit? Here, inevitably, you are up against market forces which have a protean tendency to come in all shapes and sizes:

- Informal going rates;
- Union rates;
- What the market will bear;
- The value of your own skill or expertise;
- How badly you need or want to do the job;
- How urgently the client wants it;
- Whether it is a one-off or a continuing contract.

Because freelances, virtually without exception, have worked as employees in the occupation they are engaged in, they think they have some idea of going rates. But unless they have themselves had some experience of commissioning freelances, that idea is based on an hourly rate related to the salary of employees – and it can be highly misleading. Employers reckon that the true cost of employing someone is at least twice their salary, bearing in mind holidays, employee benefits and other overheads. As a freelance you will have to carry all these costs yourself, plus the fact that by no means all your time is spent on jobs you get paid for. Nobody pays you to look for work or to quote for jobs that do not materialise, yet anything from a third to half your time is spent doing that – even once you are established. So if you base your rates on what you think are the hourly rates of employees doing a similar job, you are going to lose out badly. The best guide to what you should charge are those charges made by fellow freelances in the same line of business and you should talk to them before you start negotiating with clients.

The going rate will still have to be enough to cover your fixed and variable costs and give you enough to live on in return for your labours. If it does not, and if the rewards fall appreciably below what you could earn as an employee, you will have to think of some way of adding value – in other words, adding some twist to your service or product – that will enable you to charge more. By its very nature freelancing is often a unique or at any rate hard-to-obtain service that has a premium attached to it. Your prices should reflect that. If they do not or cannot, your activity may not be suitable for freelancing. There are things that can be done more economically within an organisation. Repetitious jobs with a predictable input of time, skill and/or materials fall into that category and, because freelancing often does not, it is difficult to give quotes or estimates for a whole job as many clients would undoubtedly like you to do. One computer consultant, for instance, in a field where pay is high on the freelance scale, says he never gives quotes because everything he does is different – so he has no historical basis on which to fix a figure. At most he will reluctantly give an estimate.

The difference between a quote and an estimate may sound somewhat subtly semantic but, though the law is not absolutely clear on this point, the Office of Fair Trading, at least, draws a distinction between these two terms: quotes are regarded as a binding figure, whereas an estimate is exactly that. If what you are giving is an estimate, you should say so clearly and preferably keep it verbal. If you are being asked to give a quote, you should be sure to leave nothing out, because the total may be all the customer will be obliged to pay you.

- Make it clear that if the client changes his mind about what he wants, there will be an extra charge.
- Set out the terms of payment– eg 30 days after completion, on taking delivery of the goods, or whatever.
- If you agree to complete a job within a certain length of time, set out the circumstances that would be beyond your control.
- Make it clear that the quote is binding on both parties – that the client cannot cancel without paying a cancellation fee.
- If you are registered for VAT, make sure the VAT element is included in the price, or that the client is aware that VAT is additional.

- If the job involves making disbursements on behalf of the client which you want to recover as you go along, specify how and when you want them to be repaid.
- State whether or not your quote includes incidental expenses and, if not, say which are excluded.

It can happen that the client has put an assignment out to tender; or that, while he wants you to do the job, he finds your price too high. The effect in either case is the same, and you will have to decide how much room you have to manoeuvre on your costs and/ or in the margin of the return to yourself. There are some circumstances in which it is worth cutting your price:

- If you have no other work on and the fee is enough to cover fixed overheads.
- If the job is of short duration.
- If you are absolutely sure the client will pay and pay promptly.
- If it will give you valuable experience in a field where there may be more lucrative opportunities.

It is never worth doing a job for less than it costs you, because if the return is that low there is something wrong with either the client or the nature of the assignment. You would be better off trying to find another one, or even taking a few days off. The best things in life are free and only the most determined workaholic would pay to work – but that is what taking on sub-economic work means.

Time-based charges and lump sum fees

When being asked for a price, should you quote a flat fee or an hourly charge? It depends on how precisely you can anticipate what is involved. If you have been given a very exact description of the job and what it entails, and have done similar things before, it would be safe to quote a flat fee. But if you are not sure of the extent of the job, or suspect it might not be straightforward, then an hourly or daily rate would be more advantageous.

From the client's point of view, the worry is that he or she might not know the speed at which you work. It would be reasonable to give an estimate of the amount of time the job will take on the basis of the information you have been given.

If problems should arise in the course of the work, it is easier to tell a client that a job is taking longer than anticipated than it is to come back for more when you quoted a flat fee.

6
Tax Benefits and the National Insurance Net

Before freelancing became as widespread as it now is, it was generally accepted by the Inland Revenue and by the courts that the label given to an employment relationship could be determined simply by an agreement between the parties to it. The reason why the courts have become involved is because there have been some instances where, despite the verbal or written existence of such an agreement, people claiming or being assigned freelance status have brought action for wrongful dismissal when a contract was terminated. As a freelance, of course, you do not have the legal protection that employees have in these matters, nor can you claim the range of social security benefits available to those who make Class 1 contributions, as explained later in this chapter. In such cases, the courts have taken the step of declaring what the relation between the parties is and overruling what it says it is or what has been verbally agreed. These judgements, though sometimes not entirely consistent, have been followed with great interest by the Inland Revenue in arriving at a definition of what in their view genuinely constitutes freelancing and is therefore taxable under the much more favourable Schedule D arrangement.

A case that is often quoted in this connection is *Market Investigations* vs *Ministry of Social Security (1969)*. In determining the genuineness of a freelance relationship, the courts took into account a whole range of questions, including:

- Was the worker in business for himself in a real and economic sense - ie was he himself running the risk of loss as well as gaining from profit?
- Was he working for more than one employer, or using an agent to procure a variety of employment?
- Did the rewards vary between busy and slack periods?
- Was he providing his own tools, equipment or premises?
- Did he have discretion as to how the job was performed, provided the results were in accordance with the employer's specification?
- Was he free to determine his own working hours?

If you can answer these questions in the affirmative, you have a strong case for being treated as self-employed by the Inland Revenue.[1] However, tax inspectors are given a good deal of discretion in how they apply these rules. In particular, they may take an unfavourable view of regular contractual relationships with a client. Even though this may be one where a service is supplied for one or two days a month only, some tax inspectors seem to take the view that this is taxable under PAYE and carries Class 2 NI deductions – despite the fact that the person supplying the service is self-employed in every other respect and is not on the client's staff or regular payroll. This is highly disadvantageous from the freelance's point of view, not only because of its tax implications – for instance, expenses cannot be charged against tax, but because the NI contributions may be out of proportion to the income received from that source.

Apart from the costly and time-consuming process of making an appeal against such a ruling, there are two options. One is to avoid formal contractual relationships and to ensure that remuneration is officially on a casual basis, whatever unofficial understanding may be reached with the client. The other, as indicated in Chapter 2, is to form a limited company and supply services through it.

The black economy

One of the popular beliefs about going freelance is that it provides a first-class trip straight to the black economy, where the tax inspector's heart does not grieve about things he or she does not see. Certainly the black economy is quite a formidable sector of the overall economic picture. According to a survey produced by the National Westminster Bank it could be as large as 8 per cent of GDP – an amazing £16 billion worth of undeclared income a year. It stands to reason that freelancing must constitute a fair share of that.

However, its very size attracts an increasing amount of attention from the Inland Revenue. The Inland Revenue are reluctant to disclose exact figures, but it is thought that there may be close on 1000 executive officers assigned to investigations in the black economy. That will make tax dodging, or tax evasion to give it its proper name, increasingly risky as well as illegal.

Tax evasion

The Inland Revenue are also reticent about how they catch tax dodgers, but some things are known about their methods. Apart from tip-offs from aggrieved ex-wives, ex-husbands or ex-business

[1] See also the Inland Revenue leaflet IR56, *Tax-Employed or Self-Employed.*

associates and employees, they work a great deal on what looks wrong at a quick glance. For instance, they acquire a general feel for the relationship between expenditure and income across a wide range of activities at various stages. Thus, travel costs are deductible from income for tax purposes and they are fairly easy to load because unless you buy your tickets through an agency receipts are not usually issued. If what you are doing does not seem to warrant the amount of travel you are claiming, however, they will not only query whether your journeys were really necessary, but will also want to look closely at your other expenditure claims. Sometimes what seem like improbably high expenses are perfectly legitimate – a writer, for instance, may get involved in heavy research and travel costs before there is any income from them, but if there is any apparent discrepancy like this between income and expenditure, you would be well advised to document your costs as far as you can.

At the earnings end, the great temptation is not to declare items of income or to understate them. However, this is not recommended and the only way it is likely to escape detection is if you get paid in cash (ie notes, not cheques) – and even then you can come under scrutiny, particularly if you are registered for VAT, of which more later. But even if you are not, anything that goes through a customer's books, or through that customer's bank account to yours, can ultimately be traced back to you. Payments in kind also have to be declared in your tax return, and if a firm makes such payments the recipient has to be shown in their books. However, if a private client pays you with a case of Scotch or a bottle of your favourite perfume it is unlikely that the tax inspector will get worked up about it – though strictly speaking even earnings like that should be declared. If you think, by the way, that the cost of the Inland Revenue's special investigations must limit their extent, don't be too sure. The haul, per investigation, was reckoned to be £135,000 a few years back – and that does not take into account the numbers of people who are persuaded to make honest declarations by the fear of discovery, the consequences of which include having to pay many years' back tax, plus interest.

Tax avoidance and allowable expenses

Few freelances who fail to declare income do so with the intention of evading tax. Mostly it happens either because they are too busy or too disorganised to keep proper records or because they think they are not earning enough, after paying expenses, to pay income tax. There is a personal allowance on which you pay no tax. It goes up each year more or less in line with inflation and at present it is £5015 for a married couple and £3295 for a single person or a wife earning income separate from her husband. It usually increases slightly each year to allow for inflation, but even if your income does fall within that bracket, you still have to prove that point to the Inland Revenue. Ridiculously enough, though, many freelances who break the law by concealing earnings, either deliberately or because they get into a muddle, could achieve much the same tax savings perfectly legitimately if only they kept a record of, and claimed, allowable deductions:

- A share of telephone and car expenses related to the proportion of business use.
- Travel.
- Postage and stationery.
- Rates, rent and utilities or a share of them if you work from home.
- Cost of goods or materials bought for processing or re-sale.
- Interest charges related to business.
- Insurance premiums related to business.
- Tools of the trade.
- Subsistence.
- Subscriptions to professional associations.
- Advertising and publicity.
- Fees for professional advice.
- Business gifts up to £10 in value for any one year.

Although the criterion is that expenses must be incurred wholly and necessarily for business purposes, some of these tend to be grey areas in nature or extent; for instance, what is an acceptable amount for subsistence, or what proportion of your telephone bill is related to your freelance activities, or even what constitutes a tool of the trade. A singer had the cost of a dress disallowed, though she clearly only needed it for an important performance in a particular concert hall and could not have used it for any other purpose. Very often what the tax inspector is prepared to accept depends on whether he or she is prepared to believe your accountant. It is most important, therefore, to choose an accountant who is experienced in representing your kind of freelance activity to the tax authorities and who can quote other precedents in your favour if a claim is challenged.

These allowances, it must be stressed, apply only if you have set up as a sole trader or in partnership. If you have opted to freelance as a limited company, you may be able to claim a similar range of expenses from the company – thus reducing its liability for tax – but you will not be able to set them against PAYE; and, as we explained previously, that is the basis on which you will be assessed, even as the company's proprietor.

Your accountant will advise you which form of entity to trade under, but it is becoming rarer now for freelances, and indeed many other kinds of new small businesses, to begin by incorporating themselves as limited companies. Changes in tax rules mean that the advantages of doing so are no longer sufficient to offset the considerable amount of additional paperwork that is involved.

Basis of assessment

Assuming you have decided to take the sole trader or partnership route, the way you are assessed for tax would be different from that of an employee (including an employee of your own company) having it deducted under PAYE. As a self-employed freelance you will pay tax in two lumps, one in January and one in July – so you will have to put money aside for that. The other difference is that you are assessed on what is called a 'preceding year' basis. Without going into too many technicalities, the effect of this is that you have a year's grace, initially, while the tax people work out how much money you have made in your first year as a freelance. Thereafter you always work a year in arrears, because it takes time to sort out and agree what you made in any given tax year, which always ends on 5 April. The tax year, however, does not necessarily have to coincide with your accounting year, which will have begun in whatever month you started freelancing. There are certain advantages, initially, in choosing the right 12-month period as your accounting year and you should get advice on this.

National Insurance

In addition to the Class 4 contribution to which we have already referred, you also have to make the Class 2 version if your income exceeds £2250 a year. The current rate is £5.15 a week. The most convenient way of paying this is through a direct debit with your bank.

You can get some benefits from Class 2, though some freelances neglect to claim them for no good reason – particularly in the case of sickness benefit. The amount paid is not large – about £30 a week at present – but the formalities are simple and, within reason, not too many questions are asked about claims for the amount of time off work. Explanatory leaflets about qualifications and claims procedures are available at DSS offices.

As a freelance you cannot claim unemployment benefit, nor do you get the additional earnings-related state pension. You can, however, get tax relief on 17.5 per cent of your taxable income at the highest tax rate on contributions towards your own pension scheme. This means that if you are paying standard rate tax of 25 per cent on assessable income of £10,000, you can get £1750 worth of contributions for an outlay of only £1312.50. (If you are over 50 even higher rates of relief apply.) The rules on National Insurance contributions are different, and in some ways less advantageous, if you are set up as a limited company.

VAT

Of the freelances who are providing a service rather than a process only a prosperous minority come into the bracket where registration for VAT is compulsory – at present, when you have an annual turnover of £35,000. The keyword, however, is *turnover* – not income or profit – so if you are buying items on behalf of a client it is fairly easy to fall into this category. For instance, a picture researcher earning a relatively modest income from book or magazine publishers, or a stylist assembling set furniture for a television production, might easily be handling quite large volumes if hirings or purchases of materials were made in their own names. If your accountant, from the description of what you do – which you ought to provide in your preliminary discussions – thinks your turnover is likely to reach the mandatory figure, you must register for VAT on a form provided by your local Customs and Excise Office (not the Inland Revenue). You will get a VAT number which has to be printed on all business stationery. The main obligations for freelances registered for VAT are:

- You will have to charge VAT on 'taxable supplies'. Although not everything carries VAT, in effect every kind of service you do as a freelance will be VAT-able, as well as any goods you supply.
- The VAT you charge will have to be paid over to Customs and Excise every month or every quarter – most people choose the latter.
- You can deduct from the VAT you hand over any VAT you have paid for VAT-able goods and services you have bought in the course of business.
- You will have to keep copies of VAT invoices issued or received in date order.
- You will have to keep your books in such a way that VAT on purchases and sales is clearly shown and to make them available to Customs and Excise for inspection when required.

There are severe penalties for late payment. In some circumstances it might be advisable to elect to register for VAT even if you are not obliged to do so by virtue of your turnover. If you buy many goods and services it may pay you to do this, thus recovering the 17.5 per cent VAT element in them; the purchase of a single expensive piece of equipment, like a microcomputer, might also warrant voluntary registration, particularly if it is likely to affect your turnover.

You will have to charge VAT to your clients, but if they themselves are registered they will not mind about that because they can simply claim it back against the VAT they have to pay on their outputs. Being registered for VAT could affect your business, therefore, only if most of your clients are private individuals who have no means of recovering the additional 17.5 per cent. Voluntary registration is, therefore, a matter of judgement. One freelance consultant chose this course on the grounds that if his clients thought he was earning less than £35,000 they might feel it reflected on his ability!

7
Just for the Record

Few freelances enjoy keeping records. They mostly regard it as a pain in the neck that they relieve by retaining copies of invoices rendered and filing as many bills as they remember to obtain and keep. For purely service activities, where transactions are fairly straightforward, this is adequate at least as a basic step. It becomes less satisfactory when there are more suppliers to keep track of, for instance, in building work, and certainly so when you move on to the scale of operations where you have to register for VAT. At the other extreme it must be said that there are freelances, mostly operating on a small scale, who keep only the sketchiest of records – or none at all – of payments or receipts; either because they cannot be bothered with the paperwork or in the hope that by lying low they will escape the attentions of the tax inspector. However, as we pointed out in the previous chapter, it is unlikely they would succeed in the latter object in the long run unless they were to manage to keep all their transactions as ready money ones. Anything that goes through a firm's books can ultimately be traced to a recipient. That even includes payments in kind unless they are small enough to be hidden.

The tax implications

There is an often-quoted rule that nobody need pay more tax than they are obliged to. By the same token the Inland Revenue are not obliged to help you claim allowable expenses, so whereas they will go to considerable lengths to track down payments made to you, the task of substantiating expenses to be set against them is up to the taxpayer. If you are unfortunate enough to come under the close scrutiny of the tax inspector, it is unlikely he or she will give you the benefit of the doubt on anything you cannot prove. In fact, in the last resort he or she will make an arbitrary assessment – usually one that is highly unfavourable to his or her victim. Thus, keeping a record of expenses and filing as many bills as you can to support them is a matter of financial self-preservation, not just one of tedious housekeeping.

At the most basic level you can hand all your records over to your accountant and ask him or her to quarry your return out of a mountain of paper. The problem with that is that it is expensive. A qualified accountant will charge you upwards of £35 an hour and a book-keeper without professional qualifications (CA, ACA or FCA) will cost at least a third of that. A book-keeper, by the way, can do a perfectly adequate job of keeping the records and putting together the tax return of a sole trader or partnership, though if you have formed a limited company its books will have to be audited by a professionally qualified person. In either case, the more preparatory work you do, the less will be involved for any third party to put your records into shape.

There are two other reasons why it is a good idea to keep proper and continuous records in date order of income and expenditure. One, quite simply, is that it is all too easy to forget items for which you do not get invoiced but which can amount to a lot of money over the course of a year – fares and postage are obvious cases – but you may also forget to keep invoices for some minor items like stationery or a book you need for your work. The Inland Revenue will accept a certain level of unsubstantiated expenditure, provided it is properly recorded and in line with the general nature and level of your activities.

Controlling your progress

A further reason why it is a good idea to keep proper records is that it provides a form of control, even at the most basic level, over how much money is coming in and going out. If that calls up visions of the complexities of double-entry book-keeping, have no fears. For most freelance activities, all you need is a simple cash book which shows, on opposite sides of a double page spread, income on the left-hand side, and expenditure on the right-hand side. It is generally a good idea to break the expenditure side into columns, analysing the main types. If you explain the nature of what you are doing to your accountant, he or she will probably suggest the sort of analysis that would be instructive in your case. For a journalist, for instance, the cash book might look like the one on page 63, with additional columns on both the income and expenditure sides if he or she were registered for VAT. These would show gross amounts for each invoice, net and the VAT element.

If a great many of your purchases are made with cheques it may be advisable to have a bank cash book showing cheque numbers against which you can reconcile your bank statements, as well as a separate petty cash book to record small cash transactions. The amounts paid in on the income side in the petty cash book would be sums you withdrew from the bank on a cheque. Details of that would be shown in the bank cash book, as with actual purchases made by cheque. For a fairly simple freelance activity, it would be in order to mix cash and cheque transactions in the same cash book, merely noting the cheque number against purchases paid for in this way and the invoice number against invoices rendered.

Even if you do not run a bank cash book, it is a good idea to keep separate bank accounts for your business and personal transactions. It costs no more and helps to keep personal expenditure apart from allowable business expenses – and, of course, business income separate from other sources of income.

You can also ask the bank to provide additional details of the items that appear on your monthly statement. That will refresh your memory about the transactions to which they relate and provide a further check against entries in your cash book when you come to reconcile the bank statement with it. There is a small extra charge for this additional information but you can also get a certain amount of back-up detail free by using your credit card. Credit card vouchers and statements are generally accepted by VAT inspectors to support claims for VAT repayment on small purchases but larger items like equipment will have to be supported by a supplier's invoice.

The amount of book-keeping you have to do increases as your activity grows in scope and complexity, but so does the amount of control you need to exercise. Initially, it is fairly easy to see at a glance whether income is matching expenditure, but later on you may want to check things more systematically. For instance, you may find that some of the analysis columns are unduly heavy and you will probably be able to relate that fact to a specific job or type of assignment, such as one that entails an undue amount of travel or input of materials. The question you then have to ask yourself is whether the income from that assignment is sufficient to cover these additional costs. Some freelances, particularly those undertaking jobs where they are reimbursed for the costs they incur on behalf of a client, keep a separate record for each assignment. This is a good practice to follow voluntarily, particularly if you are finding your income low in relation to the effort you are putting in to earn it. It may be that you are not taking all the cost factors into account in compiling your charges or that the amount of time you are spending on particular asssignments is out of proportion to the return from them where you have quoted a flat fee rather than an hourly rate.

Invoicing procedures

As far as the income side of your cash book is concerned, you should enter that as soon as you render an invoice – do not wait until you get paid. Invoices should look reasonably professional and though it is not necessary to have them printed with your name,

	INCOME
DATE	
DESCRIPTION	
SOURCE	
INVOICE NO.	
AMOUNT (CASH/CHEQUE)	
DATE	**EXPENDITURE**
DESCRIPTION (CASH/CHEQUE)	
TRAVEL	
SUBSISTENCE	
STATIONERY & POSTAGE	
PROFESSIONAL LITERATURE ETC	
ADMINISTRATION (SERVICES, PROFESSIONAL FEES ETC)	

is a good idea to buy pre-printed numbered duplicate sets such as are produced by Rediform. You can also create your own on a word processor – remember to assign a new invoice number each time you issue one.

When you invoice a client you should state the date, the details of the transaction and the name of whoever commissioned you – remember that if the recipient is a firm they may be receiving hundreds of invoices every week which they have to match up with dockets or order forms – as well as the basis of your charges. For instance, if it was an hourly rate you should state the number of hours you took and the agreed rate. If you are VAT registered (see the next section for further details), your invoice will have to show your VAT number, the net amount, the amount of VAT charged and a gross total. Finally – and this can be important – you should confirm your terms of payments: 30 days, or whatever period you have chosen. However, firms generally have set procedures for making payments. Often they pay at the end of the month or at the end of the month following the supply of goods, and there is very little the individual freelance can do to change such practices, however unhelpful they may be to his or her cash flow. The situation is somewhat easier with private clients or small customers and there, in fact, it is often a good idea to aim for cash on delivery. A great many freelances cite 'getting paid' as their principal occupational hazard.

Once an invoice is paid, you should check it off in the income side of your cash book. Thus it also serves as an instantaneous record of how much is owed and by whom.

Payments should normally be received within six to eight weeks but, sadly, it has to be said that it is not at all easy to recover small sums from those who live on the basis of 'can't pay, won't pay'. Though small claims procedures in the County Court are fairly simple, awards are not usually made on costs for claims of under £500, which means that in practice these are not worth pursuing i proving the claim is complicated. Many freelances dealing with small clients, therefore, ask for upfront or progress payments Indeed, these can be worth trying to agree even with larger clients if a job stretches out over a period of time. This is particularly important where expenditure is being incurred on a client's behal – for instance, when a graphic designer has to buy print as part o an assignment.

VAT records

If you are registered for VAT, you will be legally obliged to keep appropriate records of all your purchases – called 'inputs' in VAT parlance – and sales, called 'outputs'. All your invoices will have t show your VAT number. The procedure for making your VAT return is as follows:

- Collect all suppliers' invoices in date order and give each one a number. List in numerical order, showing date, supplier, total, amount of VAT and net. Where the VAT element is not shown separately, you can work out net and VAT amounts by multiplying the total by 7/47. This will give the VAT and the balance will be the net.
- Enter the total VAT and the total net in the VAT return form.
- File the sales invoices (ie the ones you have raised) in the numerical order you have assigned to them.
- List them all in the same way as suppliers' invoices, that is, with similar supporting details.
- Enter totals of VAT inputs and outputs on the VAT return form.

What you pay to the Customs and Excise at the end of each month or quarter is the difference between your output VAT and your input VAT. The records have to be kept in the way prescribed so that they can be checked by the relevant inspectors.

Though the collection of VAT is carried out by Customs and Excise, not by the Inland Revenue, it is likely that there is some collusion between them. If a freelance was claiming a high level of inputs and an abnormally low level of VAT-able outputs, the suspicion might arise that not all sales were being declared, unless these were primarily in the form of zero-rated goods like food.

Profit and loss accounts

When your accountant comes to compile your income tax return – assuming you are a sole trader or a partner, not an employee of a limited company – he or she will arrive at your taxable profit by deducting allowable expenses from your sales. This is very close to the procedure adopted to produce a profit and loss account which shows the performance of your business over a given period. The only difference is that there are some expenses, such as entertaining, which are a legitimate charge to the business but which, nevertheless, are not deductible in tax terms.

Your accountant will only do this once a year for the Inland Revenue, but the value of compiling a profit and loss account as a way of measuring your progress is such that it may well be worth your while doing it more frequently than that. Certainly, if your activity involves a large number of transactions, especially on the purchase side, it is vital to look at figures regularly to see how you are doing.

The exercise is not at all complicated arithmetically, provided you keep proper records. In the first place sales, minus cost of sales, give you a *gross* profit figure. The cost of sales element would be relevant if you are making a product and/or holding stocks of goods and materials to that end. For instance, if you are a freelance maker of chairs, the gross profit figure might be made up as follows:

Sales (40 chairs @ £25 each)		£1000
Cost of sales		
Opening stock	£200	
Material purchased	£150	
	£350	
Less closing stock	£200	
	£150	
Gross profit		£850

From that gross profit figure all other business expenses have to be deducted to arrive at the net profit, from which you pay yourself.

You may reflect that this is not a lot of money for making 40 chairs, though that picture could be improved if the closing stock was increased in value. The question then arises whether you could sell your chairs at a higher price – or produce more of them. These are points your accountant might well put to you, though he or she would leave it to your knowledge of the market to provide an answer. The value of the profit and loss account – and by implication the records on which it is based – is that it raises questions before they get a chance to turn into problems.

Cash-flow forecasting

An even better way of avoiding trouble by spotting problems before they occur is to compile a kind of profit and loss account in advance: in other words a cash-flow forecast. All this means is that you have to look ahead over a given period, usually at least six months, and for each month forecast your expected revenue and then deduct your expenses from it.

The figures in brackets represent a deficit and the whole exercise will give you guidance on how much you need to borrow until things take off. Obviously, the nature of the expenses will vary according to the freelance activity, but the important thing is to be utterly realistic about both income and expenditure. Sadly, the worst is more likely to happen than the best. Furthermore, even when the best happens, it may not do so at the right time; thus, a now firmly established husband and wife freelance fashion design partnership nearly went broke in their first few months, in spite of a very successful first show. They had not taken into account the fact that orders taken in March would not turn into cash until August – and they had no income, only expenditure, in the intervening period.

It is also helpful, once you have done this forecast, to compare it with what actually happens. You may have to adjust your figures up or down in the light of experience. The real object of keeping records is that it enables you to learn for the future from the past – for, as the German philosopher Hegel said, those who cannot learn from history are condemned to repeat it.

Specimen cash flow statement

Month	1	2	3	4	5	6
	£	£	£	£	£	£
Revenue	250	300	400	500	700	800
Expenditure						
Rent and rates	40	40	40	40	40	40
Utilities	20	20	20	20	20	20
Travel	25	25	25	25	25	25
Entertainment	10	10	10	10	10	10
Postage	10	10	10	10	10	10
Stationery	150	10	20	10	30	20
Advertising	100	100	100	100	100	–
Professional fees	100	50	50	50	50	50
Telephone	30	30	30	30	30	30
Materials	40	40	60	70	80	80
Interest on overdraft	9	9	9	9	9	9
	(284)	(44)	26	126	296	506

8
Getting the Work

Going freelance generally means that you have to have had previous experience as an employee in that field. There are two related reasons for that precondition. One is that the kind of work that is put out to freelances is generally what might be described as mature, falling into one of the following categories:

- A task that is an important part of what an organisation usually does, but for which the demand is not sufficiently consistent to justify hiring permanent staff – for instance, overloads of editorial work in a publishing house or many of the jobs connected with film and television production.
- A specialist assignment for which there are no in-house resources, eg consultancy in such areas as computer applications or graphic design.
- Skilled or specialised personal services, ranging from repair work to some professional fields.
- Jobs that are traditionally done by freelances, such as artistic performances.

None of these can readily be entrusted to the product of trial and error that emerges even from talented beginners. It follows that a client commissioning freelance work will be looking for evidence that the person chosen can do the job. They will seek out freelances who have worked for or with them before, or for someone they know. At the very least they will want to see examples of their work or to get the names of their other clients – the more credible the better.

Freelancing, in other words, is a contact sport and almost without exception freelances begin either:

- by working for their previous employers;
- by taking away clients they had dealt with in their previous job or at least developing contacts they had made;
- by teaming up with someone who already had a 'universe' o contacts; or
- by turning what was previously a part-time activity, in whic they already had a track record, into a full-time one

sometimes with the help of an agent who could steer work their way.

The first two of these are the most common ways of starting freelancing, but they often consist of the proverbial two swallows that do not make a summer. Your previous employer or clients may give you enough work to provide a start or a safety net for the first few months, but only in exceptional cases will the flow be extensive, reliable and consistent enough to make a living. There is the further danger that, if you rely too heavily on one source – and particularly if you work on your client's premises as well – the tax inspector may sooner or later take the view that you are not really self-employed at all, as explained in Chapter 5.

Market research

What you should do, therefore, is to think ahead with the help of a little market research. When a firm launches a new product or service, they spend a great deal of time and money assessing the scale and durability of the likely demand for it. The sort of factors they consider are:

- Who needs it?
- Why do they need it?
- How many need it?
- How long will they need it?
- What are they willing to pay for it?
- How can they be reached?
- How often do they need it?
- What is the competition offering?

Big firms go into these issues very systematically, but as a freelance there is no need to launch yourself like a new kind of chocolate bar. However, questions about the market are relevant, no matter what the scale and nature of your operations. It is therefore worth raising them with potential clients, other than the ones who have already promised you work. In some cases these may be specialist agents, for instance, for photographers, or the more generalist freelances agencies that are springing up in a number of cities as more and more people turn to freelancing as a source of income. From such soundings there may emerge ways in which your product or service could be modified to create a wider appeal, to offer something the competition is not producing, or to reach markets beyond those you originally had in mind.

You should also get some guidance on a matter which most freelances find hard to determine – how much to charge. Existing contacts are often not at all a good guide to market rates. The price you quote to friends is not necessarily the rate you should be offering to the world at large: nor, as indicated in Chapter 5, should the charges for a one-off job necessarily be the same as for a long-term contract or an assignment you need to take to get off the ground or to give yourself credibility. The best basis for pricing is the time-honoured law of supply and demand and the only place to establish that is out in the marketplace. Agents and agencies are often the best source here, because they have a vested interest in getting the best deal for those on their books.

Promotion

Many freelances do not take any formal steps to promote themselves at all. They rely on 'one thing leading to another' and on the word about how good they are spreading more or less of its own accord. Sometimes, it must be said, this process works, but it works better, more quickly and is more likely to lead you to the kind of jobs you want to do if you give it a helping hand. Here are some basic steps you ought to consider taking to draw the attention of potential clients to the fact that you are in business:

- Get business cards printed showing your name, qualifications, the nature of your activity, address and telephone number. Beware of using the word 'consultant'. It is meaningless unless you are formally qualified as a consultant – and can therefore be counter-productive.
- Get decent letterheads printed. In this case, though, it is less necessary to give details of your activity since it will probably be clear from your letter.

   If you are forming a limited company you will have to fulfil a number of statutory requirements in the information shown on your stationery and promotional literature. Your solicitor will advise you of what these are. Do not have such material printed without first consulting him or her.
- Produce a brochure that describes in detail who you are, what you do and where you can be reached. Your business card will be useful to hand out on appropriate occasions – and you should certainly always remember to carry a good supply with you – but you also need something that tells a fuller story. What this is depends on the nature of your activity and how you intend to promote it. A gardening or building service may need no more than a postcard-sized card that describes the kind of work you do and gives an address or telephone number where you can be reached – in the evenings as well as in the daytime because some clients can only ring you after

work. This can be used as a mailer to push through people's letterboxes or to display in local shop windows.

As you move upmarket, in terms of conventional ideas about job status, you will need a rather more detailed statement setting out your background and experience, the range and size of work you do, the kind of equipment you have (if that is relevant), your main past and present clients and what you did/do for them. The document should:

- not be more than four A4 pages long;
- be written in simple English, avoiding technical jargon;
- focus on a few aspects where you really know your stuff;
- pinpoint areas where you believe there is a real demand for what you have to offer;
- avoid quoting rates or prices.

Such a brochure need not necessarily be printed although, if it is typed, it should be professionally done and well laid out. If you decide to have it printed, look for a specimen of a similar piece of literature that you like and get an estimate from a couple of printers or print shops for the number of copies you want – remember that details like client lists can go out of date when considering quantities. It is also important to bear in mind that a second colour, embossing and illustrations will all cost extra money and are relatively expensive for the kind of short run that is probably all you will need.

Having got a printer's estimate, you should go to a graphic designer – there are lots of them in the Yellow Pages – and get him or her to do a layout of your text. Never leave this to the printers. The results will almost always be terrible, even if you give them an example of something similar and ask them to copy its style.

Choosing an agent

In quite a number of freelance activities work can be obtained by registering your name with an agent. The agent may be a specialist in a certain field of work, for instance, in supplying fashion models or people to cook for private parties, but in freelancing there is a growing number of generalist agencies who undertake to find anyone from a plumber to a babysitter and from a chef to an accountant. Such agencies are usually quite distinct from normal employment agencies who place temporary or permanent staff. They specialise in freelance services and indeed some of them operate by advertising these to clients and charging them a small annual retainer for the privilege of access to the workers on their books. In whatever way they operate, though, they are all bound by the provisions of the Employment Agencies Act 1973, which states that any commission must be charged to the client, not the worker. An employment agent cannot, or should not, charge you a fee or percentage for obtaining work for you. The only exceptions to this rule apply in the world of entertainment and in the performing arts generally.

Agent are entitled, equally, to absolve themselves from any responsibility in regard to the relationship between you and the client. They are not obliged to find you work, nor do you have any redress through the agent if the client fails to pay you – unless of course, the agent offers credit and collection as a service. That is one way for them to get round the legislation on charging commission to workers on their books. Most modelling agencies, for instance, charge their models when they get them work, but that charge is for conducting negotiations, doing the paperwork and the organising of bookings, not the job itself. It may be that such a relationship is either convenient or inescapable in the kind of freelancing you are engaged in and in that case you should try to find out how much the agent charges, how it compares with going rates and whether they are really providing a range of genuine services or merely getting round the law. The best people to ask about such matters are other freelances. You should also check about what happens when work comes your way that the agent was not responsible for getting. You may have a contractual obligation to pay the agent in such cases as well. If that is an unavoidable condition of getting on his or her books, try to limit the period over which the contract runs.

A type of agent of great interest to freelances in the professional and executive spheres are those who specialise in supplying contract workers. They keep registers of skilled specialists and when an assignment comes up, they send the client a shortlist to choose from, as in an ordinary vacancy. They invoice the client and pay the contract freelance on a PAYE basis, unless he or she operates as a limited company. Many freelance consultants find that being on the books of this type of agency is a useful additional marketing tool. Agencies specialising in what is called 'interim management' or 'executive leasing' in the UK include Albemarle Interim Management Services (AIMS), 18 Great Marlborough Street, London W1V 1AF; 071-437 3611; Executive Interim Management, Devonshire House, Mayfair Place, London W1X 5FH; 071-355 3437; GMS Consultancy, 46 High Street North, Dunstable, Bedfordshire LU6 1LA; 0582 666970; and PE International plc, Park House, Wick Road, Egham, Surrey TW20 0HW; 0784 43444.

One condition that many agents quite reasonably impose is for those on their books to give certain undertakings on reliability and standards of work. For instance, you may be required to notify the agent if you cannot turn up to a particular job or complete it within the time or on the terms agreed. The reason for that is that the agent's reputation and livelihood depends on the quality of the workers he or she is able to supply. Clients go through an agent not only for convenience, but for some degree of validation beyond that to be obtained from picking names out of the Yellow Pages. In the case of the generalist agencies it is for this peace of mind factor that they pay their annual fee.

A slightly different type of agent are those who place work rather than workers: literary or art agents, for instance. They charge the writer or artist a commission on the sale of finished work, having found a taker for it and negotiated terms. Here again, though, finding a good agent who will accept you – which can be crucial – is a question of asking around among fellow freelances.

Networks

Used in a technical sense, networking is a term which describes a system of linked and sometimes remote workstations, communicating with each other through information technology. It is also applied in a more general way to the notion of groups of freelances or independent consultants who agree to work together as and when circumstances indicate that this is the best way of tackling a job. The author, for instance, is a member of an informal network consisting of a printer, a designer and himself, a writer. They have produced a brochure describing the services they can offer clients. Each member operates independently, but they occasionally work together to produce corporate brochures or booklets. In that case they quote a price they agree among themselves. They also agree how the fee is to be split between them. In other cases they pass work on to each other – for instance when a client for the printer wants some writing done.

In management consultancy networks operate in another way. When an individual takes on an assignment, it often turns out that the problem has another dimension from that which was originally envisaged; what seems like a marketing issue may have a finance or human resource angle which requires different expertise, for which the freelance consultant may need to pull in another member of the network. If that role calls for contact with the client, it is advisable to tell the client that someone else is getting involved.

Another possibility may be that the job is too large for any one freelance person to handle; or simply that he or she is too busy to take the job on, but would like to recommend someone else who can help the client out.

In many cases networks are informal: groups of friends and acquaintances who pass work to each other on a casual basis, or who subcontract bits of a job. But there is also a growing number of formal networks, which in an ad hoc way, resemble consultancies. They generally have a small office with a staff of two or three people, who handle marketing and public relations. The office keeps a register of all the skills the network can put together for clients, and also keep track of where its members are so that a team can be assembled quickly. Some even bill clients and pay the networkers after deduction of a percentage to cover costs and overheads.

That saves administration for the individual, but the danger is that he or she will be regarded by the Inland Revenue as being employed by the network. Members of networks who operate on this basis will have to register as limited companies to escape the penalties of PAYE.

No list of networks exists, but local enterprise agencies or business schools may be able to point you towards local ones. In either case – whether the network is formal or informal – it is important to assess the standards of competence of the other members before joining them or passing work on. Network members are judged by the company they keep, as well as their own abilities.

Advertising and publicity

The word 'advertising' conjures up in some people's minds thoughts of expensive spreads in the Sunday supplements, which is probably why so few freelances advertise. However, advertising covers a multitude of possibilities:

- National consumer media;
- Specialist magazines;
- Local newspapers;
- Direct mail;
- Local radio.

The first of these is the most expensive and the least effective because, unless you are prepared to travel to offer your service, much of the circulation for which you are paying is wasted; there is no point in offering a Tunbridge Wells-based home security service to a reader in Inverness. To some extent this is also true of advertising in specialist magazines, though if your field is a highly specialised one, like some branches of computer consultancy, it is more likely to have an appeal that, though narrow in itself, will be broadly based geographically. That makes it the reverse of the majority of freelance occupations for which there is usually quite a large market within a defined geographical area. For this reason most freelances find that local advertising is the most effective. It is generally inexpensive, but to get its full benefits it has to:

- be in a regular spot over an initial period of at least four weeks, so that a substantial part of your market has a chance of seeing it;
- be well laid out, so that it is eye-catching within a small space;
- give essential details about your service and when and where you can be reached (an amazing number of small ads fail to give a telephone number!).

When you place an advertisement you should specify in writing where you want it to appear and, if the paper comes out more than once a week, on which days.

Direct mail – a brochure, usually accompanied by a letter to a named person – can be more effective for the simple reason that, whereas in a paper the recipient has to be looking for the kind of service you are offering and has to pick you out from what no doubt are competing ones, in a direct mail shot you have the recipient's sole attention. You can also say much more than in a small advertisement.

The temptation to say too much proves too much for many: some people overload their message with excessive detail. There is a subtle point at which information, however important, becomes tedious. Generally, that point is where you stop talking about what is likely to interest the recipient and start banging your own drum. Before you invest money in a direct mail shot, show what you have written to a few mercilessly candid friends and also get criticisms from some potential recipients.

You should be aware, though, that the wastage from direct mail shots is very high. A 2 per cent response would be regarded as good, so the selection of addressees needs a great deal of thought.

- Try to identify prospects who are known to be interested, rather than going for blanket coverage. Fifty people who attended a course on a particular management problem in which you specialise are worth infinitely more than a bundle of '1000 managing directors of major public companies' that a list broker will try to sell you.
- Aim to buy or compile mailing lists where people can be identified by name rather than by appointment.
- Sample various groups of prospects rather than putting all your eggs in one basket.

List brokers are firms that supply lists of addresses in specialised categories – businesses of a certain type and/or size, professional practices of various kinds, private individuals with known hobbies and interests, and so forth. They will sell you printed labels for a mailing, or they will undertake to do a whole mail shot for you, including printing the letter or brochure to go in it. Their rates are based on a price per 1000 addresses and you will have to undertake to use a minimum number, which may be as few as 1000, but is more likely to be 4000–5000. That makes it difficult to take a sample to make sure you are likely to get a reasonable response, but you could do this yourself simply by selecting 100 names from the Yellow Pages and doing your own mail shot. If you receive an encouraging response, you could then go to a list broker. You will find them in the Yellow Pages, under 'Advertising – Direct Mail'.

Brokers usually hold roughly similar ranges of lists, so get a quote from more than one. They will try to sell you the maximum number of addresses, whereas you will usually want the minimum number in the first instance and this is something you will have to be firm about. Recommendations are always best in choosing a supplier of any kind, so a check with your local Chamber of Commerce or Local Enterprise Agency is a good idea.

For most freelances, operating on a small scale, the more personalised the approach is, the better. Instead of blanketing an area with mail shots, try to identify very specific people, if possible on the basis of information you have previously gathered through reading, deduction, or gossip that they have a specific problem with which you can help them, and send them a personal letter and your brochure. Even if you are busy at the time with other work, this can be a highly effective way of building for the future.

Publicity

Some of the most effective publicity you can get is editorial coverage and it will cost you no more than a telephone call and the postage on a press release. If what you are doing is at all newsworthy, either as an activity in itself or because it involves some particularly interesting assignment, there is a good chance that one of the growing number of local papers – or even local radio or television – might want to cover it. Specialist magazines are also a good bet, but national media less so – they are deluged with hand-outs from PR organisations, so unless you know someone on a national newspaper who is influential enough to put your name forward, forget it. However, local papers are definitely worth a try – particularly if you are already an advertiser, though they may claim that there is no connection between advertising and editorial. They also tend to be fairly desperate for interesting local items, as some of the trivia they put out shows.

Strangely enough, though, people do read the local press and freelances report very good responses both to advertising and editorial publicity in local papers. One thing to beware of, though, is mentioning clients' names. The fact that you have just restored a painting for a named client which you think might be a Turner will certainly get a story in the papers. The client might not be amused at the possibility that burglars will be among its most attentive readers. If you are going to mention a client, directly or by implication, clear it with him first.

The best publicity of all is where a client recommends you. A speaker at a recent conference called this OPR: Other People's Recommendations. The best reward that a client can offer you (apart from the money!) for a job well done is to pass your name on to someone who might need your services. Being able to suggest this delicately is an important part of the process of self-marketing.

Over-commitment

One reason why many freelances are nervous about publicising themselves – particularly when they already have a full workload – is the fear of over-commitment. This is a real dilemma because absolute reliability in terms of time and quality is more essential for freelances than for employees. A talented but unreliable employee can always be backed up in some way. In the case of a freelance, someone in an organisation is almost totally dependent on your ability to come up with the goods, and if you let him or her down once it is unlikely that he or she will give you a second chance. Freelances should therefore beware of biting off more than they can chew, though the general feeling is that it is a life of either feast or famine: either working all night to finish something on time or waiting anxiously for the telephone to ring.

Unlike employees, freelances find it extremely difficult to control what is the right amount of work to take on and to make plans accordingly. However, that is no reason to make no plans at all and, undoubtedly, the right time to initiate promotion and advertising – though it is also the most difficult one – is when you are already busy. One reason is simply the psychological factor that a client is more likely to be impressed by someone who has a lot of work going through than little or none. The other is that promotion and publicity seldom bring immediate results. It is not a way to pay next week's bills, and probably not even next month's. It is part of your long-term plan, not an emergency measure.

Message-taking systems

Even working from home, freelances still find they spend a lot of time out of the house, seeing clients or working on-site. In that case they may leave a spouse or partner in charge of the telephone. It is important on these occasions to brief them on how to handle calls. There should be paper and a notepad by the telephone, so that details of the caller and the message are not entrusted solely to the unreliability of the human memory. Nothing is more disruptive to domestic harmony than the person you love saying in the evening of the next day, 'Oh dear, I've just remembered, I forgot to tell you . . .'

9
Briefing and Brief Taking

When there are disagreements between a freelance and the person who commissioned him or her, the reasons can nearly always be ascribed to the brief. The air is then thick with recriminatory phrases like:

- 'But I thought you meant ...'
- 'But I thought you were going to ...'
- 'But why didn't you ...?'
- 'But you never said anything about ...'
- 'But I didn't realise that ...'

The variations are almost endless and the way to avoid them is for both parties to take a lot of time and trouble over the briefing stage; and when in doubt to go back over the brief and reconfirm or revise it. It follows that the best time and place for briefing is the normal working environment and during normal working hours; not, as so often happens, in the pub at the end of the day. That may inevitably be where the briefing part of getting a commission begins, but it should not be where it ends.

In most cases the person commissioning you will have given you some idea of what he or she wants you to do before you get down to business. You should come to the first proper meeting about it having thought about what it entails and armed with a set of relevant questions. Indeed, even if an offer of work is made casually over drinks or a meal you should try to come up, there and then, with at least a preliminary set of questions about what the job is likely to involve.

The detailed issues to be settled will obviously vary somewhat according to the nature of your freelance activity, but there are a number of points that apply almost universally:

- Is the client clear about what he or she is likely to get from you? Where appropriate, show or describe examples of similar jobs you have done.
- Is there a time/money budget for the assignment?
- What does the client expect to get for his money within the time allowed? In the case of consultancy, for instance, are you

expected to implement your recommendations to any extent? If a report is required, how detailed has it to be?

- Can the client's expectations be fulfilled for the sum envisaged?
- If there is a flat fee, rather than a time rate, can you do the job for that sum without leaving yourself out of pocket?
- Does the figure include expenses, materials, etc? If not, is there a limit to what you can spend?
- Does the figure include VAT, if you are registered?
- To what extent will you be allowed to use the client's facilities (postage, telephone, secretarial help, etc) or equipment?
- Who else in the client's organisation, other than the person commissioning you, will you need to deal with and are they accessible at mutually convenient times? For instance, your work may need to be scrutinised and approved by marketing, production or accounting functionaries within an organisation.
- Should there be regular progress reviews in the form of interim reports and/or meetings?
- Where your work involves dealing with valuable items or documents who is responsible for insurance?
- In the case of research, consultancy, etc are you at liberty to use your work in other directions, for example, in a book or article?
- Who holds copyright, where that is relevant?
- Under what circumstances may the assignment be cancelled or altered by either party and under what penalties?
- Are there any restrictions on subcontracting part of the work should you be unable to handle it all yourself?
- How long after delivery/completion will payment be made? Are there any arrangements for interim payments?
- Are you being commissioned to produce an outline or interim study or is it the real thing?

The contents of such a discussion form a legally binding contract if they are agreed by both parties, even verbally, but, of course, it is a great help to have a written document to refer to if there is a dispute about what precisely was said.

It is possible to take such a course too far, though. It must be admitted that there is a good deal of informality in the freelance-client relationship, and people commissioning freelance work might tend to baulk at receiving some bulky document that attempts to cross every t and dot every i, except where large, expensive or long term arrangements are concerned. It is also inadvisable, despite the suggestions made by some freelance associations, to go into too much detail about what happens in the case of cancellation. Generally, clients cancel either because they have run out of money or because they don't like your work. In either case it is difficult to get a refund. If you feel doubtful about the payment situation, particularly on a large or long-term job, the best idea is to try for some form of progress payment.

If the person who arranged the commission does not do so, it is worth writing a short, informal note confirming the principal points discussed:

- what you are being asked to do;
- what fees and/or expenses have been agreed;
- when you intend to deliver;
- when you expect to be paid;
- when and where the next meeting is to be.

That leaves the commissioning person to agree or disagree with your recollection of what was said – and the mere act of writing it down will focus your own understanding of the commission.

Some wise words of advice on time-based charges are contained in an article in the *Journal of the Royal Institute of British Architects* (as independent professionals, many architects are, in essence, freelances): 'When proposing to charge on a time basis, always give an estimate of the likely cost and invite the client to set a budget limit. As the limit or budget is approached, let the client know. Then you will not be faced with an anguished client saying, "*How* much? I didn't think it would be anything like that."'

10
Legal Matters

One very good reason why freelances nearly always have to have a good deal of previous experience in their particular field is that they may otherwise be breaking the law in offering a service to the public. The Supply of Goods and Services Act of 1982 has been interpreted in the courts as meaning that anyone who supplies a service does so under the implication that they are competent at it. This is further reinforced by the fact that they have to exercise 'reasonable care and skill' in the execution of the task they have undertaken to carry out; that has been defined as being 'the ordinary skill of an ordinary competent person exercising the craft in question'. If you fail in this respect a dissatisfied client will be legally entitled to claim compensation from you for any damages that your lack of competence has caused him or her.

There are also two other implied provisions in the same Act which affect freelances:

- Services will have to be carried out in a reasonable time.
- The customer will pay a reasonable charge.

The criteria of reasonableness in both cases are what is normal for that type of job.

You could, of course, agree with your client that you are only a beginner and might, therefore, not do the job very well; or that you are very busy and cannot complete whatever you have been asked to do by any date you cared to commit yourself to. If you can persuade your customer to accept such conditions in writing, it may strengthen your hand in a dispute. But it could still leave you open to litigation under the Unfair Contract Terms Act of 1977, which says that disclaimers are not valid unless you can prove in court that they are reasonable in the circumstances. For instance, if a completion date or a set of costs were out of your control because you had to depend on a third party for the supply of scarce materials, that would be a reasonable explanation, provided it was made clear to the client at the time.

The whole issue of unfair contracts hinges round what you can reasonably be responsible for. Thus, if you were making a brooch containing rare stones which you did not carry in stock, you could not reasonably be responsible for their price and delivery, and a warning to the customer to that effect would not constitute an unfair contract. You could not, however, disclaim responsibility for the completed piece falling apart, far less for the fact that the stones you bought in all good faith turned out to be fakes. The criteria of reasonable skill and care also extend to knowing enough about your craft to choose materials competently. They also cover the choice of subcontractors when you yourself put out part of a job that you are doing for a client.

To some extent the provisions of these two Acts – or at any rate variations of them – are embodied in the Sale of Goods Act of 1979. This does not affect freelances so much, except for those who operate as makers, but it is as well to be aware of its provisions because these may affect you as a consumer; for instance, when you buy equipment. The Sale of Goods Act puts three main obligations on the seller:

1. The goods are of 'merchantable quality'. This means that they must be fit for the task for which you got them, bearing in mind the price you paid. Thus, if you bought an expensive drill that quickly overheated or failed to grip the bit as the parts expanded, the supplier may be in breach of the Act. One has to say 'may' because if the person who sold it to you warned you about its limitations or made it clear he or she could not pronounce on them, no offence may have taken place – though possibly the Unfair Contract Terms Act could come to your rescue.
2. That the goods are fit 'for any particular purpose made known to the seller'. Thus, if you ask whether the drill you bought is suitable for penetrating metal of a certain thickness and it turns out not to be so, the seller is in breach of the Act.
3. That the goods are 'as described'. Again, if the box you bought the drill in says on the outside that it can run for five minutes without overheating and this proves not to be the case, the Sale of Goods Act has probably been breached.

Second-hand goods are also covered by the Act, although you cannot expect them to be in mint condition. Your rights in that case would depend on how they were described, whether any defects were pointed out to you or whether they were so obvious that you should have noticed them, given reasonable care. The Office of Fair Trading recommend that when buying an expensive item second hand, you should bring along someone who knows something about it; for instance, if you are buying a microcomputer under these circumstances – and an increasing number of these are coming on the market.

If the goods fail on any of these grounds, you can take them back and claim a refund – it is the shop that sold them, not the manufacturer, who is liable. You need not accept a partial refund or the offer to exchange the item for one that works. You may even claim compensation if you can show that the faulty item has caused loss to you. Litigation is expensive, so your first recourse to put pressure on the offending party should be to the Citizens' Advice Bureau or the Trading Standards Officer of your local authority.

The Sale of Goods Act is closely related to another piece of legislation which is more likely to affect freelances: the Trade Descriptions Acts of 1968 and 1972. This makes it a criminal offence knowingly to describe goods or services falsely and consequently means that you have to be careful about how you word advertisements and brochures in which you promote your activity to clients. Claiming experience or qualifications which you do not have could, in other words, land you in serious trouble; a more likely case would be to promise a fast turn-round time, in order to get business, without being sure you can meet it.

The Trade Descriptions Act also prohibits making false statements about prices, but otherwise pricing can be a large grey area. Strictly speaking, there is no obligation on the seller to sell at a stated price. A contract is only completed when money changes hands, when the hammer falls in an auction or when a deposit has been accepted. In the latter case, you are under no obligation to return the buyer's deposit if he changes his mind, even if the money was to buy materials. You could, under such circumstances, even sue for loss of profit on other work you turned away in the anticipation of getting this assignment. In practice, if you state a price on a catalogue or brochure you should always protect yourself by saying that it is subject to fluctuations or dependent on circumstances; for instance, if you offered a freelance typing service at a rate per 1000 words, you might not be able to stick to that rate for an indecipherable manuscript. You could always turn away the business or warn the client at the time that there would be an extra charge. But if you attempted to impose it at the completion of the job, you could be liable under The Trade Descriptions Act.

On pricing, however, the biggest area of confusion for freelances lies in giving *quotes* and *estimates*. There do not appear to be any legal definitions attached to these two terms, but the Office of Fair Trading recommend that if you are not sure what the final price is going to be, you should give an estimate – and describe it as such in writing. It should be a reasonably close approximation – as far as it is within your power to provide – of what you think the price is going to be.

The Office of Fair Trading describe a quotation as 'a fixed price which should not be exceeded in any circumstances'. If your client presses you for a quotation and you find it difficult to name a firm sum because of unknown factors – for instance, how long the job will take – you can either give some parameters (for example, between £x and £y) or you can say you will do £z worth of work – which is what on present evidence you think will be required – but that you will notify the customer if you think the sum is likely to be exceeded. That, for example, is the practice usually followed by private investigators in a field in which it is notoriously difficult to predict the length and complexity of an assignment.

When giving quotes or estimates you should warn the client of any risks the job may entail for his or her property or person; for instance, when restoring a picture in poor condition could possibly damage it further. That is not regarded as an unfair contract. On the other hand, taking a risk without proper consultation with the client could leave you open to a civil action if it goes wrong. Here, again, whatever is agreed should be documented. When a dispute arises, one written word is worth a thousand spoken ones.

Leases and planning permission

In addition to trading law, another area where it is important to be aware of the legal situation relates to the premises from which you plan to carry on your business. You may have to get planning permission if you intend to do this from your own home. If you are living in rented accommodation you will also have to consult the terms of the lease in case it prohibits carrying on a trade or occupation from those premises. If you own your property there may be restrictions in your lease about carrying on a business from your house or flat. Even if you are renting a separate space from which to work, you should ask your solicitor to check whether there are any restrictions that might affect the kind of activity you plan to conduct.

Arbitration of disputes

The services of a solicitor are almost unavoidable when it comes to leases, but nothing that lawyers get involved in is ever cheap. It is fortunate that a good deal of the kind of litigation by which freelances might be affected can be conducted either by arbitration or through bringing a small claim in the County Court, both of which can be done without bringing in solicitors.

A particular kind of arbitration, known as Code Arbitration, applies if you, as the person being complained against, belong to a trade association with a code of practice that provides for arbitration as a way of settling disputes; or if you are the plaintiff and are in dispute with a client or supplier who is. Contact your local Office of Fair Trading for details of how to initiate arbitration.

Legal action for debts

Arbitration of a different kind may be ordered by the County Court in the case of a disputed claim for under £500. (A threshold shortly to be raised.) This would be the last stage in a small claims sequence which takes the following course.

If you are owed a sum of under £500 which you are unable to collect, you can bring a legal action in the County Court to recover it. All you have to do in that case is to apply for a *Request for Issue of Default Summons* from your nearest County Court, fill it in and enclose full details of your claim with copies for the defendant as well as the court. Issuing a summons will cost you 10p in the £ for sums of up to £300, with a minimum of £7 and a maximum of £43 for larger amounts.

The defendant then has 14 days in which to pay. If he fails to reply, you, the plaintiff, are entitled to have judgement enforced in your favour – which may ultimately mean sending in the bailiff to seize goods and chattels to the value of the debt. If the defendant contests the claim, there are a number of procedures to try to secure settlement out of court – chiefly, a pre-trial review of the situation in front of a registrar by the disputing parties. It is at this point that the registrar may order an arbitrated settlement if the claim is for less than £500. However, this is always preferable to going through the full court process, which is very time-consuming if you do it yourself and very expensive if you employ a solicitor. In either case, you should decide beforehand whether there is any likelihood that, having gone through all this, you will get your money; or, as the lawyers put it, whether the potential defendant is 'worth powder and shot'. The good news, however, is that the mere threat of legal proceedings secures payment in a very high proportion of cases.

Contracts

Formal contracts are something of a rarity in freelance work, but you do not need to have signed a contract to be legally bound by a set of terms. If a client, or an agency, has given you details of the job, a start date and a location, and you turn up as specified you may find you are in a contractual situation, even if you have not signed a contract.

If you have been offered a contract and not signed it because you do not like some of the terms, the time to dispute them is before you start work. If the offerer of the contract does not then reply to your objections, that would greatly weaken their case if it came to a dispute. Remember, however, to keep copies of your correspondence.

An important point to watch in freelance contracts is that the wording states that they are contracts for service, not contracts of service. Contracts of service are treated by the Inland Revenue as being tantamount to employment and would make you taxable under Schedule E, as well as being liable to make Class 1 National Insurance contributions. Contracts for service preserve your status as an independent supplier.

Part 2
Freelance Opportunities

11
Freelancing as a Management Consultant

Introduction
Anyone can call themselves a management consultant, which in theory makes it an attractive freelance proposition, especially for retired or redundant executives. However, a great many potential clients are aware that the title itself carries no real status unless the person describing himself as such is a member of the Institute of Management Consultants. That Institute is essentially a closed shop for people who have worked in a management consultancy firm, 'investigating and identifying management problems concerned with policy, organisation, procedures and methods, recommending appropriate actions and helping to implement them' as the Institute's literature puts it. Membership is, in the main, given to people who have worked in independent consultancy firms, though some exceptions are made for full-time in-house consultants.

None the less, there is a large and growing number of freelance consultants who are making a living without ever having practised formally in one of the recognised consultancy firms. If a manager can establish his or her expertise in a subject or a functional area that is in demand, his or her advice is taken more seriously, at least in some quarters, than that of a management consultant who has never been forced to practise what he or she preaches. One typical specialist area is computer consultancy or consultancy in many of the service and leisure industries, into which manufacturing firms are diversifying. Freelance consultancies are also burgeoning in specific research fields, ranging from market research in specialised areas or topics, to research on the background of potential candidates for senior managerial posts.

However, you should be aware that the concept of consultancy is increasingly moving beyond problem analysis and solution recommendation towards implementation – the criticism of consultants has always been that, having identified the problem and its causes, they walk away from actually doing anything about it. (A recent cartoon about management consultants in the *Financial Times* put it as 'We came, we saw, we invoiced.') Demonstrable qualifications, backed up by facts and figures of projects carried out to a successful conclusion – even in your own company – are an essential beginning to consultancy if you lack the formal qualification referred to. You should put together a brochure as soon as possible in your freelance career, which sets out your experience and background, quantifies your successes with facts and figures, says something about your working methods and gives names of firms you have worked for. A professionally designed and properly printed job is essential; if you are after several hundred pounds of a client's money, a photostat typescript, however neatly set out, will not do.

Most consultants get work initially from existing contacts who know of their expertise in a particular field – and quite often these are previous employers. This is then backed up by further mail shots, but the universal experience of freelance consultants is that blind mailing to addresses on bought lists does not work at all and that 'cold calling' hardly ever does. The process of client development must be aimed at personal contacts, or those gathered through a network, or picked out individually from news items in the business sections of the daily press or in specialist journals. PR is also used as a method of getting business. Local newspapers are particularly good at publicising news stories of local interest, though in talking to them about a consultancy assignment care must be taken not to breach confidentiality or even to disclose accidentally something that may be of value to your client's competitors.

The ability to communicate in writing is an important attribute for a consultant to possess, not only in order to get work but to operate as a consultant at all. Written reports and summaries before, during and at the end of an assignment are a universal requirement.

In the first place, you will have to put a written proposal to your client before your appointment is confirmed. This will set out the brief as you understand it after discussing its terms of reference with the client, what the objectives of your consultancy are to be from the client's point of view, how success is to be measured, and what period of time the assignment is to cover. For instance, if your brief was to automate a warehouse facility, you might have been asked to study the existing system, compare various solutions, select appropriate machinery, negotiate purchasing terms, train the client's staff and oversee the running-in period of new equipment for a given number of weeks. All this should be set out in your proposal, which should also clarify other matters: your fee, obviously, but also such things as the amount of in-house support you can expect from your client. Will you be able to use an office at his premises? Will secretarial help be provided? Does your fee include expenses and, if not, what items will have to be sanctioned before they are incurred?

Some consultancy assignments are divided into stages, and at each stage progress will have to be reviewed – usually on the basis of a written report. For instance, a company thinking of expanding by franchising might begin by commissioning a report on the franchise market. The next stage might be a study of whether its own operations were franchisable. If that was positive, the step after that would be to set up and run its own franchise pilot operation and to incorporate the lessons learned from that in an operating manual that would be given to franchisees once they started to be recruited. Each one of these steps would call for a breather at which progress was reviewed before any decision was made to go further. All such ways of conducting the consultancy ought to be confirmed in writing, even if a clear verbal understanding has been reached.

Computer Consultancy

Basic skills and aptitudes

Computer consultancy takes many different shapes and happens at many different levels, including some forms that are really a glorified kind of selling. The one basic skill that genuine consultants have in common is the ability to write programs, even if that only means knowing enough about it to 'bend' one of the many standard packages to the requirements of a particular user. At a higher level consultants will either have a specialised knowledge of a particular industry plus computer skills, or be able to relate computer applications to specific business or industrial problems. Yet a third kind of consultant would be someone with a very high degree of computer expertise, but no specific knowledge of any particular application. Such a person would, however, have the ability to grasp problems in isolation of their technical content and to be able to analyse them in such a way that he or she could write a specification based on that analysis. There are also various types of hack work that are sometimes mis-termed 'consultancy': routine coding tasks, for instance, which require no more than a rudimentary background in computing.

Equipment and premises

Most of the time consultancy is carried out on the clients' premises and using their hardware and facilities, though consultants have micros of their own, obviously, so that they can work out some problems at home and also keep up with new techniques. In the future, it is likely that various forms of networking with mainframe computers on a time charge basis will be available to private users, so that more sophisticated tasks can be undertaken from home.

The market

A wide variety of firms are a potential market for freelance consultancy in both the service and manufacturing sectors. That market is growing very rapidly, both with the increased take-up of computers and with existing users looking for further applications. In the UK consultancy in information technology generally is to some extent funded by a scheme which has been established to enable firms to institute computer feasibility studies across a broad range of activities, from industrial process control to computer applications in small business. Apart from accountants, architects, engineers and surveyors – in other words, those naturally associated with numerical methods – the professions have, on the whole, been slow to introduce computers, though this is now changing rapidly in legal firms and general medical practice. These are likely to be growth fields for consultancy in the future.

Finding work

There is no shortage of work and quite a number of agencies advertise for freelances in specialist publications such as *Computing, Freelance Informer* and *Computer Weekly*. Such jobs are often fairly low-grade coding tasks and, of course, the agency takes a percentage from the client – which generally means that the freelance is paid less. They are useful for filling gaps in the workload, though. It also helps to go through an agency if you want a spell abroad on a short-term basis.

Opportunities for teaching are good for people with computing skills. Apart from daytime and evening courses in the state sector, there are a growing number of private courses and schools, including those linked to sales activities by manufacturers and the larger dealers.

Fees

Typical weekly rates for an analyst programmer, whose work consists primarily of bending existing applications packages to specific uses, would be £750–£1000 per week. A systems programmer, whose work is concerned with more fundamental programming concepts, could earn as much as £1200 per week. There are also good freelance opportunities, at upwards of £800 per week, in training people to use PC software packages.

Income levels depend on the following factors:

- How established the programming language is. Expertise in any new one is always in great demand. Training rates can go well over the above-quoted figure where state-of-the-art concepts are involved.

- The length of the contract. There is a trade-off between income and guaranteed work over a longer period.
- The industry. Financial institutions, oil and communications companies pay best.
- The location. Overseas contracts in places that are not generally popular, like Africa or the Middle East, can be very lucrative.

Administration

Most assignments are medium-term contracts of one to three months' duration. Administration over the course of a year, therefore, is not large and is concerned either with making approaches to potential clients or framing proposals as a preliminary to making a feasibility study. The latter can involve a great deal of preparatory work and should therefore not be undertaken without a fee.

Fees are best negotiated on a time basis, not a fixed sum because of the difficulty of assessing how long a job might take. However, the client should be given some indication of the results that can be expected when the assignment is completed. This, of course, is easier with more routine, straightforward and lower level tasks. Here, too, it is easier to forecast completion times.

Occupational hazards

The principal hazard is that most jobs take longer than anticipated. This does not affect the fee if you have negotiated a time rate, but it makes it difficult to schedule work a long way ahead and that, in turn, can create cash-flow problems. Another major hazard is the loneliness of freelance work in a sphere where one relies heavily on brainstorming approaches to problem solving. It is also difficult to keep up with new techniques and programs if you are working on your own. For instance, there is no longer much demand for applications programmers and computer operators. It is important to keep your expertise up to date, either by trying to move into jobs where you can pick up new skills or by attending training courses. However, courses are generally aimed at a corporate market and tend to be expensive. That is one of the disadvantages of freelancing in general – you are responsible for your own career development. When your earning power depends on the up-to-dateness of your skills in areas where there are rapid changes in the kind of skills that are in demand, this is apt to be costly.

Another minor hazard is being buttonholed by people wanting free advice. What might seem to the enquirer to be a simple question can take hours of what ought to be chargeable time to resolve.

Professional organisations

It is not necessary to belong to any particular organisation to operate as a freelance but there are some where membership is useful:

British Computer Society, 13 Mansfield Street, London W1M 0BP; 071-637 0471

Institute of Data Processing Management, 2nd Floor, 21 Russell Street, London WC2B 5UB; 071-240 3304

The Freelance Informer, Reed Business Publishing Group, Quadrant House, The Quadrant, Sutton, Surrey SM2 5AS; 081-661 3996 (also operates a Freelance Informer Helpline; 0273 227244)

The most important thing, however, is to keep up to date with new technical developments.

There is also a useful book, published by *Computer Weekly*, specifically for those thinking of entering this particular freelance market – *Considering Computer Contracting* by Michael Powell.

General Management Consultancy

Basic skills and aptitudes

You need the qualities of a good manager – objectivity, analytical ability, a sense of priorities and a willingness to listen. You also have to be able to get on with people, even more so than someone in line or staff management. Bringing in an outside consultant is often taken to be a criticism of those already doing the job, or can be perceived as such. Yet it is absolutely essential that the consultant gets the full co-operation of all the people in the organisation whom he or she has to see. Often good freelance management consultants are people who have already had some previous consultancy experience. Certainly, it is desirable that they should have worked in a large company with a strong management-skills orientation, so that as a consultant you have a feeling for the essential business of keeping a consultancy assignment on track as far as objectives and time scales are concerned. Some areas of specialised knowledge are essential (for example, physical distribution, knowledge of particular processes or markets, etc). So is the ability to express yourself clearly on paper and in meetings.

Equipment and premises

You can work from home, though having somewhere you can take clients is desirable. You need properly designed letterheads and a brochure that describes what you do and quantifies your achievements. A secretary or access to secretarial services is essential; so many would maintain, is access to a fax machine.

A consultant may be brought in to advise on specific problems such as pay structures or internal communications rather than on wider issues of company policy. However, even if the assignment is narrowly functional, you will still need to know a certain amount about the general context of the business. You need to be near a good business reference library, otherwise you could incur considerable costs in reference books. Reading the main journals of your speciality as well as keeping up with the *Financial Times* is essential.

The market

The larger companies would go to one of the 'names' like McKinsey or PA Consultants. Small companies would not usually employ this type of general consultancy. Clients, therefore, tend to fall in the middle range of 100–200 employees. Some work also comes through other consultants if you have an area of particular expertise. It is also a good idea to cast your bread on the waters by passing work on to a fellow consultant, freelance or otherwise, if you do not feel qualified to handle it, in the hope that the favour may eventually be reciprocated.

Finding work

Work comes mostly, at least initially, through people you know – and it would be unwise to set up as a freelance consultant unless you have some contacts who could be sources of work. After that it is important to keep up with people and send a regular newsletter to those you have worked for or talked to. Job leads can also be found in the specialist press and by attentive reading of the business pages in quality newspapers. At least one day a week has to be devoted to looking for work – even if you have work already going through at the time. You always have to build for the future.

Fees

There are no hard and fast rules to go by, though the charges of major consultants (£800–£1000 a day and upwards) are a yardstick. It is a question of establishing the client's objectives and gauging how much he or she will gain by reaching them. If the gains are very considerable you can ask for more though, by the same token, the amount of work involved will be greater, too. The average length of an assignment is 30 days.

At any rate it is important to state terms and conditions at an early stage. Usually there is no fee for a preliminary consultation, but the clock is set running once a contract has been made or an exchange of letters effected.

Administration

The records that have to be kept are fairly simple, though there are underlying trends that have to be watched. It is possible to be kept busy earning inadequate fees, so accountants should be briefed about your objectives and what the critical ratios are. Clients are generally billed monthly in arrears on the basis of a daily charge. Careful records should be kept of any disbursements made on their behalf. Otherwise, an ordinary cash book from which the accountant can write up the VAT and tax return is all that is required.

Occupational hazards

There are pitfalls for the inexperienced in consultancy that can be overcome only by setting a series of objectives for the course of an assignment at an early stage and regularly reviewing progress towards those objectives; otherwise things can just ramble along without anything being achieved.

One particular hazard is litigation. There have been a few cases of clients initiating legal action against bad advice and some consultants are now taking out professional indemnity insurance. The problem is that anyone can call themselves a 'management consultant' and some have done so to the detriment of serious practitioners.

Professional organisations

It is important to belong to the professional associations of any special discipline to which you lay claim. Apart from that there are several more general professional bodies for consultants: The British Institute of Management (BIM), Management House, Cottingham Road, Corby NN17 1TI; 0536 204222; and the Institute of Management Consultants, 5th Floor, 32–33 Hatton Garden, London EC1N 8DL; 071-242 2140, membership of which is open only to those who have practised in a recognised firm.

Management Consultancy: Marketing

Basic skills and aptitudes

Marketing has been defined as the process of establishing a pattern in the way an organisation sells its products or services and developing a course of action that maximises effectiveness and minimises costs. Thus, it involves a mixture of analytical and creative activities; for instance, producing copy or design based on an analysis of demand in a particular market.

The whole process generally begins with a written report that sets out and quantifies the consultant's initial recommendations. The ability to write such reports is absolutely essential. As for the wide range of skills that implementing them may call for – copywriting, design, print buying, organising events, producing point of sale materials, conducting market research, and so forth – the consultant may not need to supply all of them him or herself, but should know who possesses them and how to deploy them.

A further skill that is also essential is some acquaintance with information technology. Telecommunications, for instance, play an important role in distribution.

Equipment and premises

You can work from home but appearances are important in marketing. Some kind of central *pied à terre*, even if it is only a small workspace in a converted factory or warehouse – such accommodation is increasingly available – is a good idea as soon as you can afford it. These places also often include a secretarial bureau and a photocopying service. You will certainly need to have reports professionally typed and often produced in multiple sets. For longer runs it may be advisable to have them printed. A print shop like Kall Kwik or Prontaprint can do that. Many now also have a fax bureau through which you can send out and receive fax messages. An answering machine is essential, as are a photocopier and fax if you do not have access to them. Many consultants also find a voice recorder useful to have on hand in meetings.

You will also need appropriate reference sources and directories in any areas in which you claim specialist knowledge.

The market

One reason why the last mentioned sphere of equipment is important is that it is essential to specialise, at least to begin with, in the lines of business you know best. If you have been involved in marketing in the confectionery trade, that is where you should start. Small businesses are the best bet – they have very little idea of how to buy services and are often inhibited from seeking advice they badly need because they don't know where to start.

Finding work

There are directories of members produced by the Institute of Marketing and similar listings like those in Hollis's *Press and Public Relations Annual*, but though it is worth being in such lists – especially the free ones – the best sources of work are personal contacts. You should also establish further contacts through your original contacts. Chambers of Commerce and Local Enterprise Agencies are also a potential source of work, since businesses go to them for advice. Having established contacts, it is vital to keep in touch even if no work materialises right away. You have to spend at least 20 per cent of your time marketing yourself.

Presentation is extremely important if you do sight a client. You should find out as much as possible about them beforehand and frame the questions that will enable you to define their objectives in consulting you.

Fees

Generally, there is no charge for an initial meeting, though if it results in a request to put up a more detailed proposal, there should be a fee attached – with the clear understanding, of course, that it does not bind the client beyond that. Fees are charged by the hour, per day or on a lump sum basis, though the latter creates problems in estimating how much work will be involved.

The range of fees charged varies enormously, though the way they are arrived at is uniform: a figure for how much money you aim to earn, plus overheads. An established, big name consultancy now charges its clients £800–£1000 a day, so a figure around a third of that is not unreasonable. Expenses, on a level agreed beforehand, are charged separately. If you are incurring major bills on behalf of a client, say, for buying design services, the basis of reimbursement also needs to be settled before you start paying out money. Does the client, for instance, require supporting invoices from the subcontractor?

Administration

The kind of books you will need to keep depend on the extent of the services you intend to provide, so it is important to consult on this with your accountant – and to keep him or her informed of any changes. Time sheets on clients are a good idea and getting a written commission is essential. If the client does not send you one, you should send a statement of what has been agreed, and ask for it to be confirmed.

Occupational hazards

It is important to stick to what you know best, as far as possible. Taking on an assignment in an area with which you are unfamiliar is tempting, but can lead to trouble. A freelance has to do every job taken on at least as well as an employee and is his or her own advertisement for ill as well as good. What you cannot, unfortunately, avoid sometimes are poor clients; that means not only people who haggle about fees or who are slow payers, but who ask for recommendations and then fail to carry them out. That does not mean that you don't get paid, but a bad client can be a reflection on the consultant, and for no fault of his or her own.

Professional organisations

The Chartered Institute of Marketing, Moor Hall, Cookham, Maidenhead, Berkshire SL6 9QH; 06285 24922, may award membership on application to qualified people without examination, provided they have held a suitable senior and responsible job. This is also true of a number of bodies in related fields; for instance, the Institute of Public Relations, 15 Northburgh Street, London EC1V 0PR; 071-253 5151.

What is now the leading professional qualification is awarded by the Communication, Advertising and Marketing Foundation (CAM), Abford House, 15 Wilton Road, London SW1V 1NJ; 071-828 7506.

Management Research

Basic skills and aptitudes

Some kind of background in a functional area of management is an obvious prerequisite: marketing, personnel, planning or, indeed, research and development itself are cases in point. Some companies have their own trained researchers who then go freelance. You need to know where the sources and contacts are in your specialised area, but you also need the kind of mind that can happily and fruitfully stray off the beaten track. A lot of research is concerned with pursuing apparent red herrings for at least long enough to see whether they yield a further lead. Successful researchers often have some kind of background in activities that are concerned with the association of ideas to form new patterns: publishing, writing, advertising agency work, and so forth.

Equipment and premises

This is a job you can easily do from home and it requires no more than an efficient filing system, photocopying facilities, a telephone and an answering machine. Quite often assignments are conducted on the client's premises. This is preferable if extensive telephoning is required – otherwise you will have to allow for that in your fee. Problems do, however, arise when a client wants to organise a preliminary meeting on neutral ground. Private accommodation is not usually a suitable venue for that and it tends to look unprofessional. Membership of a club can be a good investment for this purpose. Some minor, but none the less comfortable and quite imposing looking, clubs charge only a modest annual subscription.

A microcomputer, if you know how to use it, is ideal for creating the databases that allow a quick search for information and easy updating. You will also need the basic directories in your chosen specialisation and these can be quite costly – some specialist publications of this kind now cost over £100. On the other hand, if you have a good business reference library nearby, it should hold at least the main sources – though with the cutback in library funds, they are frequently now not up to date.

The market
The market depends on the nature of the specialisation. There is, for instance, little call for generalised market research but if you have experience of a particular sector, either geographically or by product, and can ally it to a news item about a venture by a particular company, they may well be interested in hearing from you. The assumption behind freelancing in this sphere is that you have a background in some management speciality and therefore have some idea of where the market lies.

Finding work
Finding work as a freelance market researcher calls for application above all of that skill itself: it is a question of reading the financial news and the trade/specialist journals in your sphere for leads to opportunities and then identifying the right person to write to about the service you can offer. Getting in touch with trade associations and Chambers of Commerce is also worthwhile. This is also one of the rather rare fields where advertising your skills in selected specialist publications can be rewarding. However, the most likely source of work initially is usually your existing contacts; quite often your last employer is among these.

Both the market itself, and the methods you apply in finding work, may require you to refer to a variety of media and sources, including foreign ones. Fluency in at least one foreign language is therefore a great advantage.

Fees
Like the work itself, these vary enormously. They depend, to a large extent, on how affluent your sector of the market is, how much competition you have and how much real expertise is required to dig out what your clients want to know. There are freelances who ask – and get – £250–£300 a day. There are others who charge less than half that. The general rule is to charge what the traffic will bear in the sector in which you are operating and to take account of special factors like speed. Expenses should, wherever possible, be charged extra though this is something that should be agreed beforehand.

Administration
The administration of charging for the assignment is simple – it is

merely a question of keeping a record of costs that are to be charged back to the client and of the time taken if the job is on an hourly basis. Keeping the database of the information in which you specialise is much more complicated and will depend on an excellent up-to-date filing system; ideally, an electronic one. You should also keep records of clients and prospects. Quite a lot of business is in the form of repeat jobs from existing clients, so it is vital to know the state of the game when you were last in touch. It is all too easy, and creates a bad impression, to have forgotten what you last did for a particular client if you have a number of assignments on the go.

Occupational hazards

One of the big problems, when you are very busy, is that you have no time to look for other jobs: you can come to the end of a lucrative series of assignments and find you have no work to follow that.

Getting paid on time can, as with other types of freelance work, be a problem: small clients often have cash-flow difficulties; large ones play for time or have extensive bureaucracies in which payment is held up simply because payments have to be approved by some third party. If you have a very strong bargaining position you can sometimes get part payment in advance.

The other hazard, arising out of that, is that the client may claim that you have not provided exactly the information that he or she wanted and will withhold part of the payment for that reason. There is very little you can do about this legally, but it is essential that you receive and agree a clear brief at the start of the assignment.

Professional organisations

There are no professional bodies for researchers as such, but it is advisable to join the one that relates to your special field. Quite often professional bodies issue directories of people providing special services and have newsletters of journals that provide job leads.

Management Information Broking

Basic skills and aptitudes

Management information and intelligence would be on a specific topic – a market or a management function, for instance. An information provider would have to have a background of knowl-edge in the topic concerned, plus experience in tracking down and putting together specific themes within it. The kind of person best qualified to do that might well be someone with experience as an industrial or organisational librarian and basic computer skills.

Equipment and premises

Possession of a microcomputer is now absolutely essential, and is obviously a great help in creating a database, retrieving information and matching it to client requirements.

The market

Companies of all sizes, nationalised industries and local authorities look for this service. In smaller companies the client would probably be the managing director. In larger organisations he or she would be a functional head, like the personnel or marketing director.

Finding work

Apart from personal referrals – you would probably have to start off with at least one reasonably established client – the best source would be professional and institutional libraries who often get enquiries that are too specific and too detailed for them to handle. Places like the CBI and BIM libraries, in particular, get many information requests of this kind. Work can also be generated simply from the process of conducting enquiries; for example, when a letter or a questionnaire goes out to an information source, a promotional brochure can be sent out with it.

Fees

These can be hourly, on a per assignment basis or in the form of a retainer. Charges are difficult to quantify exactly – they vary with the difficulty of the job, but £25–£35 an hour would be a reasonable average by 1991 prices. If the fees are in the form of a retainer, it is wise to offer some incentive or visible sign of activity; a regular newsletter about the state of the art, for instance.

Administration

The amount of administration varies with the nature of the service being offered. Where the information broker is on a retainer and has a number of clients, some kind of diary will have to be kept of when renewals are due, and there will have to be a mailing list of recipients of the newsletter or whatever other service is offered. Information and information sources will also have to be organised so that they can be accessed easily. As stated previously, this is an ideal field for the microcomputer, though it can be done with a good filing system, a well-organised mind, and the availability of a good typist.

Occupational hazards

Anybody who is offering information and advice is in danger of accidentally getting it wrong. Legal action for that reason has been rare in the UK so far, though it is quite common in the USA. Since American practices tend to spread across the Atlantic, some consultants are considering taking out professional indemnity insurance. The premiums for an occupation of this nature would probably be modest, particularly since there have been few claims so far.

Professional organisations
Information brokers would find it worthwhile to belong to the professional institutes of their speciality; and, if they are librarians, to the Library Association.

Management Consultancy: Specialist Knowledge Transfer

Basic skills and aptitudes
Although management consultancy is largely considered to be concerned with broad organisational and financial problems, it often relates to quite specific areas of knowledge. It is here that freelances come into their own, both in dealing directly with clients and as subcontractors to larger consultancy firms. Firms often do not have enough work of any particular kind in specialist areas to justify taking on their own staff.

It has to be assumed that in order to practise as a specialist consultant you have a thorough knowledge of the subject and can demonstrate a track record of achievement in your sphere; for instance, if your specialist knowledge is in magazine distribution, that you have some background in computerised methods of updating subscription lists, in negotiating special rates with the Post Office and in the pros and cons of various marketing strategies and the methods of implementing them. As in other kinds of consultancy, you also have to be able to put over verbal presentations and to write clear, well-structured and persuasive reports.

Equipment and premises
You can work from home, at least initially, and arrange to see clients at their offices. You do, however, need decent stationery and cards, an answering machine and someone who can type letters and reports to good secretarial standards. The latter should be presented in plastic binders, but there is no need to go to vast expense over them. They should not look cheap and scruffy, but neither should they give the client the impression that he or she is paying for the sizzle rather than the steak. Where speed of communication is essential, you might have to consider installing

fax. You might also find it a good marketing point to demonstrate computer literacy by using a word processor – apart from the fact that such a machine will probably enable you to get by without a secretary.

For your own promotional purposes, you should also have folders containing details of past work you have done, and offprints of any articles about you and your work.

The market

The growth in management consultancy has come about because clients increasingly use consultants not only to advise on organisational problems, but also to carry out feasibility studies and to look after specific functions and assignments – essentially as subcontractors in areas where in-house skills are lacking; for instance, to investigate the viability of entering a particular product or geographic market and to establish what skills and resources they need to do so.

Finding work

Most people start by approaching firms they know – not only because of the value of personal contacts, but because they already have some insight into the circumstances and the kind of help they require.

After that, finding work is a matter of using initial contacts to build further ones and keeping a close eye for possible work leads on the business sections of the national press and on reports and information in the trade press. Making yourself known by drawing successful and interesting assignments to the attention of editors can also be very effective – but you should get clearance to do so from your clients first, because of the confidentiality factor.

Fees

Consultancy fees are usually on a daily basis and range between £200–£400 per day. It works out much cheaper to use a freelance than to go to a management consultancy firm, where the client is charged with overheads as well as the individual consultant's time. A good consultancy firm will charge about three times that and more and the client should tactfully be made aware of that if he or she quibbles about rates.

The usual procedure is to prepare a preliminary study and a short report, spelling out what is involved and roughly how long the job will take. Preparing that study will take two to three days and this raises the difficult issue of how much preliminary work you should do for nothing. That is very much a question of individual judgement.

The general feeling is that if the initiative has come from you – that is, if you have made the proposal that an organisation should use your services as a consultant and they respond to that – it has to be regarded as a promotional cost. If they have contacted you in the first instance, they would expect to be charged, though not for a preliminary discussion.

Administration

Records relating to each job will have to be kept. You should also notify your bank manager of the nature of your business because payments from clients, though often quite large, can be episodic. If you are appointed to a consultancy on a contractual footing, you should take out some form of indemnity insurance to protect your liability against giving wrong advice.

Occupational hazards

The chief hazard is that you have to spend about 50 per cent of your time chasing work. It can be a costly process, involving travel, a good deal of informal wining and dining which is not tax deductible, and putting together presentations to prospects about half of whom then fall by the wayside.

Professional organisations

There are no professional organisations for freelance management consultants, though there are some informal local networks. Try your local enterprise agency or Chamber of Commerce for information on them.

There is a growing number of organisations and enterprises who offer, through advertisements in the press, what is essentially an agency service for independent consultants. The basis of payment is usually an upfront joining fee and a percentage of the contract value of any work that is obtained through the organisation. None of them has been in operation for long enough for any opinion to be formed about them, but as a general principle it is unwise to part with money upfront on any business venture unless there is a reasonable hope that it can be recovered out of profits within two to three years. So the first question to ask is whether promises made to this effect can be substantiated, for instance from the experience of others using the service. Other key questions are:

- How is the organisation marketing the services of its members?
- What sort of work has it been able to obtain for them and in what fee ranges?

- Are commissions payable only on work that is obtained directly and attributably through the service?
- Who does the client pay? If it is the agency, you may be treated by the Inland Revenue as its employee and be taxed on a PAYE basis. Another question to be raised where payment is made to an intermediary is when he or she pays you. It ought to be on completion of the work, or within 30 days of that, *not* when the agent is paid by the client. The intermediary ought to be taking the responsibility for collection, and the risk.

12
Business Services

Introduction
Peripheral business services like PR, research, publicity and other activities that are not essential to corporate survival tend to be the first to be cut back in a recession, all the more so since they usually lack powerful patronage in the structure of office politics. The need for the work to be done does not, however, go away and when this is perceived the tendency is to put it out to freelances rather than to re-hire – quite often to the people who were doing it before and who are now operating as freelances. When things get really difficult, large companies will cut even into functional areas like accounting and sales. This can be an opportunity for smaller firms to pick up the services of freelances in areas where expertise is badly needed, but where volumes are not large enough to enable them to hire it for themselves on a full-time basis.

One reason why business services can be hard to justify within a company is that, although there is a demand for them, it is not sufficiently large to be economic. However, when these are shared between several clients they can be very lucrative for a freelance: thus, an activity carried on for two different firms will double the revenue without notably increasing costs. This can, however, leave a problem of confidentiality, for instance, in something like the preparation of market research. Clients should never be given the feeling that you are serving two masters, even when this is to some extent an inevitable consequence of working as a freelance.

Approaches from potential clients mostly come through contacts and recommendations, but there are ways of facilitating the process. It is, for instance, worth putting your name with organisations like Chambers of Commerce and Local Enterprise Agencies who may be contacted by firms who need various kinds of services. You should also have a brief descriptive brochure explaining what you do, listing your credentials and giving the names of any clients who would be willing for you to mention them.

Ideally, the way to grow to a point where your service is producing a viable income is gradually to increase your client base. Where this is not possible or proves to be difficult, the answer is to add on value which will enable you to charge more. Thus, a translator may branch out into interpreting or into a specialised area like translating technical literature. Other services may be marketed across a variety of clients. Private investigation, for instance, is a growth area despite the changes in the divorce laws and the consequent reduction of investigation into marital break-up. It has moved into the business field where personal security and industrial counter-espionage are now providing lucrative and interesting high-level work. It is essential, however, to graft expansion on to a subject you already know. The potential of either course of action should be studied before you start as a freelance. Though a business plan taking you several moves ahead is essential if you need to borrow money, it is equally important if the investment is merely your own time and skill.

Export Sales Representation

Basic skills and aptitudes

Since freelance representatives work wholly or largely on commission, the obvious prerequisite is selling ability: a mixture of confidence, good contacts among buyers and enough product knowledge to answer basic questions about what you are selling. As an export salesman you ought to know at least one major European language: Spanish, French, German or Italian are the preferred ones. You also ought to be reasonably conversant with customs and shipping procedures because it is quite likely that some of your clients will need help with documentation. The mere fact that they are employing a freelance representative is an indication of the fact that they are less than completely familiar with exporting. To facilitate their understanding they may require you to produce reports. They will certainly expect you to make judgements on the creditworthiness of the customers to whom you are selling. Finally, you will need a fair degree of organising and administrative ability in order to plan your trips in the most cost-effective way; and you will need to be prepared to travel – not necessarily for long periods at a time, but certainly for a large part of the year in total.

Equipment and premises

Whether you need a car for your work depends on your territory and the nature of your representation. In western Europe, though, you will probably be doing at least some of your trips in that way. Apart from that you will need a telex or fax, an answering service, an office from which to organise your paperwork and possible storage space for samples. Since you will be out of the country for extended spells, this is one freelance activity where you will need to employ staff, or at any rate a member of the family, to handle calls and pass on urgent messages. A good deal of secretarial work may also be involved to book appointments and make travel arrangements.

The market
As an intermediary you have to resolve two marketing problems. First, there is the question of finding takers for your services, of which more below, but in essence it is a matter of seeking out firms and manufacturers who cannot afford a sales force of their own, either in export generally or in a particular territory. Second, you have to be reasonably sure that there is at least a potential sale for what they are producing – both for their sake and yours. This will involve a certain amount of preliminary research into demand and into competition in terms of quality and price.

Finding work
Most of your clients will be firms with a turnover of £500,000 or under, who would not find it economic to employ their own sales force. The most attractive propositions here are in industries with a lot of growth potential, so it is worth keeping an eye on the trade, technical and business press, as well as fairs and exhibitions, for interesting new arrivals on the corporate scene who might be open to an approach. However, building up a list of firms to represent ought to be a systematic process of putting together coherent and related groups rather than a ragbag. Too many random agencies could involve you in uneconomic journeys to scattered calls. The other trap to beware of, particularly when you are trying to put together a group of agencies at the beginning, is taking on firms whose product, for one reason or another, has very little chance of making an impact. The effect of taking on no-hopers or what you suspect might be a low-quality weirdo is to detract from the better lines you are carrying. Yet a third problem is carrying directly competing lines; you may end up by pleasing neither principal. No one will think the worse of you if you deliberate before taking on an agency and look carefully at such factors as their general reputation for quality and efficiency of supply and their policy on credit and collection.

Fees
Generally, there is a commission based on percentage of turnover: 10 per cent is normal in many forms of enterprise. In order to make export representation even viable on this basis you must start with at least £400,000 worth of turnover and you will not begin to show a profit until you exceed £600,000. The reason is that travel and

accommodation costs alone will be very high. You must ensure that commission is paid on invoice – not on payment by the customer. Ideally, of course, a retainer from one or more of the people you represent is worth negotiating, since you will incur costs before you get paid.

It is important to clarify beforehand if there is anything you are required to do in addition to selling. Some principals expect freelance reps to mail sales material to customers and to be responsible for pressurising slow payers. If such additional services are called for, you will have to follow the custom of your own particular activity about whether this is subject to an extra charge or comes within the commission percentage.

Administration

The amount of administration is much greater than if you are employed, partly because you will not automatically have access to the same channels of information about customers and products, such as turnover figures per account or territory, or letters from principals to customers. Communication with those out in the field, often a problem within organisations, becomes doubly problematic when you are working outside, so you will have to make sure the channels are drawn up in such a way that you are kept informed of all the things you need to know to do the job effectively. You will also have to plan your own trips a long way ahead. Journeys become longer and more complex if you carry a larger number of lines. You may also have to organise participation in trade fairs and other selling occasions, and become involved in principals' general promotional activities.

Occupational hazards

Psychologically, loneliness is the biggest hazard facing the export rep, though those who have been doing the job for a long time tend to build up their own overseas friends and contacts. The other side of the coin is that you tend to lose touch with friends and even family at home. It is important to take active steps to keep your UK social life going – not always easy when periods in the UK are filled with making plans for further trips, meetings with principals, and so forth.

From a business point of view one of the biggest hazards is that there can be a penalty in success; once you build turnover up to a good level, your commission figures may well tempt a principal into thinking it was time he appointed someone of his own – just at the point, of course, where the business is beginning to look profitable for you. For this reason it is important to have contracts for at least a couple of years, with at least six months' notice and, if possible, automatic renewal facilities unless there is formal notification to the contrary. At the other end of the scale, you are at the mercy of principals who may not really be committed to export; you and your customers come last in the scale of priorities, which makes it impossible to build up turnover to viable levels. Ultimately, also, you are dependent on the honesty of principals and the efficiency of their accounts department in calculating the turnover and hence the amount of your commission.

Professional organisations

A useful trade body is the Institute of Export, Export House, 64 Clifton Street, London EC2A 4HB; 071-247 9812. In practical terms, though, a course in business studies is more likely to be relevant.

Accountancy

Basic skills and aptitudes

Although limited companies have to have their books audited by a qualified accountant – that is, a member of one of the UK's recognised institutes of chartered accountants – no such conditions are laid down for looking after the financial records of self-employed people operating as sole traders or partnerships, nor do you have to have any particular qualifications to prepare VAT returns. It is, however, generally advisable to have had some experience of working in an accountant's office to learn the basics of preparing management accounts and to be able to advise clients on what books and records they are likely to need.

Preparing tax returns is a somewhat greyer area. Strictly speaking, here again there is no statutory requirement for formal qualifications and a simple tax return calls for no more than an ability to collect and marshal the information you have asked the client to produce for you. However, at a slightly higher level of sophistication, it helps to have taken the exams of the Institute of Taxation (ATII). Apart from giving you a deeper insight into taxation principles, it also enhances your credibility with the tax inspector.

Equipment and premises

Apart from a filing cabinet, a calculator, a personal computer and the annual purchase of some basic reference such as *The Stoy Hayward Business Tax Guide*, no equipment is needed.

The market

The obvious markets are conventional small businesses, but they are only part of a much larger picture of self-employed individuals, employees engaged in part-time earning activities, doctors, small professional practices and partnerships of various kinds, and, indeed, the whole panoply of entrepreneurial activities spread across the Yellow Pages and newspaper classified advertising.

Finding work

As with many other skill-based services, a lot of work comes in by word of mouth, spread by satisfied clients. However, the process can be initiated by putting your name down with Local Enterprise Agencies who deal with hundreds of entrepreneurs in the course of the year. If you are living in a city you could easily put your name down with more than one such body because freelance accountancy is an occupation where it is easy to be mobile. Citizens' Advice Bureaux are also a possible source of work, since they are often approached by private individuals who have got their tax affairs in a tangle. Private local agencies of the kind referred to in Chapter 8 (page 71) are likely to bring you more affluent middle-class clients, both private individuals and those running small businesses.

Fees

It is best to charge an hourly rate, based somewhat on the difficulty of the task concerned. For ordinary book- and record-keeping the fee is £16–£20 an hour, and for preparing a tax return or a set of management accounts around £25–£35 an hour. This is very competitive compared to qualified accountants who charge anything from £60 an hour upwards. Indeed, the extremely high fees charged by professional accounting practices in themselves offer growing opportunities to freelances.

Administration

Some administrative ability is obviously required because the ability to analyse financial information and organise what is sometimes an exceedingly untidy set of facts and figures into a tax return is essential to the job. You have to be able to keep clients' records in a competent fashion, or to show them how to do this. A freelance accountant himself needs no very elaborate records other than a diary of reminders about when particular items need to be attended to on behalf of clients.

Occupational hazards

One of the big problems about working by yourself in an area that can become quite technical is that there is no back-up when you have to go outside your personal expertise; for instance, on a tax question or the lay-out of accounts in a type of business with which you are unfamiliar. The tendency for professional accounting practices to become bigger is partly due to the fact that they need to call on an ever-growing circle of technical skills as legislation becomes more complex. As a freelance you are moving in the reverse direction, though this is not harmful provided you understand the implied limitations. The fact that your work is likely to be concerned with routine financial matters means, however, that it has a strong element of seasonality: March, April, May – the months around the end of the tax year – are by far the busiest. It is difficult to space out your work unless your skills fall into specialist areas that will give you a reasonable cash flow throughout the year.

Professional organisations

There are none for freelances though, of course, there are professional institutes for chartered accountants in England, Scotland and Ireland. Some freelances belong to the Institute of Taxation, 12 Upper Belgrave Street, London SW1X 8BB; 071-235 9381. Membership is by examination.

Word Processing

Basic skills and aptitudes

Secretarial skills can be expanded fairly easily into word processing ones at day or evening courses, though you can also take a direct route into word processing without previous typing experience. An increasing number of such courses are being provided by local authorities, and they are also offered by private sector colleges and educational institutes. In either case, before committing money and time to training, you should find out how much 'hands-on' experience will be provided. There ought to be at least one keyboard and screen to every two people on the course.

Equipment and premises

You will obviously need a word processor – now generally a microcomputer with a word processing program – plus printer. Amstrad sell a complete system from £350 plus VAT, while a more sophisticated machine that runs IBM programs costs in the region of £750–£1250. You can also effect savings by shopping around, but most of the experts reckon that this is a false economy unless you already know a lot about microcomputers. Otherwise, it is worth paying a little extra for the initial advice, aftersales service and help over teething troubles that you should get from an established dealer – and that you will not get if you are 'buying a box'.

In making your choice, you should be clear in your mind about the range of tasks you want the word processor to perform, because that will determine the software you need to go with your machine and also the capacity of the hardware. It may, in fact, turn out that you do not need a word processor at all, but merely an electronic typewriter with a memory and a few words of display. In this, as in other freelance fields, the best plan is to hold off making a major financial commitment until you are sure it can pay its way.

The market
Word processing can be most effectively used by firms or organisations who have to send out multiple copies of personalised letters; for instance, recruitment agencies who may need to reply to large numbers of applicants in response to a job advertisement or a charity making an appeal to a group of prospects on a mailing list. Word processors are also ideal for recording, storing, maintaining and classifying mailing lists; for producing drafts of documents that need updating and revision; and, increasingly, for putting texts on a disk which can then be linked into a typesetting facility.

Finding work
Work mostly comes from existing contacts, possibly previous employers, and by word of mouth. Advertising is not effective because of the diffuse nature of the market. However, an intelligent reading of the local press for news items that might indicate a firm is embarking on an activity that calls for the services of an external word processing person can produce results.

Fees
There are various methods of charging, according to the nature of the task being performed: storing names and addresses on a mailing list, printing and storing letters, producing addressed envelopes, typing drafts of a document, creating various classifications in a list, and so forth. The simplest course of action, however, is to quote an hourly rate – at least £12 an hour. The client should be charged for stationery, since this can be a hefty additional cost.

Administration
The main factor is the kind of housekeeping that is associated with microcomputers – marking the contents of disks and creating files from which information can be readily retrieved.

Occupational hazards
Although computers are supposed to take the tedium out of routine tasks, there are some jobs that remain obstinately boring

and dreary. One of these is creating and maintaining mailing lists and for that reason it is the kind of function that may be subcontracted; and because it is not inherently difficult it is hard to justify the premium charge that it ought to carry. At the same time, freelances who have bought a microcomputer may find it necessary to take on drudgery tasks to help pay for the machine.

The other hazard is ergonomic. Comfortable seating and the correct lighting are essential if you have to sit in front of a screen for hours. In general, it is thought that five to six hours a day working directly on a word processor is about as much as anyone should do. There are also fears, unsubstantiated as yet, that the foetus may be harmed if a pregnant woman spends hours at a VDU screen.

Professional organisations

There are quite a number of users' clubs related to particular makes of hardware. These are encouraged by manufacturers and are mainly for computer buffs, though they do on occasion serve as a grapevine for news of work.

Freelancing in Public Relations

Basic skills and aptitudes

Although there are other forms of freelance PR than writing – photography, preparing illustrations and organising promotional tours, events and receptions all come into that category – most PR activities involve some writing. A journalistic background – the ability to write usable press releases, at any rate – is essential. So are good contacts with journalists. You have to know people to ring up and also to put the story to them in such a way that they will want to use it. This requires an ability to see the news angle in what might otherwise appear to be – and often is – a somewhat routine piece of information.

Equipment and premises

Most PR freelances work from home, with the aid of the usual items of journalist's equipment – an answering machine, a word processor, fax and a photocopier or access to one. Some people take desk space in an established PR agency – these agencies use freelances extensively – but this may not be a good idea. For one thing an agency that has desk space available is probably not a thriving one. Furthermore, it is difficult to keep track of costs, especially on major items like telephone bills and on shares of overhead costs. If you go into a desk space arrangement, it is essential to sort out beforehand who pays for what.

The market

Few companies use PR freelances direct, though if you know people in marketing departments you can get assignments to write brochures, manuals and advertising copy or to publicise particular occasions on the basis of personal contacts. It is more usual, though, to freelance for a PR agency.

Finding work

In approaching agencies with whom you have not previously worked, it is obviously important to define what you do. It is useful to have a specialisation. Computers, telecommunications and video are 'hot' at the moment and there is also a lot of interest in lifestyle and leisure subjects. Apart from knowing people in agencies, there are several ways of marketing yourself. Direct mail shots to PR and advertising agencies can work if they are good and arrive at an opportune moment. Lists of such agencies are contained in Hollis's *Press and Public Relations Annual,* in the *Advertiser's Annual* and in *The Creative Handbook.* You need to aim your approach at the special field of the agency concerned, which is usually stated in such directories. It is also a good idea to keep an eye on PR staff ads in magazines like *Campaign* and *Marketing Week* – they will sometimes take on a freelance to tide them over if they cannot find someone to fill a more permanent position – or they might decide that a freelance is the better option.

Fees

Fees depend somewhat on how well known you are, how urgent the job is and to what extent you can more or less guarantee national media coverage of some kind. In the latter case you can get £250 plus per 1000 words as a writer. Otherwise, you will be more likely to receive either a flat fee per job or payment by the day at anything between £100 and £200. It is sometimes possible to get an advance of half to one-third of the agreed amount.

Administration

Whatever is agreed about terms should be confirmed in writing: the price, what is to be delivered, the expenses limit and what is regarded as a fair charge to expenses. It is also important to make sure that the brief is clear and that it is understood by both parties. Brief notes of meetings with clients should be kept and sent to the client if he or she does not send them to you on his or her own initiative.

Financial records are fairly simple. A cash book showing income and expenditure, coded by client, is sufficient.

Occupational hazards

All news media are bombarded with PR handouts of various kinds and it is not at all easy to get coverage for things that are not obviously newsworthy. The biggest hazard is to convince clients that you are working for them when they are not getting coverage, despite your efforts.

Professional organisations

Many PR people belong to the NUJ if their background is in journalism. There are no obvious advantages in that from a job-getting or negotiating point of view, but most feel that it increases their credibility with clients. This is also true of membership of the Institute of Public Relations, 15 Northburgh Street, London EC1V 0PR; 071-253 5151.

Market Research Interviewing

Basic skills and aptitudes

Market research interviewing requires no particular qualifications though it calls for good powers of observation, particularly of the social nuances that would, for instance, distinguish a genuine yuppie from someone who merely wants to look like one. The reason is that market research is concerned with finding out what a social cross-section of consumers think about a product or service that is either already on the market or is being considered for launching. It may also be concerned with examining attitudes to issues or even trends, such as how people feel about smoking or about the EC.

Market research organisations compile a detailed questionnaire to test public reactions to such matters and the idea is that research interviewers, invariably freelances, are asked to seek out and question people who will provide a fair sample of the population. The completed questionnaires are returned to the market research company who collate the results, analyse them and then present a report to their client. The researcher may be asked to find a certain class 'mix', or be directed to seek out households with specific characteristics; for example, women under 35 with a child at school in a middle-class neighbourhood. There are also more difficult – and therefore better paid – types of research interview, where questions are put to executives or members of professions that are con-nected with their job.

For the latter type of interview some background or training in the field in question is generally needed. But in the majority of cases, the main qualifications are good health (a fair amount of standing at street corners or walking around residential areas is entailed), availability at short notice and sometimes at odd hours and absolute integrity. That is not just a question of not 'fiddling' the questionnaires by sending in entries for people who have not been seen. It also means adhering strictly to the sequence of questions set out and never prompting the respondent, even by a gesture or tone of voice. The validity of the whole exercise depends on the neutrality of the interviewer.

The skills, therefore, are not those of a journalist or a TV interviewer, though tact, perception and the ability to get on with a wide variety of people are essential. You also have to be fairly thick-skinned, at least up to salesperson standards.

Market research interviewing calls for some training and this is given by the firms in the business, though it is fairly brief. The drop-out rate is said to be quite high – as high as 50 per cent.

Equipment and premises
No special equipment is needed, though in rural areas a car is essential.

The market
There are about ten major market research companies and quite a number of minor ones. If you are interested in applying to them for training you should write to: The Market Research Society, 15 Northburgh Street, London EC1V 0AH; 071-490 4911. They will put you in touch with the one nearest your home, though it must be said that because of the close relationship between market research and advertising, most of the large companies are, like advertising agencies, in the London area.

Finding work
Once you are established as a reliable interviewer, work will come in from the companies. The large ones have contracts with clients which ensures a steady flow of work for researchers. Many interviewers work for more than one firm which is, of course, an almost essential prerequisite to being recognised by the Inland Revenue as a self-employed person rather than one who is, to all intents and purposes from the tax point of view, a contract employee.

Working for more than one market research firm obviously raises problems of confidentiality. As an interviewer you are bound by a strict code of conduct that prohibits you from disclosing one client's business to another. Indeed, you are also prohibited from disclosing to the interviewee anything about the product or service for whom the research is being done. In most cases, you are not told the name of the client by the research company in any case.

There is now a growing tendency for market researchers to be treated as employees by the Inland Revenue.

Fees

Consumer interviews are paid at a rate of between £25 and £35 per day, plus expenses. The same rate applies if you are called in for a briefing before you embark on fieldwork. Some companies pay you during the brief three- to four-day training period, but most only cover expenses because of the high drop-out rate previously referred to.

Depth interviews, or industrial ones conducted with senior executives or professional people, are rather better paid. Whereas most of the people doing consumer interviews are housewives earning extra money, depth interviewers are full-time freelances who can earn £10,000–£12,000 a year.

Administration

A fair amount of paperwork is involved. Keeping a record of hours and expenses is easy, but you also have to check very carefully the documentation that comes in from the companies. The questionnaires can be lengthy and complicated and, human error being what it is, you need to see that everything you are supposed to receive is included. Sometimes you are asked to complete two or three questionnaires and send them back to the company for checking before you proceed any further, so that they can see whether any changes need to be made in the type and sequence of questions. Whatever their requirements, it is essential that completed questionnaires are returned as soon and as safely as possible. Some researchers recommend that you should get a postal receipt for anything you return. You should never leave that part of the job to any third person, whatever procedure you adopt.

Occupational hazards

Interviewers do not always appreciate that the work may take up time in the evenings and at weekends (because these are the only times when certain types of people can be found). It may also be difficult on occasion to find the kind of respondents specified in the brief. That may involve long, unproductive hours knocking on doors and trying to find the class/age/occupation mix that fits.

Working outdoors and standing on the streets in mid-winter manipulating paperwork in the wind and rain is not something for which everyone is suited. Outside urban areas, the job could mean considerable travel. Working in a 50-mile radius is not uncommon, and notice of an assignment can be short. A manufacturer facing an urgent problem over a product can call on the services of a research company at a few days' notice.

Professional organisations

Membership of the Market Research Society (for address and phone number, see page 120) is open to individuals sponsored by two members. There is a small annual subscription which also covers insurance, some tax advice and provides a newsletter. Members are listed in the Society's yearbook, together with a note of their special fields of activity.

Conference Organising

Basic skills and aptitudes

Although this is a freelance activity that calls for a high degree of organising, administrative and planning ability, it needs less experience than many of the other occupations described. There are no formal qualifications required and anyone with a clear head who has been involved in conference organising as an employee ought to be able to make a fair shot at it, provided he or she establishes from the outset with the client who exactly is responsible for which aspects of the event. Previous experience with even a couple of conferences should highlight what the main problem areas are likely to be and how to avoid them.

Equipment and premises

Much of the planning work can be done from home, but you should be aware that the cost of implementation can be considerable. A conference run as a commercial venture – not all are: there are also in-house conferences by firms for their own staff and/or customers – will call for a mailing of anything from 5000 pieces upwards to attract a worthwhile audience. Lists of potential delegates can generally be bought from brokers, but this still leaves the organiser to make arrangements for the stuffing of thousands of envelopes and the printing of an equal number of letters and brochures. Telephone bills also run very high. It may therefore be necessary for the organiser to run a substantial part of the venture from the client's offices, using facilities such as photocopying, fax, the mailroom, in-house printing and meeting rooms.

The market

Numerically the market is very large – it is reckoned that there are some 50,000 conferences and workshops organised in the UK per year for audiences of 25 or more people, and that the market is growing by 12 per cent annually. Organisations involved in holding conferences range from political parties and learned or professional societies down to medium-sized firms. Occasions range from the propagandistic and the dissemination of information (such as press conferences and product launches) to those with an intrinsic and direct commercial objective (for example, explaining a sophisticated new tax avoidance scheme to accountants who are willing to pay a large fee to listen to expert advice).

Finding work

Firms who handle their own conferences are well aware of the amount of executive time it takes. It has been reckoned that a conference of 200 people requires 300 senior staff hours to organise, and in fact there is an irreducible amount of work involved in the planning and marketing stages, irrespective of the number of delegates. Thus, an approach from a competent freelance is usually welcomed, if it comes at the right moment. This is partly a question of keeping your ear to the ground, looking out for firms in your neighbourhood who are launching a new product or who may have some specialised information which they want to market. Most commonly, though, work comes by word of mouth. If you are interested in conference organising, put the word about.

Fees

Though, as stated earlier, there is an irreducible amount of administration involved at the planning stage, no matter how many delegates attend, once bookings are received, the amount of work is to some extent directly related to the numbers involved. Some organisers make a capitation charge. If you pitch it high enough, this can be very profitable in the case of larger conferences, but it means that you share the risk if the take-up turns out to be disappointing. Before accepting a capitation-based formula, you must therefore be reasonably sure that the client is investing sufficient money and effort on marketing the conference. The alternative is to charge an hourly rate, plus expenses. A flat fee is not a good idea unless you are reasonably certain about exactly how much work will be involved.

That is in any case an important point to try and settle because it depends on what aspects you are to take responsibility for. Generally, it is the client's job to define the objectives of the occasion (though you may find that he or she is hazier about this than you would expect) and to find and brief the speakers. The organiser may be responsible for all or any of the following: advising on marketing the conference, writing the brochure, organising the mailing, finding the venue, setting up the catering procedures, ensuring the availability and testing of audio-visual facilities, handling the bookings, looking after signposting at the venue, arranging the preparation of delegate packs, and administering reception and ticketing of delegates. Who is responsible for which of these duties needs to be clarified from the beginning.

Administration

A considerable amount of administrative time and skill is involved – indeed, conference organising is essentially an administrative job, in which every step has to be confirmed in writing, if possible, after due consideration of all the things that could go wrong. For instance, will the delegates be able to find the venue? Will the space booked be available on the day? A considerable amount of financial housekeeping is involved if you are looking after the money, with careful notes being kept of a wide variety of expenses as well as receipts. Because of the amount of preparatory work that arises, long lead times are necessary. It takes at least three months to arrange all the details for even a small conference, from briefing to D Day. An international one will need to be planned a year ahead.

Occupational hazards

The chief hazard is that of things going wrong. There are boring speakers, which the organisers can do little about, though it is a good idea to try and persuade the client not to schedule the drier topics straight after what for some delegates might be too liquid a lunch. Apart from that the possibilities for foul-ups are, unfortunately, endless. But they can mostly be avoided by good planning, related to action for contingencies.

Professional organisations

The Association of Conference Executives United Kingdom (ACE UK), Riverside House, 160 High Street, Huntingdon, Cambs PE18 6SG; 0480 57595.

Organising Professional Library and Information Systems

Basic skills and aptitudes

There are two aspects to this kind of work. One might be termed simple library maintenance: arranging books, periodicals and catalogues from specialist suppliers and updating whatever system has been installed or already exists under which members of a professional office can look up sources. It may also involve ordering new materials and logging their arrival – books in particular – circulating journals and making sure that borrowings are returned:

very much the kind of thing that a librarian in an ordinary lending library has to do. Work of this nature does not require special knowledge, though obviously a general training as a librarian would be a great asset.

A more sophisticated extension of this work is the development of information systems and this may require a knowledge of the subject matter itself. For instance, an architectural librarian might be called on to supply a list of all floor covering materials for a partner and this would call for a knowledge of the building industry, or at least of the information sources within it. The same would be true in a legal library, where the librarian might be asked to supply a list of cases similar to one under discussion. In information librarianship a knowledge of new technology and the ability to compile and retrieve from databases on a microcomputer is essential.

Apart from the usual librarian skills of tidiness and logicality, there is a further very important aptitude involved if you work as a freelance, and that is adaptability. It is not a question of forcing your system on a captive customer as it can be in an ordinary library. Rather, it is a matter of studying how information is already organised, improving it where necessary but in the main working within a framework that is already there. If you try to impose your own different system, users may not find what they are looking for when you are not there.

Equipment and premises

Because of the importance of information technology, a microcomputer is a useful investment – for instance, for creating indexes or compiling lists. However, most professional offices have them, so a step lower down the investment scale might be to take a short course in business applications. It is said, however, that manuals for the standard programs have now been improved to the point where you can buy your own microcomputer and teach yourself. It is possible to buy a second-hand make of one of the commoner models for about the price of an electronic typewriter. But defects in second-hand PCs are hard for the uninitiated to spot. Unless you know its provenance, the general opinion is that you are better off buying a new machine. You also need to subscribe to the journals and directories in your specialist area. Some of these can be very expensive.

The market

Larger professional offices tend to have their own full-time librarians and the smallest ones generally do not have a large enough flow of information to justify even a part-timer. To make using a freelance librarian worthwhile for either party he or she has to come round at least once a week for three or four hours. Medium-sized practices in law, accountancy, architecture and related building professions, consultancy of various kinds, finance and private banking keep the kind of extensive records that call for professional organisation.

Finding work

Most freelances start by having one or two existing clients – possibly including someone they had previously worked for as an employee. Work tends to come from a mixture of word of mouth recommendations and judicious mail shots to potential clients. On the information broking side, if you have a speciality you get work from other specialists who have been retained but who have no knowledge of a specific field in which you may be a known expert. No directory of information brokers exists in the UK as yet, but there is one published in the USA: *The Directory of Fee Based Information Brokers*.

Fees

Library maintenance fees range between £12 and £16 an hour but the situation in information broking is more fluid. It depends on the nature and difficulty of the task and what you judge to be the resources of the client: you could probably charge an accountant or financial institution more than an architectural practice, for instance.

Administration

Since materials and publications are generally ordered on behalf of clients and on their account it is simply a matter of following their purchasing procedures. Your own consist of keeping records of hours spent and expenses incurred. A good deal of administration is called for in library work, however, mainly in the way of setting up and keeping records of things like journal renewals.

Occupational hazards

Very little is known about fee scales and the tendency among librarians, a retiring lot not given to pushing hard on financial matters, is to undercharge for services which can be quite invaluable to the client. It is also difficult to develop a sensible strategy for getting clients. The temptation is to take anyone who comes along, whereas the right balance would be one of jobs you liked doing with those that are well paid. Many freelances end up with quite a number that are neither, and find it difficult to drop them when something better comes along.

Professional organisations

Most professional librarians belong to ASLIB (the Association for Information Management, 26–27 Boswell Street, London WC1N 3JZ; 071-430 2671) which issues regular bulletins to members and holds conferences on new developments in the field.

Private Investigation

Basic skills and aptitudes

There are no specific skills involved in being a private investigator, though it helps if you have some knowledge of the elements of civil and criminal law and of the techniques of questioning people. Private investigators have no legal status, so their rights in that respect are only those of ordinary citizens.

The kind of person likely to be successful in this sphere is someone with a background in work related to it: the police (though far fewer policemen enter it now because of the boom in the private security business, and this increases the scope for others), business, the services, insurance investigation and experience in legal offices and the courts.

There is a professional qualification which can be obtained by examination in subjects such as law and the rules of evidence; this is membership or fellowship of the Institute of Professional Investigators.

Equipment and premises

You need a small office at which to see clients to achieve any degree of credibility, but apart from that very little is required in the way of equipment other than an answering machine, a typewriter or word processor, a car and a camera. You also have to invest in some decent stationery which your local print shop can run up for you.

Unless you are a skilled typist yourself it is advisable to try and get a part-timer to do this. Inevitably private investigating calls for making reports to clients. Apart from the fact that typing is not a productive use of your time, it will look better if done professionally.

The market

Forget about glamorous, Raymond Chandler-type assignments. Certainly for someone starting up a lot of the work is very routine stuff. The most common jobs are process and writ serving (for debts, affiliation orders and even parking offences) and status investigations for credit ratings. The latter would typically involve going to a shop that is trying to establish credit accounts and confirming that what they have told suppliers about premises, number of employees and ownership is true. This is not a long

process – nor is writ serving – and you can get through quite a lo
of such work in a day, though it's not well paid. A trade protectior
society might pay as little as £5–£8 for each report.

At higher levels a private investigator would be dealing with sucl
matters as vetting appointees to sensitive jobs, tracking dow
information leaks and industrial espionage between companies
finding missing persons and locating witnesses to accidents
Obtaining evidence in divorce proceedings, at one time the brea
and butter of private investigation, is no longer in demand becaus
of the changes in divorce law.

Finding work

The best sources of work are local: solicitors, companies, det
collecting agencies and finance firms. Nationally, it is worth makin
contact with trade protection societies and with other investigators
The main ones are listed in the *Directory of Registered Members* (
the Association of British Investigators, though these only repres
ent a proportion of the 3000 or so private eyes who are thought t
be operating in the UK now. Investigators in other parts of th
country may direct jobs to you if they are local to you and do nc
warrant travel time and costs for them or their client.

Press advertising does not usually pay, though a Yellow Page
entry is worthwhile. An initial mail shot to the type of clients liste
above is expensive, but is generally regarded as the best way c
getting the word about that you are in business.

Fees

There is no laid down scale of charges. Depending on location, th
generally accepted rates are £20–£25 an hour, plus expenses
Estimates are not normally given because of the difficulty c
quantifying beforehand how long a job, like finding a missing perso
or tracking down a bugging device, will take. The usual procedur
is to agree an upper limit with the client and to ask for furthe
instructions if you look like exceeding it – and at the same time t
give some idea of the chances of a successful outcome.

In the case of small companies and private individuals, it i
generally advisable to ask for some payment in advance.

Administration

Apart from keeping general records of costs and revenues you als
need to run worksheets for every job. These should give the client'
address and telephone number and details of any special require
ments on matters like confidentiality. You will need to log cost
related specifically to that job and also the hours to be attributed t
it. Precise times should be stated and the purpose to which the

were devoted. It may be necessary to produce such details as evidence in a court of law or at an enquiry.

Occupational hazards

Contrary to the popular view of it, the work is not dangerous, though process servers, like traffic wardens, run the risk of being insulted – and sometimes assaulted. The rule is to defend yourself only from physical attack, and to resist the temptation to respond physically to verbal abuse. Private investigators have no legal status and must not represent themselves as having any official authority. Thus, they can only ask questions and not demand answers.

This can obviously put at risk the accuracy of the information they pass on to clients. It is advisable to take out professional indemnity insurance to cover that situation – and it is a mandatory condition for membership of the Institute of Professional Investigators.

Professional organisations

No external qualifications are required to become a member of the Association of British Investigators (ABI House, 10 Bonner Hill Road, Kingston upon Thames, Surrey KT1 3EP; 081-546 3368). You have to be a detective or a detective agency and have been in business for at least two years to apply. To be accepted you have to produce references about where you have worked and what you have done and pass an entrance examination. There is a small annual subscription, for which you receive a regular newsletter and an entry into the members' directory. Enquiries from members of the public are channelled to the appropriate member.

The Institute of Professional Investigators Ltd (31a Wellington Street, St Johns, Blackburn, Lancs; 0254 680072) also publishes a journal with interesting, state-of-the-art articles; and as indicated earlier it conducts an examination system to maintain standards among its members.

13
Home and DIY Services

Introduction

Services supplied to the home are mostly, though not exclusively, concerned with the care and maintenance of buildings, attention to utilities like plumbing and electrics and repairs to a wide variety of items, ranging from household equipment and gadgets to cars. There is also scope in the growth of some personal services like home beauty care and even looking after occupants' pets while owners are away. All of these constitute a rich area of opportunity for freelances for two reasons. The first is the growth in the number of possessions – it must not be forgotten that, despite the unemployment figures, the majority of the working population is better off than ever. The second is that there are not enough tradesmen to go round who are willing to work reliably at a reasonable price. Anyone who has ever tried to get a car repaired at a busy period, or tried to get building work done can bear witness to that.

Significantly, this is a sector that has attracted attention from one of the fastest growing areas of self-employment: franchising. There are several franchisors who have been extremely successful in providing services to householders in such spheres as plumbing and drain clearing, car tuning, damp proofing and home cleaning. The lesson in that success, as far as freelances are concerned, is that franchises offer one advantage that it is difficult for the sole operator to match – a known name with a proven record. Many private householders are reluctant nowadays to open their doors to unknown contractors. The reasons are partly to do with security, a factor that weighs particularly heavily among older householders. Connected with that is the reassurance that appears to come with a known name. Every week there are stories in the papers about customers whose ignorance, timidity or stupidity is taken advantage of by cowboy operators. Placing work with a known company, even though its operatives may be virtually independent, as franchisees are, is often a preferred course which outweighs factors of cost.

However, this is not a situation where freelances should feel that being unable to beat the competition, they should join it. On the other hand, there are two leaves that are worth taking out of the franchise book. One is to keep your activity clear and simple and not to stray outside a definable field of competence. The other is to put that simple message over in your publicity and to make sure it is seen by possible customers – not only private householders, but also local agencies, estate agents, Citizens' Advice Bureaux, and so forth. That is essentially what franchisors have found to be a successful procedure – the amount of expensive national advertising they do to get their name around is, in many cases, quite modest.

On price, freelances should be able to enjoy an advantage. Without the overheads of an employer with staff and an office and without having to pay a royalty to franchisors (which in some cases can be quite high) the margins should be enough to quote competitively, particularly as most transactions will be in cash.

The opportunities to operate in the black economy are very considerable – although not desirable – which may be one reason why activities in what must be a major freelance field are not well publicised. Certainly, those who are successful seem to enjoy a standard of living above the sometimes modest levels described in the ensuing descriptions of just a few of the many possibilities.

Car Repair and Maintenance

Basic skills and aptitudes

Although numerous courses are offered in technical colleges leading to NVQs and such awards as BTEC, SCOTVEC and the City and Guilds examinations, the essential ingredient in working as a freelance is to have worked in a garage and to have had first-hand experience of repair and maintenance on a wide range of cars. It is working on that wide range of makes that gives the professional the edge on even the most skilled DIY performer on his or her own car – particularly in view of the number of foreign cars, sometimes with unintelligible manuals. However, basic mechanical aptitude is certainly a great help and those who have it could probably pick up the rest by working in a garage for a few months.

Equipment and premises

The range of car makes also means that you have to have a wide range of tools, some of which can be very expensive. It probably costs as much as £1800 to tool up properly but you can pick up second-hand ones quite cheaply if you have time and patience. Finding suitable premises, however, is very expensive and most freelances are mobile. A van with a lift-up tailgate is a great help if you cannot work from a garage-type pit, but failing that you can achieve most things, sometimes with a little discomfort and a certain amount of squirming, by using a commercial jack and stands. Most customers have garages with power sources, otherwise you may need some kind of generator.

The market
Good commercial garages are rare and becoming rarer; and if you have a foreign car it may entail long journeys to get to one, particularly if you live outside a city. Therefore, the scope for freelance work is very considerable, not only among private car owners but for small business fleets. However, it is best to stick to a manageable radius, otherwise you can end up spending an undue amount of time driving from one job to another – unless, of course, you have your own workshop, by which time you are more likely to be an employer yourself rather than a true freelance. There are also ways in which the market for your expertise can be widened; for instance, in advising customers on the purchase of second-hand cars or preparing their own cars for sale.

Finding work
Although advertising in local papers and through newsagents, leafleting householders, and so forth bring a good response in terms of quantity, the quality may be dubious. It turns up, apparently, a fair proportion of people who quibble about reasonable charges, who are reluctant to pay bills and who possess ancient, rusty wrecks that are not economically worth repairing – though it is hard to convince their owners on this point. Word of mouth recommendations from satisfied customers are best and it soon spreads if you make it clear that you would be grateful if your name was passed on to their friends.

Fees
Hourly rates of around £14–£20 per hour are usually the best way of charging, unless the job is something routine and predictable, like servicing. Quoting a flat rate for a task that turns out to be more complicated than you thought at first can leave you out of pocket. When a customer wants to know approximately how much an hourly rate job is likely to cost, make it clear that it is an estimate not a quote. Sometimes it is possible to agree to refer back to him or her if it is likely to be exceeded by much, but with car repairs, as with surgery, it can be hard to stop in the middle.

Administration
You have to keep copies of all bills, which can cause problems if you have to run out to the wholesalers for a part in the middle of a job

It can be solved by opening an account, but it is difficult for freelances to get credit facilities until they are established. Paying by credit card, however, can be a useful way of keeping a record of purchases because these will come with the statement, though in a very abbreviated form.

It is best to keep a small stock of everyday parts, if you can afford it, and to carry them with you in your van – otherwise you can waste a great deal of time driving back and forth to wholesalers and hanging around while you are there.

Another important administrative tool is a diary, because once you are known, you will have to start operating a booking system. It is also essential to have either an answerphone, or someone to answer the telephone while you are out.

Occupational hazards

Apart from the problem, common to many kinds of freelances, of getting paid, one of the chief hazards is the weather. Generally, freelance vehicle repair and maintenance has to be done outdoors because, although many clients have garages, the light is not usually good enough to work by. That also means that in the winter months work is very restricted. A particular hazard in this type of freelancing is the very high cost of the insurance you have to carry if you test drive other people's cars – as inevitably you will have to do.

Cooking and Catering

Basic skills and aptitudes

Though quite a lot of the younger freelance cooks and caterers (a term that includes those who prepare pâtés, cakes, etc for speciality food shops and restaurants) have a cordon bleu training, it is by no means essential. Indeed, in spite of the activities of food writers and the growing number of consumers with educated tastes in food and wine, the preferences of the majority of the public remain conservative. Prawn cocktail, steak or some kind of roast, a choice of fairly familiar vegetables, a fruit salad and a cheese board remain the popular choice of British business people, though certainly they are less prepared to put up with badly cooked meals than was once the case. This does not mean that a cook should not be able to turn out a gourmet meal on occasion, or that a foray into French or Italian dishes is unwelcome. It merely puts into perspective that to make a success of cooking freelance, you have to be a competent cook but not an artist of the kitchen.

With the notion of being a good cook go a number of attributes that are essential for anyone who wants to cook professionally: the ability to control several operations in the kitchen simultaneously, having a feel for quantities and measurements that are 'about right' when you get out of range of what the cookery books tell you, a chemist-like knowledge of what happens or should happen when you mix ingredients together and an eagle eye for quality in your supplies. With all that goes a gift for absolute unflappability over matters like guests arriving late, a dish going wrong or having to make last-minute improvisations to cope with extra numbers or to conceal some minor kitchen disaster.

A prerequisite that is neither a skill nor an attribute is to get permission from your local environmental health inspector if you are going to prepare food at home. That would normally be the case if you are supplying restaurants, but if you are asked to cook for a special occasion you may also want to do parts of the meal well in advance and possibly at home: the cold starters and puddings, for instance. The environmental health inspector will be concerned with the cleanliness of your premises and whether you have adequate facilities in relation to your scale of operations for keeping supplies under conditions that make them fit for consumption.

Equipment and premises
Your need for equipment and premises also revolves around the nature and scale of your activities. If you are cooking boardroom lunches – a favourite sphere of freelance work – everything will be available on the spot; or if it is not, your client will generally allow you to buy or hire what is needed, provided you can make a good case for it. If you are mainly cooking from home for special occasions or preparing dishes to order for restaurants and delicatessens, you will need a large cooker and deep freeze as well as commercial food processing machines. You may also want supplies of crockery, cutlery, glasses, and so forth, but in most large towns it is possible to hire both these and various bits and pieces of catering equipment. The general advice of the experts is never to buy anything unless you are absolutely sure that you have a continuing use for it.

If you are being asked to freelance for a company, you still have to check that all the supplies and equipment you need are there and that the freezer and stove are big enough to handle the anticipated throughput. As far as equipment, crockery and cutlery are concerned, it is wise to make an inventory before you take over – especially if these include valuable items. In the latter case someone will have to be responsible for checking them regularly.

In most cases you will need a car with an ample boot – preferably an estate car. There are suppliers who will deliver but in most cases you will have to look after this aspect yourself.

The market

There are agencies that handle assignments for freelance cooks and caterers. No central list of them is available but the department teaching cookery or catering at the nearest technical college or polytechnic should be able to give you a name. The agent charges the client – not the cook – so it will not hurt you to get on their books. The assignments that come up vary widely from helping out with a private dinner party to going abroad for a week or two with people who have rented a ski lodge or beach house, but don't want to go near the kitchen.

The biggest growth area in private cooking has been in boardroom catering. A loophole in the legislation makes entertaining one's own staff tax-deductible, whereas taking outsiders to lunch or dinner is not. It is also increasingly costly to take business guests out for a meal – it is quite easy to run up a bill for £80 for lunch for two in a good restaurant. There is, therefore, a double incentive to set up in-house catering at board and even executive level – especially since the tax people find it virtually impossible to distinguish whether a meal has been eaten only by the company's own staff, or whether guests have participated.

The other growth area is in supplying finished products to food shops and restaurants. There is a very limited range of mass-produced, often imported pies, pâtés and other delicatessen items. If they want to be different from the supermarkets, good shops either have to produce such items themselves or buy them in from freelance suppliers. This is also true of bread and cakes. There are several successful freelance bakers in London, whose customers are selling as much as they can produce.

Finding work

An agent will do the marketing for you. Generally, they will want to know your experience and background, because there is no sense in sending someone to cook for a wedding when they have never handled groups of more than six to eight people. They will give you a trial and check discreetly with the client to see how things have worked out.

As far as boardrooms are concerned, contacts are obviously extremely useful and the way in which most freelances start. If you have no contacts – though you should surely be able to think of someone with a position in business or the professions whom you have entertained at some time and who can give you a lead – try writing direct to the managing directors of local companies, again stating your experience and background. You will have to send out a lot of letters, though. If you get one reply out of a hundred you would be doing well – but one contract a week is enough to get you going.

Selling to shops, wine bars and restaurants simply involves visiting and telling them what sort of food you make and asking them if they are interested in trying it for sale. Better still, take them a sample – they will certainly want to taste before they buy. After that, practice varies. Some will take goods on firm account, others on a sale or return basis. The former is obviously better and you should try to get firm sale commitments if your goods are selling well.

Fees

The important point to remember about fees is that cooking will only take up part of your time. The shopping, preparation and administration involved in a quite ordinary two-hour executive lunch will take three hours on top of that. Therefore, unless you can clear at least £35 for your work and preferably more, it is hard to see how this form of freelancing could be made to pay. That is a point you will have to sell corporate clients, especially as all the costs of food come on top of that. The trouble is that people in such positions have little knowledge either of the work it takes to prepare a meal or of the cost of food. They may, however, have a knowledge of the cost of wine and that at least gives you a starting point. But unless you can make £12–£15 an hour, forget about cooking as a freelance activity unless you are doing it just to make some extra money.

As far as selling finished products is concerned, that is simply a matter of charging the going rates. Look at what similar speciality items cost, rather than at the mass-produced ones whose prices you will probably not be able to match. The shopkeeper/restaurant/wine bar owner will have marked the counter price up by anything from 30 to 50 per cent; so the display price less that percentage is what you can hope to make. You should remember, though, that as well as ingredients you should count the cost of gas and electricity.

Administration

Administration is fairly simple if you are supplying shops. It is then just a question of keeping a record of costs and revenue. You should keep your private food purchases separate from your business ones, although sharp practitioners are able to 'lose' some of the former in the latter and from a tax point of view are then able to eat 'on the firm'.

It becomes much more important to keep business and private transactions separate if you are catering for a client. He or she will not take kindly to your 'fiddling' private purchases on his or her account and the temptation to do so should be firmly resisted. You should keep careful records of all purchases made on behalf of clients, though it becomes difficult to keep them apart if you are buying for more than one client from the same supplier. You will have to insist that the client keeps separate accounts for each of them and that supplies are boxed up separately. They will have to be checked on receipt or delivery, which adds point to the statement that only part of your time is taken up with actual cooking.

The question of leftover food or supplies is something to negotiate with your client, though it might be tactful to leave that issue open for a while. Once he trusts you not to over-buy on purpose, the path in such discussions will be infinitely smoother and you will very probably benefit handsomely from the crumbs that fall off the boardroom table. You should also clarify from the outset who is responsible for non-cooking duties, like table setting and cleaning up after the meal. Some cooks will not undertake such tasks.

Bear in mind that as a professional caterer you are entitled to buy food supplies wholesale. A letter from your client stating your professional role is generally sufficient to establish your *bona fide* with the wholesaler. You will find the difference between wholesale and supermarket prices surprisingly great, though you will have to commit yourself to buying wholesale quantities, like 7 lb tins of tomatoes!

Occupational hazards

The chief hazards in freelance cooking occur in the kitchen, over timing and ingredients. You may get away with a burnt offering in the tolerant bosom of your family, but never when you are cooking for money. You should also make sure that you are insured against the risk of accidentally giving your customers food poisoning. It can happen in the best regulated circles, as a case against British Airways/Concorde once showed. It cost BA a lot of money, and a private individual simply cannot afford that.

Contract Gardening

Basic skills and aptitudes

You need a knowledge of planting and propagation techniques and some understanding of the principles of garden design – otherwise your status is really only that of a garden labourer. You have to be able to tackle a wide range of tasks which embrace both skilled and unskilled work. A typical assignment might be restoring a ruined lawn which involves a sequence of high mowing, applying weed-killer, feeding and seeding bald patches and possibly returfing. The job thus entails a mixture of physical strength and horticultural knowhow.

Equipment and premises
Most people with large gardens have a range of tools in their shed or garage, though not necessarily the right ones for the job. You should carry your own – apart from anything else, it looks more professional. Ideally, you should have two lawn mowers, a bill hook, a ladder, a range of digging tools and powered clippers and saws. You obviously need either an estate car or a van to carry them, and a big, dry shed to store them in.

The market
The typical client is a successful business or professional person in the 30–40 age group who has bought a large house with a neglected garden which he or she doesn't have time to look after without help. At the other end of the spectrum there are elderly people who are no longer able to take care of their gardens themselves. Some business firms are also set in grounds that need regular professional attention from someone who can offer greater skills than those of an odd-jobber.

Finding work
Initially, most work seems to come from friends and their contacts. Local newspaper advertising tends not to be productive – people are cautious about letting strangers loose around their property, especially while they are not there. For the same reason putting notices in shop windows does not pull in many clients – though it helps if you know the shopkeeper and he or she can vouch for you if a customer asks. It is a good idea to have local references that potential clients can ring up. Local job agencies can also be a useful source. A number of these provide on-demand services to householders for anything from babysitting to cleaning.

Another way of getting work is to have leaflets printed and drop them into any houses whose gardens are obviously in need of care. There again, to state that local references can be supplied will reassure the nervous.

Fees
These can be as much as £8 an hour, though £5 an hour, plus materials, is more usual. The purchase of materials can be a useful source of extra revenue if you can negotiate trade prices with suppliers. For this reason it is a good idea to make it clear that you

will purchase plants and other materials after discussion with the client. The discount given by nurseries is, however, fairly small – about 10 per cent.

Some contract gardeners find it better to quote a price per visit or per job rather than an hourly rate. It saves argument – if the client is not around while you are doing the job they will have no idea how long it took anyway. It also puts you more into the class of a professional service rather than an hourly labourer. The only difficulty in that case is that with a lengthy job you should negotiate at least an interim payment, otherwise you may run into cash-flow problems. Indeed, with a new and unknown customer, it may be worth trying to secure an advance payment as well.

Administration
Very little is needed apart from a cash book showing receipts and expenditure, and an efficiently kept diary.

Occupational hazards
The most obvious one is that gardening is not an essential service like calling in the plumber when there is a burst water pipe. Clients have time to shop around and the gardener is one of the first services to go if money is short. The other big problem with contract gardening is the seasonal aspect. From April until about November there is always a lot to do, but the mid-winter months, especially January and February, are virtually dead.

Getting work is also very slow when you first start. It is not advisable to take the plunge into freelance contract work – assuming you have any choice as far as earning a living is concerned – unless you have a few good clients lined up first.

Professional organisations
A diploma in horticulture is very useful if you want to go into the business seriously. It also impresses corporate clients, like businesses who want their grounds maintained. A national diploma in horticulture (NDH) can be taken by correspondence with the main professional body, the Royal Horticultural Society, 80 Vincent Square, Westminster, London SW1P 2PE; 071-834 4333. An examination is also offered by the sister Scottish body, the Royal Botanic Garden, Edinburgh EH3 5LR. These institutions will also provide details of full-time or part-time courses elsewhere in the country.

Freelancing in the Building Trades
The large-scale but sporadic nature of building work means that it

is and always has been a natural area for freelances – particularly as skilled men can earn more hiring out their services as subcontractors than by working on a contractor's payroll. The extent of freelancing in the construction industry has meant that the Inland Revenue has made special provision to deal with it by issuing a subcontractor's tax certificate in approved cases. The effect of this is that the contractor then pays you a gross amount, rather than deducting PAYE. In return you have to give him or her a tax exemption certificate (called a 715) which he or she then sends to the tax office each month. Your tax liability is assessed largely on the basis of these returns, and on self-employment terms.

The conditions of eligibility for a subcontractor's tax certificate are fairly stringent. In particular, you have to have had a satisfactory record of employment or self-employment for a continuous period of three years in the six years before you make your application. Short breaks in employment will not count against you but they must not add up to more than six months in total. An exception is made if you were working abroad, but in that case you will have to provide evidence of that fact.

By 'satisfactory record of employment' the tax authorities mean that during the qualifying period you have fulfilled all the expected requirements in the way of making tax returns and National Insurance contributions. People who have been in full- or part-time education, and cannot therefore meet the three-year requirements, may get a special certificate that confers many of the benefits of the full-scale subcontractor's tax certificate. Your local tax office will be able to give you all the details.

Basic skills and aptitudes

There are no hard and fast rules about qualifications to freelance as a building tradesperson. A physically fit and skilful DIY enthusiast who is also a quick worker could probably make his way in a world that seems to suffer from labour shortages even during recessions. The only real restrictions are the legal ones described in Chapter 10: that is, that there is a duty on those offering a service to be able to carry it out in accordance with normal standards of competence. Most building tradespeople offer either experience or formal qualifications as proof of that. Such proofs may be demanded by contractors, but are seldom required by private individuals who are only too glad to find someone to do building jobs honestly and competently.

For those who want to strengthen an interest and skill in DIY matters by taking a building course, these are offered by quite a number of technical colleges and lead to NVQs and to such qualifications as SCOTVEC (in Scotland) or BTEC and the City and Guilds of London Institute (CGLI) awards in England.

Equipment and premises

The tools of the trade are an obvious requisite and so is a van. In some cases it may be necessary to hold a modest stock of materials, particularly when there is a constant demand for items for which there is also an inducement to bulk purchase. Wholesalers give trade terms to bona fide building tradespeople, so having cards or even purchase order forms printed is a good and very modest investment.

Materials, equipment and a van may call for dry storage space, though it is usually possible to rent that very cheaply.

The market

The market for building work is very large. Britain has the highest proportion of owner-occupiers in Europe and in one area alone – that of damp proofing and timber protection – the annual value of work done is said to be £200 million. Sources of work, apart from building contractors, are architects, housing associations, estate agents, property managers and private houseowners.

Finding work

Local newspapers, Yellow Pages and cards in shop windows are a favourite source for totally independent operators, but a great many freelances prefer to rely on contractors to find work. The reasons are that many clients go to a builder in the first instance, that the builder does the negotiating and much of the paperwork in preparing estimates and quotes and takes the responsibility for extracting money from the client. Clients for their part often prefer to deal with a main contractor as well, rather than a name in a shop window. If you can validate your experience and the quality of your work by named references, so much the better, because many clients are justifiably nervous about building trade 'cowboys'. For this reason it is likely that franchising, which ideally gives the consumer the protection of a nationally known company (Dyno-Rod is a good example), may become a more widespread way of providing a building service to the general public. Becoming a franchisee also has some advantages for the freelance from the point of view of marketing.

Fees

Fees vary widely according to the part of the country and the degree of skill you can offer. In the London area, however, a freelance labourer can earn £50–£60 a day and a tradesperson upwards of £100. The mark-up on materials bought wholesale can be a further source of income.

Administration

At the very least you will have to keep a proper record of income and expenses, so that you can keep the simple records required for the subcontractor's tax certificate. If you are registered for VAT – that is, if your turnover is in excess of the figure laid down in that year's Budget (it goes up slightly each time but it is £35,000 at the time of writing after a 40 per cent jump in 1991) – you will have to show VAT paid and charged in your books.

A lot of freelances in the building business try to avoid paying VAT, but it should be noted that it relates to turnover not profit, or even income. The snag about buying materials, therefore, is that it is liable to bring you into the bracket where you are obliged to register.

The more you do, the more administration you are likely to have to face. Thus, if you work independently rather than, or as well as, for contractors, you may have to prepare estimates and possibly even written reports and contracts. You will also have to issue invoices and statements and take all action to secure payment – including, on occasion, taking steps for recovery through the County Court as indicated in Chapter 10.

Occupational hazards

Outside work is apt to be affected by weather, and winter conditions can be very unpleasant. Safety is a constant problem on such work as well, and you need a head for heights because even a two-storey domestic dwelling means having to work on scaffolding 15 or 20 feet above ground. Apart from that, the principal hazards are getting paid. Bankruptcies among small builders are the highest for any single business sector and you should never undertake extensive work without getting progress payments, whether from a private client or a contractor.

Contract Cleaning

Basic skills and aptitudes

Contract cleaning is mainly of the heavy duty kind – periodic cleaning of fabric and carpets in private houses and cleaning of large areas in offices and supermarkets. There is a tendency to regard such work as a dirty, low-grade job which is why it is not widely popular. On the other hand, the demand for it is considerable and the rewards are relatively high for a job that does not require a vast amount of skill and where industrial cleaning techniques can be picked up in a week or so's training.

Equipment and premises

The two main items are an industrial vacuum cleaner and a steam cleaning machine, costing around £200 and £1200 respectively. You also need chemicals and a few basic cleaning tools. The initial setting-up costs should not come to more than £1600 or so, though this does not include the cost of a van and such office essentials as an answerphone and a typewriter or word processor, or the cost of brochures and other promotional materials.

The market

Shops, offices and private houses are the main sources. Businesses are increasingly turning to contract cleaners rather than using their own staff.

Finding work

Advertisements in local papers are reputed to bring excellent results, as are selective local mailings. Some cleaning contractors even employ door-to-door salesmen who work on commission, but that makes it difficult to keep prices competitive, as costs do not go down with increases in customers. There are, however, savings to be made in contracts to clean larger areas in shops and offices, so personal approaches to potential customers are worth making where there is a positive reaction to an initial enquiry.

Fees

In private houses the average charge is £12 a room and £18 for a larger area, such as a hallway. Fabric cleaning can increase this by 30–40 per cent depending on the difficulty of the task. A good operative can earn £70 a day without too much difficulty. A contract to clean a supermarket or an office can be worth as much as £400 a week for a couple of hours' work a night.

Administration

Little administration is required though you need to keep a diary if you are running contracts. In that case you will also need to raise invoices. Private cleaning work is almost invariably on a cash basis.

Occupational hazards

This is a year-round business with virtually no hazards involved. The only problem is that private customers use cleaning services once a year or less, which means you have to promote yourself regularly. There is also competition from several well-established franchises who have the benefit of a name behind them. The activity of franchisors in this field is, however, a good sign of its potential.

Security Installation

Basic skills and aptitudes

Installing burglar alarms and security devices is essentially a branch of electrical work: a great many of the people in it are, therefore, trained electricians. The alarm points are around doors and windows, and a certain amount of carpentry ability is therefore also useful.

Equipment and premises

There is no need to carry a vast amount of stock, though you should have enough spares to deal with emergencies and break-downs. A large storeroom at home, equipped with a workbench and good lighting, is sufficient. The secret, as in so many other forms of business, is to keep it simple. Security is a boom business in which new products are constantly coming on the market, though in reality there is little to choose between them. The only really important factor is reliability. For this reason it is worth sticking with two or three manufacturers whose products you really know and only to accept innovations if they are recommended by wholesalers on the basis of experience.

There are two other reasons for this. One is that you are generally expected to follow the practice of the big installers like Banhams and to guarantee the installation against breakdown. If you choose equipment that has not been properly tested, it is you, not the manufacturer, who has to pay the penalty. The second is that if you install a wide range of devices it follows that you have to carry a corresponding range of spares. Professionals are rarely gadget-happy. That is a mark of the amateur.

The market

The market is enormous – and growing, especially in domestic installations. Each burglary is an indirect advertisement for the need to install security systems.

Finding work

Most work eventually comes through referrals from satisfied customers, though there are obvious advertising channels – local Yellow Pages and newspapers, even door-to-door leafleting. It is also worth notifying architects and builders of your services, and police crime prevention officers too, as they maintain a register of firms that install security devices. Their approval could be crucial in the first instance, because what people who have valuables to protect are afraid of are installers who are less than totally honest. It is not unknown for some of them to be both poachers and gamekeepers.

Fees
The big security and alarm firms charge a minimum of around £800, usually calculated on the basis of a flat fee, for the whole installation in the average three-bedroomed house. A freelance without the overheads of a firm is reckoned to be able to halve that figure and still show a handsome profit. It has to be taken into account, however, that a preliminary survey is necessary to ensure that doors and windows provide a tight fit for the alarm devices and that wiring can be installed without difficulty. Guaranteeing the system can also be a cost which, though not obvious at first, can become quite large if the equipment is faulty, or a mistake has been made in wiring it up. Distinctly coloured wiring is generally used to make fault finding easier and keep it apart from other systems in the house.

Administration
Because maintenance and after-sales service is an important aspect of security installation, you need to keep records not only of the costs and fees for each job, but also of details of the equipment that was used and who supplied it. Such documentation is, of course, of enormous potential value to criminals and some professionals advise that such records should be kept in a simple code.

Occupational hazards
The spread of DIY security kits is a threat to the professional installer, though many of them are reckoned to be almost useless. The growth in the market has also attracted competition from electricians, though here again professionals claim that electricians are not qualified to advise on the selection of a system or correct installation procedures. A further hazard, shared with many other skilled trades, is that of being asked to give quotes, spending the best part of a morning – or in the case of larger jobs a whole day – giving advice and then finding the work going to someone else: a moonlighting electrician already on the job or a DIY-minded householder.

Architectural Design

Basic skills and aptitudes

Being an architectural designer is not the same thing as being an architect. By law you are only allowed to call yourself an architect if you have been registered as such, having taken the professional examinations. However, on a smaller scale an architectural designer can offer a very similar range of services – that is, he or she can prepare sketch schemes and get planning permission from the local council for them. Architectural designers are generally people who have worked in architects' offices as unqualified assistants and have seen their employers do many things they could do themselves.

Equipment and premises

You can work from a large room at home, but having a small office looks more professional, especially to clients. You need a drawing board, good lighting, and probably a dyeline printer – the cheapest usable variety costs about £1000 though they can be leased. You need access to a printer/copier because in each case multiple copies of plans are required – for instance, three for the local council for planning permission plus further copies for builders, tradespeople and for the client.

The market

The market is mainly small jobs like dining room or kitchen extensions and attic conversions.

Finding work

Quite a lot of work comes through builders and it is important to point out to your contacts among builders and other tradespeople the mutual advantages of working together – you are in a position to put work their way as much as vice versa. Estate agents are also a source of work and so, strangely enough, are qualified architects. Large and even medium-sized firms get quite a number of jobs offered to them that are too small for them to take. And now that architects themselves are allowed to advertise, they feel less sensitive about competition from their non-qualified brethren.

Fees

You can charge a percentage of the contract value as architects do. Another option is to charge on a time basis, which is the fairest way if you are going to be involved in doing work other than just designing. For instance, the client may ask you to supervise the work of contractors. A third alternative is to base your charges on the area of space your plan covers.

Administration

The great thing is not to become involved in paying contractors on the client's behalf. Apart from the risks involved, it greatly increases the administration. It will also certainly put you in a VAT bracket. However, you do need to be a good administrator because of the amount of documentation involved in dealing with the local council. Records should be kept of all clients' instructions and whatever you have been asked to do should be put in writing.

Occupational hazards

The usual one is extracting money from clients, and many designers demand a split fee, half of which is payable on preparation of plans and the second half for the drawing of details. Apart from that the chief hazard is the sheer complexity of the building regulations and the fact that building control officers in different authorities tend to interpret them differently. It is also advisable to take out professional indemnity insurance. Claims for professional negligence are becoming a big hazard in architectural practice, and there is no reason to think that they will not extend to non-professionals.

Electrics

Basic skills and aptitudes

You do not have to be qualified through one of the craftsperson's courses but it obviously helps. The best training is to have worked alongside an experienced technician. Domestic work, however, is not beyond the capacity of a good DIY person. It involves rewiring, the provision of lights and sockets and tracing simple faults in the system.

Equipment and premises

A complete set of tools costs about £400 and for the professional electrician they are best obtained from a wholesaler. The wear-out factor is high. Most things in your toolbox need to be replaced at least twice a year. A van to carry larger items like ladders and a workbench is also necessary.

The market and finding work

The market is virtually all householders in your district. In addition to installation work there is also the repair of domestic appliances. During the guarantee period these are generally maintained by the manufacturers. However, the call-out fee is high and after the guarantee expires householders would get a better buy from most tradespeople. Regular advertisements in local papers and notices in shops are cost effective. It is also a good idea to have a visiting card printed so that satisfied clients can pass them on to others.

Administration

It is essential to keep all records, bills and receipts. Having an account with a wholesaler will save you a good deal of record-keeping, though he or she will probably not be willing to open one until you have established yourself as a customer doing a reasonable amount of business. Payment from customers should always be secured as soon as the job is done. Do not accept cheques unless backed by a cheque card.

Occupational hazards

Not getting paid is the chief problem. If the client is a new one it may be advisable to get a deposit before you start. There is also the problem that some jobs are uneconomic, which explains why some manufacturers charge quite a high call-out fee irrespective of the nature of the job. Whether you intend to follow this practice or treat minor jobs as a goodwill offering is a matter of personal choice.

Beauty Therapy

Basic skills and aptitudes

In the first instance you need to know about the body and how it works – muscle, skin, metabolism, etc. That is the basis for being able to recommend and apply make-up and, of course, to give massage treatment. Although there is no law that says you have to have formal qualifications, they are necessary if you want to be taken seriously. A Diploma in Beauty Therapy is given at a limited number of colleges, taking you through a course recognised by the British Association of Beauty Therapy and Cosmetology or one of the other professional bodies mentioned later. The course takes at least six months and is expensive at between £1400 and £1600.

Equipment and premises

Start-up costs for exercising machinery and other equipment can go as high as £7500, but you can get by with a foldable massage table and a range of facial creams and oils. The former is essential because you cannot give a massage, at least not a reputable one, on a bed. To some extent the equipment you need will depend on the range of treatments you propose to offer and course tutors will advise you on this. It is also a good idea to look at some professional beauty salons and consider the range and make of equipment they contain.

The market
Freelance beauty therapy involves going to clients' houses, so it follows that they are either young mothers who can't get out, career women who do not have the time for treatment during working hours, or older women who prefer to be treated in privacy.

Finding work
Although a lot of work comes by word of mouth and many beauty therapists are former beauty salon employees who take their clients with them, selective press advertising can also be effective. National glossies, however, have too wide a catchment area – it is no use spending a lot of money to take a small ad in *Harpers & Queen* when you operate out of Lincoln and can only treat people in that area. Local glossy magazines, of which there are quite a number, are the best medium.

Fees
Fees vary widely but the main factors that you have to take into account, to arrive at an hourly rate, are the cost of product and travel, telephone, publicity and the depreciation of equipment. The norm is about £9–£11 an hour which leaves you with about half that as the net amount.

Administration
You need to keep a record of costs and also a diary for forward bookings, but otherwise there is very little administration involved because most transactions are in cash.

Occupational hazards
Beauty treatment inevitably involves very intimate contact similar to that between doctor and patient. As is the case with the doctor, it is absolutely essential to dress and behave professionally. This is one of the things taught in the college courses. However, women therapists generally avoid giving massages to men at home even if they are apparently on a bona fide basis.

Another hazard is that of skin allergies or adverse after-effects from massage. Clients should always be asked beforehand of any conditions that may affect the treatment you want to give them. It is also worth looking into the possibility of taking out professional indemnity insurance from your broker.

Professional organisations

Several bodies award qualifications, including:

British Association of Beauty Therapy and Cosmetology (BAB-TAC), Suite 5, Wolseley House, Oriel Road, Cheltenham GL50 1TH; 0242 570284

International Health and Beauty Council, 109a Felpham Road, Felpham, West Sussex PO22 7PW; 0243 860320

14
Photography, Illustration and Design

Introduction

Many kinds of enterprise need creative services at some point, but only the largest can afford to employ full-time staff for this purpose. Even those who use design regularly, for instance to produce promotional literature, now prefer to go outside, partly because such work comes in short, intense bursts and partly because it gives them more freedom of choice. In-house creative people go stale after a while and even at best it is hard to avoid a certain sameness if similar work is presented to the public too often. For their part, designers, photographers and those in other creative occupations also need the stimulus of a wider range of assignments than any one employer can usually give them. In some cases the answer is to attach yourself to a design consultancy as a freelance. There are, however, those who prefer to remain completely autonomous.

In this kind of work nothing impresses clients as much as the credentials of a successful record, and this is most likely to come about when you are in sympathy with what you are doing. If you are thinking of going freelance, you should begin by looking around for clients who you think would like your work. That is not only a matter of personal contacts, but also of studying media that publish the kind of thing you yourself like and can do. It is in these offices that your portfolio is most likely to make an impact.

Taking round a portfolio is a time-consuming business and not everyone is effective in marketing their own work. Quite apart from identifying the right outlets for it, there are also negotiations over fees and copyright and this is where having an agent can be useful. It means that the commercial side, which can on occasion involve hard and even acrimonious bargaining, is divorced from the personal and artistic rapport which is so important in working with a client on the creative side.

However, employing an agent is expensive and the less established you are, the higher the charges are likely to be. A bad agent can be a costly millstone and before committing yourself to anyone who asks to represent you – flattering though such an approach may be – you should check him or her out, preferably with other freelances. Also, any agent's contract should be shown to a competent solicitor. There have been cases of freelances who have unwittingly sold themselves into something very like slavery for the term of a contract from an unscrupulous agent.

Photography

Basic skills and aptitudes
There are a fairly large number of professional photographers around, most of them operating as freelances. The *British Journal of Photography*, the leading professional magazine, has a circulation of around 10,000, but there is also a huge army of amateurs, many of whom are highly skilled technically. *Amateur Photographer*, the leading consumer magazine, goes to over 85,000 readers every week and it is significant that its assistant editor has written a book on freelance photography; in other words, there are a lot of amateurs who have, or aspire to, semi-professional status. What is needed to succeed at a professional level goes beyond skill and technique – essential though that is.

You have to be clear about the market you are aiming at, ideally a specialisation of some kind (the main areas are social, commercial and business, advertising, and industrial and scientific photography), and to be able to market yourself. This involves not only initiative and the ability to sell yourself, but also the ability to seize, or inveigle yourself into, opportunities and to be able to work quickly when the shots present themselves. You also have to be able to get on with people. With rare exceptions loners do not succeed in commercial photography. Only about 20 per cent of your time is spent photographing. The rest is taken up by dealing with subjects, clients, suppliers or competitors.

Equipment and premises
Anyone contemplating earning a living as a freelance photographer would presumably already own much of the equipment, the cost of which can run into thousands of pounds. The problem thereafter is to keep up with the constantly changing technology – great improvements in technical quality seem to occur almost as rapidly as they do in microcomputers, and, of course, the microchip has had a great impact on the photographic equipment and accessory scene. Not all of them, however, need to be kept up with in terms of buying the latest thing on the market, and indeed the avalanche of new products has greatly increased the opportunity for buying second hand what would otherwise be extremely expensive.

Second-hand goods are advertised in the various specialised

journals, as are studios and darkrooms available for hire. You can, however, work equally well from home if suitable spaces are available. A studio needs special preparation. It does not necessarily need to be the conventional darkened room with lots of bright lights – some of the most successful photographers use daylight, as you can see from looking at their work – but you do need a large space with diffused natural light which takes away the shadows. Diffusing screens can be bought which do that job. Artificial lighting is provided by special tungsten lamps and there are also various flash effects which are much more refined than those in the ordinary run of commercial cameras.

Many photographers also do their own processing, at any rate for black-and-white film. That obviously means having a blacked out space large enough to work in, with room for enlargers, processing drums and preferably a good water supply. The alternative is to use a processing laboratory. That has certain advantages in cost benefit terms because when you are processing your films you are not out there taking pictures or getting business, but you also lose a good deal of the creative input that makes photography so rewarding, and you are at the mercy of the laboratory both in the quality of what it does and the time it takes. There is, incidentally, an Association of Photographic Laboratories which supervises standards of service and quality and to which most of the labs used by professional photographers belong.

Apart from these facilities you will also need to invest in administration and presentation. You will need to present a professional-looking portfolio and to set up your office systems: an answerphone and a typewriter or word processor are essential. You will almost certainly also need a car.

The market

Though the investment in equipment, materials and premises is larger than for many freelance occupations, the market is potentially very large. It begins with taking pictures of events like weddings for private clients, through to contacts with local newspapers and then on to national ones. Apart from that there are literally hundreds of magazines, from general consumer media to those catering to special interests. A look round your local WH Smith will give you some idea of the range, but they probably only stock about half of what is available: a full list is published in *British Rate and Data*. Apart from working directly with papers and magazines, there are also picture libraries and photographic agencies through which you can offer your work – not only to the media but to other consumers of photographs, like advertising and PR agencies.

Finding work

One way to get into freelance photography – and it is probably the one usually chosen by those who take a formal course at one of the several polytechnics who offer it (see the *British Journal of Photography*, or *British Qualifications*, published by Kogan Page, for details) – is to begin by working as a freelance assistant to a photographer. There are a number of agencies who handle freelance assignments, but the one that most freelances put at the top of their list is AFAEP (the Association of Fashion and Editorial Photographers). This is a professional association rather than a commercial body, and one of the things they do is give regular introductory courses on what freelance photography involves. They also maintain a register of freelance assistants and members regularly telephone to ask for names on the register. They do, however, apply some quality checks to your work before putting you on the register.

Working as an assistant – in the case of AFAEP, to some of Britain's top photographers who are members – you will learn an enormous amount about the technical side and probably make some good contacts, though not much money. There are, however, other ways of getting work. At a local level, putting on an exhibition of your work in a library generally attracts local media attention and most librarians are amenable to putting on exhibitions of this kind. You will, of course, have to pay for framing and other aspects of display. This is also true of competitions. They are generally worth going in for, not only because of the possibility that your work may be published but because art editors visit the major ones in search of new talent.

You can also approach art editors yourself. The usual way is to send a portfolio, or take it in yourself after making an appointment. It should be professionally presented and should consist of not more than 20 pictures, chosen for their relevance to the paper or magazine you are approaching – black and white or colour, as appropriate. If you are sending the portfolio rather than bringing it along yourself, make sure that all the pictures are captioned and that you enclose a stamped addressed envelope – some papers and magazines will not pay return postage on work sent in on spec.

If you cannot face making the rounds of possible clients yourself, the alternative is to use an agency. A list of these is given in the *Writers' and Artists' Yearbook* or in the yearbook of BAPLA (the British Association of Picture Libraries and Agencies). Agents take your work round art editors and picture libraries for 50 per cent of any sales they make. They will require rather more than 20 pictures because of the range of outlets they cover. It is best to go and see them, form your own impression of who you are dealing with and find out whether they think they can do anything with your material – if they can't, this might give you serious pause for thought in your plans to become a freelance photographer.

Practice and acceptance in the market are worth any amount of paper qualifications. There are quite a number of correspondence courses and they do a good job up to a point; for instance, the BFP School of Photography course, which specialises in training freelances, is highly spoken of by experts (address: Focus House, 497 Green Lanes, London N13 4BP; 081-882 3315) and their course, devised by the Bureau of Freelance Photographers, is not expensive; but it will not guarantee you work, never mind a living.

Fees

Fees vary enormously according to the circumstances, and the medium. An assistant will get from £30 to £50 a day and a single picture will bring anything from £25 to £70 in black and white, although famous name photographers and scoops will pull in much more – as much as £1000 per day. A freelance with a name in his or her field would expect to charge £250–£400 a day plus expenses on a commissioned assignment. A lesser known but established freelance would expect a fee of £150–£200 per assignment. In the case of new customers, it is advisable to negotiate a fee beforehand – sometimes they have very little idea of how much work can be involved in getting the right picture.

The big money is in advertising photography. One well-known design photographer recently earned £18,000 in a single week taking photographs for a catalogue put out by a furniture manufacturer; but that was a rush job, which involved working 18 hours a day for a week.

Administration

The admin side of photography is rather more extensive than in many other kinds of freelance work. The trouble is that you not only have to keep books with fairly long schedules of expenses which your accountant may ask you to break down into materials, travel, equipment, etc, you also have to keep files of your actual photos. It is very easy to get into a muddle and not know where to put your hand on a picture that a magazine wants to buy, so you have to keep your records in such a way that you can find what you want quickly.

You will need a system of filing by topic, by date within topics and cross-referencing where the picture was published, if that was the case. Some photographers also like to keep a record of technical data, in case they get a similar assignment. This is exactly the sort of problem of storing and accessing data which a microcomputer could handle, and though no program had been written for photographers' files at the time that this book was compiled, it is quite possible that it will only be a matter of time before this happens. No doubt when it does it will be an event that will get at least passing mention in the *British Journal of Photography*.

The very high costs of materials and equipment may mean that it pays you to opt for voluntary registration for VAT. Although the compulsory level is £35,000 (it has tended to increase in line with inflation at each Budget), you can opt for the status of a taxable trader. That means that you have to charge your customers VAT, but you get 17.5 per cent back on all your taxable purchases. It involves keeping careful records and making a quarterly return to Customs and Excise, but many freelances find it worthwhile in spite of the extra hassle.

Even though you get the VAT element back on your purchases, it is still worth considering, on larger or more expensive items, whether you should rent rather than buy, unless you are sure you are really going to get your money's worth. Remember that bills have to be paid in cash and that it is very dangerous to tie up too much of that valuable commodity in hard-to-realise assets.

Occupational hazards

Apart from the near certainty of high costs and the endemic uncertainties of the freelance life, one of the main hazards of photography concerns the question of copyright. Strictly speaking, when a freelance is commissioned by an editor or other client, the copyright belongs to that client only if he or she stipulates that the commission entitles them to it. However, this has become something of a grey area and the practice has grown up that copyright in a commissioned assignment always belongs to the commissioner. Whether you can get away with retaining copyright depends largely on how strong a position you are in, but it is painful to see a picture you took on an assignment for which you might have been paid £100 appearing in other magazines in the full knowledge that your client is probably making far more money out of it than you ever did.

However, if someone uses one of your pictures which they have obtained direct from you, the position is quite clear; they are only entitled to reproduce it for the one purpose for which they have sought permission and, one hopes, paid.

Professional organisations

There are several professional organisations, but the best-known ones are:

Association of Fashion and Editorial Photographers, 9 Domingo Street, London EC1Y 0TA.

British Institute of Professional Photographers, 2 Amwell End, Ware, Herts SG12 9HN.

Many photographers also belong to the National Union of Journalists (314 Gray's Inn Road, London WC1X 8DP). There are mixed opinions about how useful the NUJ actually is, for instance in disputes over money and copyright, but the Press card which membership confers can get you into newsworthy occasions for which you might be denied access as a member of the general public.

Technical Illustration

Basic skills and aptitudes

You have to have disciplined technical drawing skills, at least up to good A level standards. Beyond that you need experience at the commercial end, either in a drawing office or in some kind of creative or design agency. There are one or two courses for technical illustrators. Details are shown in *British Qualifications* (published by Kogan Page).

Equipment and premises

The main requirements are really good lighting, a drawing board and the usual range of drawing supplies. The biggest item of expenditure is the second: a drawing board can cost as much as £800, though there is a market in second-hand ones. Some trade magazines for the graphic design industry carry classified advertisements for second-hand equipment. They are listed in *British Rate And Data* which is carried by most large reference libraries.

The market

There is quite a large potential demand for technical illustrations not only among magazine and book publishers, but also from advertising agencies and companies producing technical manuals. The main reference books for these sources are *The Creative Handbook* (for design and advertising agencies), *Writers' and Artists' Yearbook* (for book publishers), *British Rate and Data* (for magazine publishers) and local Yellow Pages for companies that might need manuals illustrated.

Finding work

Most work comes from existing clients – either directly or because they recommend you to their contacts. You also have to spend

quite a lot of time marketing yourself unless you are lucky enough
to find a reliable source of continuing demand – which in freelance
work is almost a contradiction in terms. It means writing on-spec
letters and going to see people with your portfolio. If you find
someone who likes your work ask them, tactfully, if they also know
of anyone else you could talk to.

It is also worth reading specialist magazines for possible leads,
particularly publications like *Campaign* and *Marketing Week*. If a
company has switched advertising agencies, for instance, it is quite
on the cards that they will want to produce new artwork across a
whole range of products. On-spec approaches which indicate that
you have taken an intelligent interest in the sort of work that might
need doing are always more likely to be successful than simply
writing in out of the blue. This also applies to approaches made to
local companies. Look out for pieces of information in the local
papers that might indicate a need for your work: a big export order
– the sort of thing that gets into the local news – may call for
manuals to accompany the equipment.

Fees
Fees, it has to be said, are not exceptional: about £15 an hour,
including travel. Advertising agencies are least concerned about
what you charge, book publishers the most price-conscious. If the
job is a big one it is a good idea to provide an estimate and agree it
with the client.

Administration
Apart from a simple cash book you only need a job record: a book
in which the date of the commission, the name of the client, the
object being drawn, number of drawings required and the invoice
date are entered. If you are working on a per hour basis, you should
also show the time given.

Professional organisation
Institute of Medical and Biological Illustration, 27 Craven Street,
London WC2N 5NX.

Occupational hazards
Work is somewhat susceptible to general economic conditions and
you have to spend a good deal of money and energy chasing it
When it does come in, it is often wanted in a hurry – you might have
to sit up all night to get it done on time. A longer-term risk is the
advent of computer-aided design (CAD). At present it is still much
cheaper to produce a one-off drawing manually than to program a
computer, but production drawings are largely computerised

already. Learning how to design with a computer may be the best form of training one can undertake at the moment.

Freelance Illustration

Basic skills and aptitudes

An art college education is not absolutely essential, though obviously you need to be able to draw really well and to have an individual style; in other words, you need something more than technical ability, though you do also have to have an understanding of the technical processes involved in turning a drawing into a printed image – for instance, an awareness that very fine lines will get 'lost' when reproduced on certain kinds of paper. You also have to have the ability to work quickly and reliably to deadlines which, in the case of newspaper or magazine work, can be set at short notice.

There are, however, two main advantages of an art college background. One is that it is a useful source of contacts – these days agents and art editors stalk the shows of the more fashionable colleges in search of new talent. The other is that it teaches you to distance yourself from your work and look at it critically. This is something you have to be able to do if you want to keep your style and approach fresh.

Equipment and premises

You can work from home, but you should have a well-lit, good sized space to do it in. Busy illustrators are often working on different stages of several projects concurrently. You need plenty of good, clean space for storage of finished artwork and of the various types and sizes of paper stocks you should carry – paper usually has to be bought in lots of 25–30 sheets at a time. A plan chest is a good buy – they can sometimes be found second hand in the classified pages of artists' magazines or in *Exchange & Mart*.

Another near-essential is a camera, since you often need an image for reference; and since you can only get really good results by doing your own black-and-white developing, you should also have a space which can be used as a darkroom. Many illustrators also use a camera to make colour transparencies as a permanent record of their work.

Beyond this there are many gadgets which it would be useful to have – photocopying machines, for instance, or a Grant projector or doing enlargements and reductions. Fortunately, the spread of print shops and reprographic bureaux now makes it possible to have access to such devices as and when they are needed, rather than investing in them yourself.

The market

Publishers, magazines, newspapers and advertising agencies all use freelance illustrators. Much of the work for publishers is doing book jackets, though the vogue for illustrating texts as well has crept back, perhaps because of the success of *The Country Diary of an Edwardian Lady* and other books which have been 'packaged' for the gift market in a similar way. In this, as in magazine work which generally consists of illustrating an article or a feature, the illustrator has to pick out the salient – but also the visually significant – elements in the writing. That, of course, involves reading the text, or at least some of it, and lengthens the actual working time you spend on the assignment.

Newspapers are more likely to use an illustrator for reportage – for instance, in a courtroom where cameras are not allowed, or in a restaurant where the patrons might not necessarily care to be photographed. Advertising agencies like visually bland but commercially strong images, though there are certain artists who manage to transcend that. The American artists Steinberg and Tomi Ungerer, for instance, have produced some highly individual and even disturbing images for advertisements.

Finding work

In the first instance work is generally found through illustrators' agents. They take your portfolio round art and creative directors and charge between 25 and 30 per cent on commissions that result. A good deal of work comes from existing clients once you are established and they may also recommend your work to others. Always try to get a byline on your work.

A list of illustrators' agents is available to members of the Association of Illustrators. If you are good at selling yourself, have a convincing portfolio and the time to make visits to art directors, you can, of course, bypass them and save yourself quite a lot of money in commissions. On the other hand, agents have a better idea of what art directors like which kind of work than most individuals.

Fees

Fees vary widely, depending on how large the circulation is of the medium for whom you are doing the illustration. A book jacket in colour might bring around £150–£300, though you have to take into account the fact that you will have to read the text first and do some roughs before you do the final artwork. A black-and-white line drawing would fetch a fee of £30–£70. In both cases there might be reasons for working at the lower end of the scale. For instance, a publisher producing a couple of thousand copies of a hardback would not be able to afford as much as a paperback house doing runs which can be hundreds of thousands. In that case you have to make a decision about how badly you want the money – or how much you like the job or the person commissioning you.

Whatever the fee, the copyright remains with the artist unless you specifically assign it – in other words, the client cannot use it for any purpose other than the one for which it was commissioned without negotiating a further fee. Strictly speaking, he or she cannot even use it on his or her own promotional literature, though it might be unwise to make an issue on that kind of point.

Even if you have assigned the copyright, however, the artwork still remains your property.

Administration

You need to keep records of income and expenditure in the form of a simple cash book. You should support the latter with receipts wherever possible. If you are doing a wide variety of work it may be advisable to keep a job file, listing the client, the fee, deadline, date of commissioning and date of despatch. Fees, incidentally, usually include expenses unless they involve out of town travel.

Occupational hazards

Illustrating is a highly competitive business and the market is limited – firms that need a lot of artwork quite often have in-house illustrators, though the trend towards using freelances is growing. At one end of the scale the hazard is not getting enough to do. At the other it is taking on too much. If you become very popular and successful, you can be overwhelmed with work. It is possible, by working flat out, to earn over £1000 a week. The problem is that after a while you become stale and your work begins to show it. At that point clients turn to a fresh source. Illustration is in some ways a fashion business and, as in fashion, a style can become stereotyped.

Professional organisation

The Association of Illustrators (1 Colville Place, London W1P 1HN; 071-636 4100) is open to all illustrators and art directors on payment of an annual fee. They issue a monthly newsletter, maintain a register of approximately 1000 members and, as previously stated, keep a record of agents.

Graphic Design

Basic skills and aptitudes

A design training and some practical experience is essential. A knowledge of print buying and production is also useful. Relatively large sums can be involved in producing the finished article, and there can be considerable savings in making the right decisions about printers and processes.

Equipment and premises

At a basic level you can get by with just a drawing board, sheets of Letraset and the usual armoury of pens and pencils, but this will not take you much further than marking up copy and specifying type for setting: routine stuff and not well paid. You can even specify enlargements or reductions on artwork for the printer to follow but it is not as satisfactory as doing it yourself; it can be risky too, because it involves an element of guesswork. To do better than that you have to be able to visualise scale and size changes yourself and this requires suitable equipment like a Grant projector. They cost upwards of £1000, though they sometimes become available on the second-hand market.

The growth of instant print shops has taken some work away from graphic designers, but it also means that the largest ones have made some of the more sophisticated pieces of equipment available in the high street. Some of them, for instance, have machines for producing PMTs (photo mechanical transfers) from artwork. That means that you can prepare camera-ready copy for the printer.

The market

A very wide variety of small businesses and professional offices need the services of graphic designers to prepare letterheads, business cards, brochures and logos, particularly as there is a growing tendency for some professions to be allowed to advertise. At higher levels design can extend to establishing corporate identities across a whole range of interfaces with the public and with customers; including, in the case of manufacturers, packaging and ultimately product design.

Finding work

Although in the end the most effective source of work is recommendation from satisfied clients, there are a number of ways of priming the pump. Both the Chartered Society of Designers (29 Bedford Square, London WC1B 3EG; 071-631 1510) and the Design Council (28 Haymarket, London SW1Y 5SU; 071-839 8000) maintain registers of designers and their specialities which are sent out to potential clients in response to enquiries. The *Creative Handbook* (published by Thomas Skinner Directories, East Grinstead, West Sussex) also includes lists of designers of various kinds. Putting your name about with your local Chamber of Commerce is reported to be effective, especially outside London, and it is worth leaving your card with local print shops.

After that, a great deal depends on personal chemistry, on the quality of your portfolio and your ability to make a convincing presentation to your prospective client.

Fees

For most jobs fees are charged in three stages: for doing rough layouts and visuals, for producing a final sketch and for doing the finished artwork. The first two of these stages may require quite lengthy consultation with the client, depending, obviously, on the complexity of the job. A bill is sent out at each stage and most freelances charge on an hourly basis, though they may not express it as such in the actual invoice. Again, charges vary enormously with individual designers and to some extent with how much they think the client can afford, but few work for less than £25–£30 per hour at 1991 rates. The only exception is in doing subcontract work for design firms, when lower rates may compensate for regular work and slightly less responsibility. Expenses, obviously, are billed extra.

You can enhance your income very considerably by getting involved in choosing and briefing printers. This is certainly a service graphic designers ought to try and develop, because most clients are putty in printers' hands and you can almost invariably save them money, get a much better quality job and make a healthy percentage for yourself by doing the print buying, especially on substantial jobs. A fairly small business can require 10,000 and more copies of a brochure or even a colour calendar, with a unit cost around £1 a copy.

You can either charge direct for your time as a print consultant or you can actually become a print broker, paying the printer yourself and recovering costs, plus your own percentage, from the client. The problem here is obviously that you need prompt and absolutely reliable payment from the client. It is not a service that should be undertaken unless you are sure of who you are dealing with. Even then, some kind of stage payment is advisable – say, half on sending the camera-ready copy to the printer and half on delivery. You should also be aware that getting involved in print broking will probably mean that you will have to register for VAT, payable by traders whose turnover exceeds £35,000 a year.

Administration

The amount of administration you need depends very much on whether you get involved in print buying. If you are registered for VAT you will need to make quarterly returns of sales and purchases. At the most basic level, that involves keeping a book showing the invoice number, client, amount, VAT, tax point, total including VAT and date of payment. You will also need to keep a record of all business purchases and other expenses and whether or not they bear VAT. Some surprising ones do not – for instance, stamps are exempt.

If you are not registered for VAT a simple cash book, with analysis columns breaking down the main items of expenditure (materials, travel, postage, stationery, etc) will be sufficient. The best plan is to discuss with your accountant how he or she would like you to write up your books to simplify the task of making your tax return.

Occupational hazards

Apart from the universal problems of late payment, the loneliness of working alone (unless you share premises with other freelance designers, an increasingly common practice and one that can in itself be a source of work passed on by other specialists – and vice versa), the biggest difficulty is bad briefing from clients. British firms are very unsure what designers can do for them, fail to ask the right questions and are then unhappy with the result for the simple reason that they have not specified their needs. You should always try to establish what market your client is trying to reach (and even professionals like an accountant or a solicitor are marketing their services in some way), how much they want to spend and what they expect for their money. Some people have very naïve ideas about that and regard designers' charges as excessive – even when their own prices or professional fees are much higher!

Professional organisations

Both the Design Council and the Chartered Society of Designers (addresses already given on page 162) maintain registers of designers. The Chartered Society of Designers also produces a number of practical booklets on the business side of design as well as guidance on fee structures and conditions of engagement.

Fashion Design

Basic skills and aptitudes

The vast majority of fashion designers have come through one of the 62 fashion design courses given in art schools and technical colleges. They turn out some 1500 graduates a year and since there are very few vacancies for employees in the industry, freelancing is the only option for the vast majority. A fashion course will introduce you to design basics and the assumption is that, to have taken it at all, you will have manual dexterity in executing your own designs with reasonable speed. You will certainly need that to succeed as a freelance, but you will also need a critical eye for detail, the ability to spot fashion trends before they hit the street and a good deal of business acumen in buying services and materials as well as a gift for, or at least no inhibitions about, selling.

Equipment and premises

You can work from home, but it looks amateurish if you have to show business customers your work there. Most freelances have a small studio of some kind and at least one commercial sewing machine. There is a good second-hand market in these. You also need some display space, a couple of dummies (also readily available second hand) and good lighting. A lot of studios are in traditional 'rag trade' areas because of the proximity of buyers, but this is not essential provided you are in a reasonably trendy or up-and-coming part of town.

The market

The big market is among retailers from individual shops to department stores – including the buyers of foreign companies who maintain bases in London as some American ones do – but many designers start out by selling to the general public. Street markets where stalls can be rented for a few pounds a day at weekends are a favourite method for this.

Finding work

There are agencies for the work of fashion designers who take their work and portfolios round to potential customers, but they charge from 30 to 50 per cent commission. The heaviest weighting is on new work from an unknown, which is the hardest to sell. Many designers do their own selling. Intelligent buyers are always looking for interesting new work: you need to have design portfolios and finished garments to show the standard of workmanship.

Fees

Fees vary wildly. A minority earn six figure sums, but the average income is said to be £13,000–£17,000.

Administration

The high rate of business failures in freelance fashion design is due as much as anything else to the fact that administration is more complex than many designers realise at the outset. You have to prepare costings and cash flows carefully from the very beginning, to control outworkers and be able to keep track of garments sent out for finishing. It is highly advisable to find an accountant with some knowledge of the fashion business so that you can set up your records in a way that will enable you to monitor your progress. This is not only important from a financial point of view, but so that orders can be executed on time and to specification.

Occupational hazards

The biggest hazard is that, however good and efficient you are, the fashion business is notoriously fickle. As in the pop scene, you can be the flavour of the month for a while and then be supplanted by someone with a new idea. Unless you can be continually innovative as well as reliable and proficient, life as a freelance designer is totally unpredictable. So also are the fortunes of manufacturers and retailers. Bankruptcies are common.

Technical Draughting

Basic skills and aptitudes

Very often draughting work is meant to be reproduced. Therefore a knowledge of basic print processes and their implications in terms of drawing styles and materials is useful. Academic qualifications are not necessary, though experience in a drawing office is. In any case most people who have done work of that nature would have had some kind of technical drawing qualifications.

Equipment and premises

You obviously need a good drawing board, though again anyone who is contemplating freelance work in this sphere would probably own one of these. Apart from that, little initial investment is required, though you obviously ought to have a range of drawing tools and materials.

The market

Magazines, book publishers, advertising agencies and producers of technical manuals are all potential clients.

Finding work

Initially it comes, like so much freelance work, through personal contacts. Thereafter it is a question of trying to develop a contact network: phoning round people one knows, trying to get recommendations and references and taking one's portfolio round. Putting your name down with potential sources of enquiries like Chambers of Commerce, Local Enterprise Agencies and small firms information services is also important, and there are a number of specialist agencies who supply freelance draughting personnel.

The best people to ask about them are other freelances because some agencies are obviously more effective in getting work for the people on their books than others.

Fees

Book publishers do not pay well – the rate there can go as low as £8–£10 an hour. Magazine rates are rather better and advertising or PR agency fees are around £20–£25 an hour. Materials are charged extra, if they can be shown as specific items – like buying sheets of Letraset, for instance. Travel times should be charged at the same rate as hours spent at the drawing board. Some costs can be quite substantial – for instance, if you have to have lettering or captions set by a printer. It is essential that all expense claims should be supported by an invoice.

Administration

It is fatally easy to get muddled up between several jobs both as regards the client's brief and the costs incurred. The best way to avoid this is to set up a job record book and to keep a separate page for each job. It should show the date on which instructions were received, the required completion date, the subject, the client contact and telephone number, the time taken, expenses incurred and the date on which fee and expenses were paid. Costs and fees can then be entered into a cash book.

Although fee income may not take you over the threshold above which you have to register for VAT, it is very possible that if you are making disbursements on behalf of clients you could get into the VAT-able category because the criterion is turnover, not fees or profits. If that is a possibility you should register for VAT right away because you should be charging it on your invoices. If you fail to do so, there is a risk that Customs and Excise will try to recover it from you and it will be virtually impossible for you to extract VAT from clients after the event.

Registering for VAT requires more rigorous book-keeping than if you are outside the system and you have to make a quarterly return of inputs and outputs to Customs and Excise. On the other hand, it enables you to recover the VAT element on all your taxable costs which in the case of a draughtsperson could be considerable.

Occupational hazards

By its nature sitting at a drawing board is a solitary occupation. In an office you can maintain human contact with the people around you, so working on your own does create problems of loneliness. You also have to be able to work at speed. Book publishers work over fairly extended periods, but magazines often operate on tight schedules. So do advertising agencies, especially the less well-organised ones that pay less attention to planning ahead. Agencies, though the best payers, also tend to be among the slowest and it is not advisable to pay out too many large sums on their behalf to printers and other suppliers. Unless you can contrive to get paid in advance – which seldom happens – you should arrange for more substantial amounts to be billed direct to the client. That must, of course, be agreed beforehand.

There are, of course, cases where you never get paid at all and usually the amounts are too small to pursue through the small claims procedures in the County Court. Such a situation is more easily avoided by working through an agency, though, on the other hand, the fees tend to be smaller because the client has to pay the agency as well as the draughtsperson.

15
Freelancing in the Crafts

Introduction

The crafts cover an enormous range of activities. Whole books could be – and have been – written about the major ones, though they emphasise how to do it rather than how to make a living at it. Many of them are a hobby rather than a potential source of income. Those that fall into the latter category are, however, also those where the strongest level of support can be expected from the Crafts Council and the separate but kindred body, the Rural Development Commission (formerly CoSIRA). The latter deals with enterprises in rural areas and small county towns in England. It also has sister bodies in Scotland, Wales and Northern Ireland.

The crafts that come under the umbrella of the Crafts Council include: bookbinding, fashion accessories, glass, lettering, metal, musical instruments, ceramics, textiles, toys and wood. The Rural Development Commission's technical services extend to: farriery, forgework, furniture making and antique furniture restoration, pottery, saddlery, harness and saddlework, thatching and upholstery. However, though it helps to be in a mainstream craft, skill is not the whole story. There are other dimensions as well.

Basic skills and aptitudes

When a skilled amateur told a professional freelance cabinet-maker that he thought he himself could achieve similar results, the professional's reply was, 'I'm sure you could – but could you do it as quickly?' In other words, you need speed as well as skill, and that is a matter of practice as well as manual dexterity – knowing where you can cut corners and take risks, for instance.

Although freelancing as a craftsperson is a lonely occupation it is not simply one for pure backroom boys or girls. You need to be a good communicator, verbally, graphically and sometimes in writing, as well as a good maker. Getting and developing commissions calls for an ability to make presentations to clients and to establish a clear brief about what they want. Writing ability – not literary skill – up to the level of producing a report comes in when you confirm what has been agreed verbally; if the client does not produce such a document, the craftsperson certainly should.

On top of that you have to be able to cost out your work and to be numerate enough to trim a brief to the amount of money the client has available. Where no commission exists and where you are producing a one-off object on spec to try to sell to a retailer, you also have to be aware of the market in terms of the nature of the thing you are proposing to offer, and its price.

In other words, to function as a freelance craftsperson calls for a whole range of skills beyond the obvious question of how good you are as a maker. The last one, marketing, is the most important of them. If you have a unique product that a lot of people want, you can get away with a great deal, but few craftspeople are in that happy position.

Equipment and premises

You can work from home, if you have a space suitable for your occupation or if you are producing on a very small scale. There are, however, various arguments against it. For one thing, if what you do creates a hazard (eg from chemicals or fire) or makes a noise, you will have to apply for planning permission to use your premises in that way. Strictly speaking, you should do it in all cases where you intend to use a residence for non-domestic purposes, but in practice very few people bother unless what they do is going to be obtrusive for neighbours. Of course, if you are on a lease you will have to inform the landlord in almost any circumstances. You should also let your insurers know, since your policy only covers ordinary domestic risks.

Because of these complications and because a great many crafts require access for materials and finished goods, storage space and a working area where dirt, dust and noise does not matter, craftspeople generally prefer to operate from a workshop. It also looks more professional, when seeing clients, than working out of a back room at 77 The Laurels.

Small workshop spaces are not easy to find at an affordable rent, but the problem is getting a little easier, because of the growing trend towards small, one- or two-person enterprises. In quite a number of locations, redundant industrial buildings are being converted to house individual workshops; and, unlike the traditional chilly space under a disused railway arch, they are properly serviced by the developers with gas, water and electricity. Having previously been industrial buildings, as they often were, they also tend to have decent lifts and goods access if they are on more than one floor.

The best people to ask about small workplaces are now not so much the estate agents, but Local Enterprise Agencies, the Rural Development Commission offices in England (or the Scottish

Development Agency in Scotland; the Welsh Development Agency in Wales and the Local Enterprise Development Unit in Northern Ireland) and Small Firms Centres. In areas of high unemployment it is worth asking about the availability of grants or loans. A useful free booklet on this subject is produced by the accountants Binder Hamlyn: *Government Help for Your Business*. (Write to Binder Hamlyn, 25 Milton Road, Swindon, Wilts SN1 5JA.)

There are also some advantages in setting up in an Enterprise Zone. There are a number of these in the UK, mostly in areas of high unemployment. Although they were established originally to encourage larger-scale manufacturers to provide jobs, they have been tilting more towards the small enterprise and converting disused factories into individual workspaces.

They have a number of advantages for someone setting up in business; there is an initial rate-free period and a relaxation of some of the more onerous bureaucratic controls. On the other hand, they tend to be stuck in depressed areas, with few customers in the immediate vicinity.

Wherever you decide to locate, the best plan initially is to have a tenancy agreement that can be terminated at short notice and without penalty. Once you are established you can make arrangements over the longer term, but until then it is unwise to make extended commitments that it will be costly to get out of. This also applies to equipment; never buy it or commit yourself to a leasing arrangement that may cost you money to terminate until you are absolutely sure that you can make it pay its way. Hiring can be expensive – and in some cases there may be no facilities to do so – but it should always be considered first. Exceptions to that rule are, of course, less expensive but necessary items like a typewriter and a camera for photographing your work, though most people already own these.

The other option is to buy your equipment second hand. Most of the specialist magazines and trade papers relating to a particular craft carry advertisements for second-hand machinery. Sometimes it is antique, clapped-out plant, but quite often it is being sold by liquidators of failed companies or by craftspeople who have either decided to call it a day or gone on to use some superior machine. There are, however, some amazing buys even in the first category: a specialist printer recently bought for the merest song a press that could fold as well as print cardboard. The owners had thrown it out in favour of the new technology but the specialist printer recouped its price in printing packaging material for gift firms in a matter of weeks.

Nevertheless, there is a strong element of *caveat emptor* in buying second hand. There is some protection for buyers in the Sale of Goods Act which states that goods must be 'as described' and 'of merchantable quality', but it still pays you to examine them very carefully and to ask about age, availability of spares and/or service, output given reasonably skilled operation, and about defects that are not immediately obvious. It is a good idea to take a witness along in case arguments arise later.

You are allowed to write off the cost of capital equipment against tax at the rate of 25 per cent a year, but apart from any grants and subsidies that may be available locally on buying equipment, there is one form of government grant that is definitely worth applying for, if you are eligible. That is the Enterprise Allowance Scheme. If you have been unemployed for 8 weeks, and can put £1000 of your money into your venture, you can get £40 a week for 52 weeks from the Department of Employment. That will certainly help with equipment rental costs, though you can use the money any way you like.

There are, however, schemes run through the Crafts Council – and also again through its sister bodies – which are directly designed to fund equipment and related costs. There is a setting-up scheme which provides up to 50 per cent of the cost of fitting out a workshop and a maintenance grant to subsidise some of the initial running costs.

Because crafts are generally attended by personal enthusiasm on the part of the maker, it can be easy to deceive yourself about the size of the market for what you are doing. This is less likely to happen if you have previously worked as an employee in the field where you intend to freelance – indeed, your former employer may well become one of your customers – but if you are launching out into the blue, market research is essential. How you conduct that depends on the nature of the craft you are engaged in: it may be a question of talking to shops, to manufacturers for whom you intend to freelance as a subcontractor or – much more difficult – to private individuals who you hope will be your customers. That research has to cover not only demand, but also the price that people will pay for what you do.

Local Enterprise Agencies are worth talking to here and, if you live outside urban areas, the Rural Development Commission or its sister bodies in Wales, Scotland and Northern Ireland. The Rural Development Commission's officers will be happy to talk to you and comment on how your proposed venture might be modified to meet the greatest demand. Initial consultations are free.

Finding work

Ultimately, the best form of promotion is good work that you have done but you cannot rely on that solely. Fortunately, the Crafts Council is a great deal more active than most such associations on the marketing side. In the first instance, you should be sure that you are on their Register of Craftspeople. This is a card index of makers divided according to craft and county and is an unselected list on which all makers known to the Council are represented. The next, and more desirable stage up, is their Index of Selected Makers. To get on that – there are about 470 names on it at present – your work has to pass the scrutiny of the Index Section Committee. Once that happens your details will be entered in the Crafts Council's files and computer database. The Index of Selected Makers is the prime reference source for prospective clients, but even if you do not get on it, there are plenty of other steps you can take to publicise yourself. For instance, the Crafts Council publishes *Crafts* magazine and a map guide featuring selected craft shops and galleries and supplies up-to-date details of forthcoming craft events, fairs and markets throughout Britain.

It is certainly worth taking part in these, but before taking the plunge or even showing your work to craft shops in your area, it may be worth taking it round to Contemporary Applied Arts, 43 Earlham Street, London WC2H 9LD; 071-836 6993. They will give you an opinion on whether it is good enough to find a niche commercially.

Another good way of finding work is simply through local publicity. This is more difficult in metropolitan areas, where editors get more news than they can handle, but outside them the opposite tends to be true and copy is extracted from even the most unlikely sources. Local radio and even TV stations are also interested in anything that has local news value. The audiences for these are generally much larger than for written material, especially during hours when most people are at home.

Finally, there are local directories, Chambers of Commerce, even the Yellow Pages. In many cases it costs nothing to be listed but the benefits can be very substantial. Another group of people who can be useful in publicising craftspeople's work are trade associations connected with particular materials; for instance, the Copper Development Association.

Fees

In view of the variety of crafts and the enormous range of materials that are potentially involved – anything from precious metals to wood and clay – it is better to look at fees from the point of view of general principles than specific sums. Charges can be on the basis of an hourly/daily rate or related to individual objects, but in both cases the fundamental questions are: How much do the materials cost? How much should you add on for overheads, like rent, rates and services? How much is the competition charging? How much can the client afford to pay? How much do you need to make to produce an adequate income? On top of that you will have to consider, when discussing fees or prices, what extra costs will be involved. Will you have to travel to London for meetings? Are you going to have to make regular long-distance telephone calls to go over details with the client? Who is going to pay for delivery? It may be that in the light of such questions either your concept or the client's brief will have to be altered to fit the available resources.

Further guidance on costing and pricing work is given in Chapter 5, but the important thing to remember is that as much as possible about payment should be cut and dried before the job is begun:

- The brief or specification – ie what the client is paying for.
- What payment was agreed – including VAT.
- What extras and expenses you can charge for.
- When payment becomes due, either as a single sum or in stages.
- Whether the client is buying copyright or merely the object you have produced. Most makers hang on to the copyright or at least insist on a royalty if the client reproduces their work for re-sale.

Administration

Few craftspeople like the idea of administration and paperwork, but unfortunately there is quite a lot involved. In the first place reliability is very important for a freelance. You should never take on more work than you can handle, so you need to keep two diaries: one on your desk and a pocket version to carry around with you, with entries being transferred from one to the other, as required. Once you start doing a lot of work you will probably need some kind of wall chart that will provide a schedule of jobs at a glance. If you are subcontracting work to other freelances – and this is quite common – you also need to know about their availability. If you are using particular materials and supplies, you will have to keep track of their current prices and the most reliable suppliers. Once you are set up in business you should get in touch with them and make sure they send you their sales literature which will have to be filed in some accessible way. Clients quite often want to see craftspeople at work, and indeed the general look of a studio may be a factor in making a commissioning decision. An office that looks like a tip could count against you in that situation.

Once a commission is under discussion you will have to keep a record of meetings and confirm them with the client if he or she does not do so. Some kind of voice recording machine – they can be bought for under £40 – is a good buy, either to put on the table at meetings or to summarise afterwards your memory of what was said. The latter course is better, otherwise you will have to listen to a surprising amount of rhubarb to get at the few facts you need. Apart from investing in that, you will also need some decently designed letterheads and visiting cards. You could also get invoices printed for you, but unless you are fairly sure you will have a flood of business, it is better to buy these ready-made. Packs of quite professional-looking pre-printed invoices in duplicate can be bought from business stationers.

Before you get to the invoicing stage – that obviously comes at the end of the process – there is a continuing but necessary amount of administration to keep track of. The most important element is to establish and set down a detailed brief. How much detail it will involve varies from case to case, but the following essentials are common ground

- Dimensions
- Materials
- Colour
- Delivery dates
- Delivery location
- Maintenance.

Before these stages are reached, however, there may be a call for approval of a sketch design or a prototype with an abort provision built in. In that case your diary or wall chart will have to track the points at which you have to refer back to the client before making a further move. But even if he or she does not want to hear from you until the job is finished, it is essential to keep him or her informed if you are going to be late – or even early.

Early delivery, though it seldom happens, can be inconvenient if a client has no storage space or is not yet ready. Late delivery can invalidate your contract. If time was an essential item in the client's requirements he or she would be within his or her rights in refusing delivery when it was unreasonably late.

As far as book-keeping is concerned all you need to worry about is keeping regular, accurate and up-to-date records for expenditure and receipts. Your bank manager's or accountant's advice should be sought here because it is easy to overlook vital items, like rates. The important discipline is to enter up the cash book, showing income and expenditure, daily if at all possible.

In addition to a cash book it is also a good idea to keep a record of costs on each job: materials, labour, travel and overheads. That

will help you to give increasingly accurate estimates as your
freelance work grows.

Occupational hazards

Most of the occupational hazards have already been touched on
under previous headings. Apart from those that are common to all
kinds of freelance work – loneliness and chronic uncertainty about
where the next penny is coming from – the big question mark is
always about the market. There is a close kinship between many
crafts and hobbies – an unpalatable fact which craftspeople refuse
to face at their peril. So is there really a big enough demand from
people who are willing to pay a realistic sum of money for what you
do? Contemporary Applied Arts and indeed shops or agents you
want to sell to should provide an answer, but it is one you should
seek before you start out.

Another hazard relates to copyright. In the first place you will
have to be absolutely clear that you are not infringing anyone else's.
Second, you should note that when a client commissions work he
assumes that the copyright passes to him. This is actually a grey
area in the case of a great deal of commissioned creative work,
including journalism, because some authorities hold that rights not
specifically granted are withheld. The trouble with a maker or any
other kind of creative person maintaining that position is that the
person commissioning, assuming he or she has the resources to
exploit your copyright, also has the means to fight off a legal action.
The best plan, therefore, is to agree with the client beforehand
exactly what rights he or she is buying.

Another hazard which craftspeople have in common with other
freelances is that of clients of the 'can't pay, won't pay' variety. One
fairly obvious way of dealing with this problem is not to deliver until
payment has been received, but that is not always practicable,
especially in the case of commissioned pieces that are hard to place
elsewhere. There is not a great deal you can do unless larger sums
of money are involved that justify pursuing the matter in the small
claims court: about £250 is probably around the minimum. The only
answer, in the case of an expensive job – expensive either in time or
in materials – and an unknown client is to ask for stage payments.
If the client is reluctant and you have that uneasy feeling about him
or her, it is often best to turn the commission down.

One reason why the client might refuse to pay, or might withhold
some of the money due, would be if the work was defective in some
way. Under the Sale of Goods Act you are liable to make good such
damage, though you can limit your responsibility by building
'defects' period into your agreement. If it was unreasonable it might
not, however, protect you in the courts and the appearance of such

a clause tends to alarm clients at the outset. So do make provision for payment should he or she refuse to accept the goods. To envisage such a possibility might be taken to be something less than a token of confidence in your own abilities.

Professional organisations

There are a great many organisations to which craftspeople can either belong or turn to for help and advice.

Contemporary Applied Arts, 43 Earlham Street, London WC2H 9LD; 071-836 6993

The Crafts Council, 12 Waterloo Place, Lower Regent Street, London SW1Y 4AU; 071-278 7700

The Crafts Council of Ireland, Thomas Prior House, Merrion Road, Ballsbridge, Dublin 4; 010 3531 6797368

Local Enterprise Development Unit, LEDU House, Upper Galwally, Belfast BT8 4TB; 0232 491031

The Rural Development Commission, 141 Castle Street, Salisbury, Wiltshire SP1 3TP; 0722 336255

Scottish Crafts Centre, Acheson House, Canongate, Edinburgh EH8 8DD; 031-225 4152

Wales Crafts Council, 20 Severn Street, Welshpool, Powys SY21 7AD; 0938 555313

The Craft and Design Department, Welsh Arts Council, Holst House, Museum Place, Cardiff CF1 3NX; 0222 394711

Repair and Restoration of Valuables

Introduction

Whether as investments, status symbols or from what seems to be a widespread instinct to collect or preserve family heirlooms, interest in antiques and pictures has never been greater. Quite often, though, they are in poor condition through age or accident and there are then considerable problems about getting them repaired. This is not just a matter of technical knowledge, but is due to the fact that such objects were made at the time by highly skilled craftsmen operating on comparatively low wages. The costs of equivalent work now would be prohibitive, even if the skills were widely available – which they are not.

Thus, the big problem for freelance restorers of all kinds is that the value of their input – many hours or even days of repairing a damaged porcelain figure, for instance – is often almost as great as the intrinsic value of the work. It is seldom worth repairing anything except the simplest damage on an object worth less than £250 or so on cost grounds, though sentimental value can outweigh such factors with private individuals.

Dealers, from whom most commissions come, are not usually swayed by sentiment. They tend to want a quick, and sometimes bodged, job – except on really valuable pieces – which will enable them to effect a quick sale. This is where the restorer's professional pride and conscientiousness may clash with commercial consider-ations and it is an issue on which you will probably have to make up your mind from the very beginning, because there is a certain amount of competition from those who are prepared to compromise on matters of artistic integrity in order to earn a living. If that course of action is forced on you there is, however, a potentially profitable way of doing the kind of job you would really prefer to be doing. Quite a number of restorers buy the occasional piece for themselves and do it up for re-sale. Indeed this is one of the rare kinds of freelancing where you can become your own customer when work is slack.

Picture Restoring

Basic skills and aptitudes
Strictly speaking, anyone can set up as a picture restorer, though you need a knowledge of paints and pigments, excellent eyesight, infinite patience, manual dexterity, some painting ability of your own (to handle re-touching) and, of course, more than a passing acquaintance with art history. There are courses for picture restorers – a full list can be obtained from the Conservation Unit, Museums and Galleries Commission, 7 St James's Square, London SW1Y 4JU; 071-233 3683. The course offered by the Courtauld Institute is generally regarded as the most prestigious one and is therefore very difficult to get into. It also takes three years and grants for it are reputedly hard to come by. A lot of people, in fact, get into restoration from a fine arts or chemistry background and go to work as an apprentice or assistant to a restorer before setting up as a freelance.

Equipment and premises
You need a fair-sized studio with good natural lighting and high-grade artificial lighting for the winter months. Materials are expensive – though, except for solvents, you don't use a lot of them. This fact, however, makes it difficult to buy cheaply in bulk.

The basic equipment you need is also expensive; an easel, a hot spatula, an instamatic camera, an ultra-violet light source and a binocular microscope are essential and will cost around

£1200–£1500 new. Some materials, like canvas for relining, can be purchased as specific orders come in.

The market

There are a vast number of works of art around that need cleaning, restoration or repair. Museums and galleries have their own restoration staff, but work comes in from dealers, framers, private collectors and sometimes from other restorers if you have a speciality. Some restorers, for instance, specialise in modern paintings. Water colours, drawings and paper restoration generally form a subject of their own. Dealers are the best source, though.

Finding work

Recommendations from satisfied clients are best, but for the newcomer that creates something of a 'chicken and egg' situation. Some restorers advertise in places like *Country Life*, though this is regarded as not quite the done thing by those who regard restoration as a profession rather than purely a business. The best thing is to go and see dealers and show them before and after photos of pictures you have worked on. Museums and galleries are also a source of work because they get a lot of enquiries from private individuals which they pass on to outside restorers whom they know can be relied on to do a good job (though inevitably some museum restorers are also fairly keen moonlighters!).

If you are very confident of your ability to spot saleable pictures you can buy works in need of restoration and do them up yourself. To do that, though, you need to have at least £1000 to invest. You cannot normally buy for less than that a picture which will produce an adequate return for the risk and the costs of restoring it yourself. On the other hand, restorers do have certain advantages in the art market, like knowing what kind of surface will clean up well and easily. Some pictures are best left in their existing state. Cleaning would show up their defects, or they are simply too delicate for such treatment.

Fees

Restorers generally charge an hourly rate – around £15 an hour for a trained and qualified, but not an experienced, restorer. Successful restorers can earn more than £25,000 per annum, but £18,000 is a good average and £10,000–£12,000 is as much as you are likely to make initially. In fact, restorers say that it takes two to three years before you make a living wage.

It is difficult even for experienced restorers to give an exact quote to a client because often the problems do not become evident until you have begun to work on a picture – in the case of an oil painting, stripping off the varnish. It is best to show the client what needs doing and then to quote only in a range. In the case of a big job it would be advisable not to talk fees at all until a written report has been prepared and the work agreed with the client, subject to price. However, major jobs – over £500 – are rare and quite a lot of work is done for around £100.

Administration

Apart from basic books and records (see Chapter 7), you need to keep a job book. That should show:

- A description of each picture brought in
- Its approximate date
- Owner's name, address and telephone number
- Treatment required
- Quote
- Completion date
- Delivery instructions, if any
- Collection/delivery date
- Invoice date
- The amount of time taken over the job.

If you send pictures out on subcontract – for instance, for framing – there should also be a record of who they were sent to, the agreed price and the completion date.

Occupational hazards

The biggest one is accidentally damaging a picture. Leaving a quick-acting solvent on while answering the door can produce instant disaster. One restorer told a horrifying tale of carving up a £3000 drawing which a colleague had carelessly left face down on the table where she cut her mounts. A professional negligence policy is essential.

It is difficult to insure against theft because of the varying values you may have on your premises at different times. Clients should be asked to make their own arrangements and a declaration to that effect should be prominently displayed on the premises.

Another problem that occurs with some private clients is that they either fail to collect pictures or leave them for unreasonably long periods. Some restorers advocate that you should ask unknown clients to sign a declaration giving you the right to recoup your costs by selling any picture left with you for more than a certain period of time.

There is a physical hazard which affects restorers who wear plastic contact lenses. They may be attacked by strong solvents and it is wise to check with your optician under what circumstances you should resort to ordinary spectacles while working. New materials like solvents come on the market all the time, and indeed keeping in touch with new technical developments, while at the same time earning a living, is a problem for freelances in this field. There are, however, regular conferences where new advances in the state of the art are discussed. Restorers find that it is essential to attend at least the major ones to keep up with their subject.

Professional organisations

The main one is the Association of British Picture Restorers, Station Avenue, Kew, Surrey TW9 3QA; 081-948 5644. This has around 200 full and associate members and, though it does not maintain a formal register, the names of suitably qualified restorers are put forward in response to enquiries. Full membership is granted subject to approval of work by the ABPR committee.

The International Institute for the Conservation of Historic and Artistic Works is at 6 Buckingham Street, London WC2N 6BA; 071-839 5975. There are no conditions for Associate membership and the Institute publishes a quarterly containing mainly technical articles, *Studies in Conservation*. They also issue a twice yearly set of *Art and Archaeology Technical Abstracts*. As its name implies, the Institute's coverage extends to artistic works across a wider field than painting alone. It also organises international conferences. These are highly regarded by the experts and have the further attraction of being held in glamorous locations with interesting museums.

Picture Framing and Frame Mending

Basic skills and aptitudes

You need manual dexterity at the level of a competent DIY craftsperson but, as examples of competently executed but artistically hideous framing demonstrate, taste, judgement and a feel for what looks right have to be added to skill in cutting mounts, frames and glass, replacing mouldings and covering over lost areas of gilding. To some extent taste, like physical skill, is something you are born with, but you can also develop it by going to galleries and museums and seeing how the pictures there are framed. Styles in framing vary from one period to the next, as do styles in the paintings themselves.

Equipment and premises

At the top end you can invest in sophisticated tools and presses for making mouldings and cutting frames and mounts which can cost you £3000–£4000. It is best to start with basics, though, and gradually to build up from there as your skill increases – particularly as second-hand items can be picked up over a period of time. You can do competent work with no more than a good mitre box, a powerful stapling gun, a professional duty glass cutter and a couple of large, stable tables as working surfaces. Also, of course, you need good lighting and plenty of storage space for materials. If you are repairing frames you will need to invest in gold and metal leaf. The former, though bought in almost tissue paper thicknesses, is expensive.

The market

Private individuals, dealers in pictures of all kinds, and antique shops put framing and mending out to freelances. Very few employ full-time staff of their own for this purpose.

Finding work

Visits to such establishments and personal contacts with friends and acquaintances are enough to bring an initial response. Thereafter how much work you get depends on how good you are. The demand for framing and frame repairing services by art dealers and print sellers is considerable.

Fees

Most framers quote a flat fee, but base it on labour and the cost of materials. Labour charges average from £10 to £12 an hour and materials bring this up to £15–£18 an hour.

Administration

Only basic purchasing and sales records need to be kept, for which an ordinary cash book will suffice, but the range of materials needed means that purchase entries can be quite lengthy. You will also have to come to a conclusion fairly early on in your freelance career about how much stock you are going to carry in the way of materials. There are only a limited number of art suppliers who carry anything like a complete range of framers' requirements outside London, which means you may have to weigh up the pros and cons of buying to specific commissions – and making trips to suppliers to get your materials – with the strains on cash flow of carrying larger inventories.

Occupational hazards

Wastage in picture framing can be high – an error of a few millimetres can render hours of work worthless. For this reason some framers recommend getting crucial bits of cutting done by specialists, though this obviously cuts into their own profits. Large quantities of glass represent a physical hazard when working at home and there may also be difficulties about getting garbage collectors to accept waste of this kind as falling within the province of domestic refuse.

Antique Furniture Restoration

Basic skills and aptitudes
You need manual skills – specifically a talent for woodwork, plus a fine arts background. Furthermore, because a restoration job is seldom confined to one particular aspect, you also need some ability in handling other dimensions of it – metalwork, for instance. Courses in restoration are given at West Dean College, West Dean, Chichester, Sussex PO18 0QZ; 0243 63 301. Some practising restorers also take pupils.

Equipment and premises
This is a form of work which is fairly demanding in terms of space – not only for working surfaces, which need to be generous, but also for storage. Access must be easy and entrances large enough to take big pieces without damaging them.

Good lighting is essential because colour matching processes are often involved. Some of the tools, like a bandsaw, can be noisy, so if you are working from home, this is one occupation where you will need to apply for planning permission.

Equipping a workshop properly can cost from £3000 to £5000, but it can be done for less. The assumption is that anyone who was contemplating this way of working freelance would already be doing some form of cabinet making or restoration as a hobby and would therefore have some of the tools already. However, specialist tools are expensive and by no means easy to buy. Most restorers use antique tools to some extent because for some jobs they are the only ones that are available and also because they are generally considered to be better made.

Antique tools used to be cheap – you could pick them up from cabinet makers who had retired or from the deceased's estates. In recent years they have become collectors' items and increased in price accordingly. The country's leading dealer in antique tools and an authority on the whole subject is Roy Arnold, 77 High Street, Needham Market, Suffolk IP6 8AN; 0449 720110.

The market
Museums are the best customers for high-quality work. Dealers tend to be highly conscious of their profit margins and to want work in a hurry, though they are less concerned, or purport to be, about

standards. Collectors and also ordinary people with good pieces, often left as heirlooms, are also likely customers.

Finding work

The best source of work is word of mouth recommendation, especially from museums who may not only send you their own work but also recommend you to private people who come to them for advice. Once your name gets around, jobs tend to come in, though not in an even flow. The problem then is that if you go and get it by making personal calls on potential clients, such as dealers, there is less time for careful supervision of the work you have. This is also true if you take on staff. Generally, they require supervision and this can be to the detriment of your own restoration.

A possible additional source of work is to buy in pieces yourself and fix them up, though this requires a knowledge of the antique furniture market and its fashions, which restorers do not necessarily have. Another option is to run courses. If you are skilled in some speciality and are a good teacher, there is quite a demand for such courses among other professionals, and also beginners who want to get into this form of earning a living.

Fees

These are generally charged on a time basis to cover costs, overheads and to produce a margin of profit. However, in practice many restorers have to be elastic, within reason, about how much they charge – or run the risk of losing a job. The basis of charging a museum or a wealthy collector for an important piece is often treated differently from repairing an heirloom for an ordinary family. A further factor may be whether or not the assignment is an insurance job, where money may, within reason, be less significant than if the client has to fund the repair out of his or her own pocket. Generally, an estimate is given within a cost range and the client is contacted if the job looks like going over the figure that has been given.

Administration

This can be kept to a minimum, though you do need a cash book with some simple analysis columns: tools, overheads, car expenses, insurance and VAT. You also need to keep an order book, showing the name of the customer, when the piece came in, what needs doing to it – and when by – and what the estimate was. Actual and estimate costs are also worth keeping track of, to make sure your prices stay in line with costs.

Occupational hazards

The worst one is the conflict of interests that tends to arise between your own standards and commercial considerations, not only in terms of the pieces you take on but also of the quality of the work you do on them. Dealers, as mentioned before, want everything in a hurry and, apart from the element of artistic compromise that this may entail, it can also lead to making mistakes if you try to bodge work.

Mistakes are seldom fatal in the case of wood – you can always repair them yourself – but they can be very time consuming. Actual breakages are a more serious matter, and as antique furniture often includes delicate materials such as glass or marble, they can be very expensive since they generally have to be put right by a specialist in that type of repair.

Another hazard is that because pieces are seldom uniform in their materials you tend to become involved in restoration about which you do not have much experience; for instance, desks often have leather surfaces and it is not only the wood but also the leather which requires attention. That can create complications and can turn a profitable job into a marginal one.

Professional organisation

The British Antique Furniture Restoration Association (BAFRA), 37 Upper Addison Gardens, London W14 8AJ; 071-603 5643, monitors standards and is also a source of work, as enquiries are often routed through them. Membership requires references from museum officials or serious collectors and may also entail inspection of your workshop or premises to make sure they are up to professional standards.

Pottery and Porcelain Repair

Basic skills and aptitudes

Pottery and porcelain objects are moulded and, usually, decorated. Repairing them therefore calls for skills both in modelling and in painting and drawing. You also need an understanding of the properties of various types of clays and glazes and, of course, a good deal of knowledge about the history of pottery and porcelain: the styles of various periods and even of different factories and the artists employed by them. Not surprisingly, many freelance restorers come through art history courses and conservation departments in museums. Some have worked for other restorers and picked up skills along the way. Others have attended the year-long course in the subject at West Dean College in West Sussex or the conservation course at the Institute of Archaeology (31–34 Gordon Square, London WC1H 0PY; 071-387 7050).

However, even if you have attended a course – some are given informally by practising restorers – you still need prolonged exposure to the realities of studio work. And apart from actual skills you need certain physical and mental attributes, particularly good eyesight and patience.

Equipment and premises

Some restorers use an oven to re-fix glazes and to harden any clays that have been used. An ordinary kitchen oven will do for this, since it is done at low temperatures, but not one that has previously been used for cooking, since any impurities will foul the glazes. Others work on cold cure principles, but in both cases the basic tools are similar. You need an air brush and the compressor that provides the pressure for it – you can, in fact, run more than one air brush off the same one; also a dental drill. Apart from that, you need non-machine tools, like a wide range of files and spatulas; adhesives and resins; and a broad spectrum of pigments. The costs of some of these materials are fairly high, but they are only used in small quantities.

A compressor costs about £200–£300 and you can buy a second-hand dental drill for around £100.

The location of premises is not important though they should be reasonably acessible to a customer base – they will not drive miles out of their way to find you. That means you can go for fairly low-cost accommodation, though it has to have good lighting and plenty of storage space both for objects still to be repaired and for those which are still awaiting collection. You also need plenty of good, firm working surfaces. Formica is best because it is easy to clean and formica tops can be fitted on to ordinary wood tables. Massive Edwardian monstrosities are good for this purpose because they are strong, well-made and still relatively inexpensive compared to their much less stout modern equivalents.

The market

Private individuals are probably a better market than antique dealers. Dealers seldom buy damaged pieces unless they are very rare because their value in that case declines sharply. They are, of course, subject to accidents like everyone else and also they occasionally buy pieces without realising they are not in perfect condition. Simply in numerical terms there are many more private individuals with damaged pots of value – at least to them. There are very few households that do not have at least one possession that comes into that category.

Private collectors, unlike dealers, will buy damaged pieces out of interest, and, since they don't intend to re-sell them, they are less concerned about the cost of repair, within reason. That is also true of museums.

During slack periods, some repairers buy damaged pieces in sales and auctions and do them up themselves for re-sale to dealers and others.

Finding work

Most jobs come through personal contacts and recommendations. A satisfied customer is always a good advertisement. It is a good idea to keep in touch with museums – though quite often they have their own conservation departments – because private individuals often approach them for advice on getting antique repairs done. Advertising in trade and collectors' magazines is said to be useful and so is simply going round dealers yourself or doing a mail shot to them.

There is also scope for free publicity in repair work. Local newspapers particularly are avid for local interest stories. If you have a particularly unusual or important piece it is worth notifying the features editor.

Fees

Most people who bring things in for repair want an estimate. Restorers base their prices on an hourly rate related to what they would like to earn, plus what is needed to cover overheads, but estimating off the cuff is difficult: a job can be more complex than it looks – rarely less. You also have to be realistic about how quickly you can work. If you are considerably slower than others you cannot pitch your prices as if you worked at the same speed.

The best plan, if the job looks at all complex, is to ask customers to leave it and come back for an estimate. That is usually verbal, and though an estimate, if described as such, is not legally binding you should inform the customer if it is likely to be substantially exceeded.

Insurance can also be a problem. Rates on fragile objects are very high and it is advisable to ask the client to effect their own insurance on any work they leave with you. Some restorers also stipulate that completed work must be collected within a fixed period of time. This is partly to protect cash flows, but also to minimise the risks of things being damaged. The longer they are left lying around, the greater the risk of that happening.

Administration

Though restorers, like other freelances, prefer to keep administration down to a minimum, a certain amount of it is inescapable because of the number of objects from many different owners that pass through their hands. Accounts can be kept in the form of a simple cash book showing income and expenditure and organised on lines laid down by your accountant, but beyond that you also need some kind of stock book. That should show such details as:

- Customer's name, address and telephone number
- Description of the object
- Nature of the work required
- Estimate or quote
- Date to be collected
- Details of work needing to be done on it by a third party outside your premises
- Signature of owner/person collecting on completion.

Payment is generally made at the time of collection – in fact, you should not let an object go without payment unless the customer is someone who cannot pay in this way: a museum, for instance. That should be made clear at the time you give your estimate. Some restorers, in fact, insist on part payment in advance on major repair jobs that are likely to take up a lot of their time.

Occupational hazards

Working with solvents and resins can present health hazards to people with allergies. Hygiene conditions, such as washing hands after dealing with solvents, must be strictly observed. People with contact lenses must be particularly careful, not only about corrosive fumes, but also about getting minute particles on them from airbrushing.

The other hazard is financial and it is simply the fact that the amount of work done in restoring an object may not bear much relation to its value. This has the effect of restricting the income you can realistically expect to earn.

Professional organisations

There are no associations for restorers of pottery and porcelain as such, but membership of the International Institute for the Conservation of Historic and Artistic Works is generally considered worthwhile. For details see the entry on Picture Restoring, pages 178–181.

16
Performing Arts

Introduction

The performing arts and their related fields cover a wide spectrum of activities – not only music and drama, but things loosely connected with them like sport or fashion modelling and, of course, the media techniques by which they are disseminated. Although these are big industries in money terms, there is very little in the way of a career structure among the performers and to some extent the technicians. They are, therefore, traditionally areas where freelancing is the rule and where a talented few are in constant demand, but where a great many are really casual labour. In much film and TV work, for instance, production companies are set up on an *ad hoc* basis for the duration of a particular project and disbanded at the end of it, together with the staff that have been hired to do the job.

Quite frequently, in fact, money cannot be raised and the freelances who have already been engaged for the task find themselves back on the streets or, to be more precise, in agents' offices or in the London pubs where much hiring is done informally on the basis of contacts between acquaintances who have worked together before. To bring some order into the situation, the Broadcasting, Entertainment, Cinematograph Technicians' Union (BECTU, formerly ACTT), the film and TV trade union which operates a post-entry closed shop, and without whose members it is impossible to make any kind of film or video, insists that production companies deposit two weeks' wages in the bank in advance. That way members are sure of getting some money, but BECTU's stranglehold on the industry also makes it impossible to get technical jobs in it without a BECTU ticket. Getting that appears to be remarkably close to a Catch 22 situation – you cannot get work without a ticket and you cannot get a ticket without experience. That at least is the theory, though in practice BECTU is usually prepared to offer membership once you get an assignment. Equity, the actors' union, has a similar grip on stage and operatic performers, without having been as successful in negotiating terms for its members as BECTU has.

Freelancing at the performing end is fiercely competitive. Top names can make a great deal of money – for instance, a star actor can get a six-figure income from films, stage appearances, commercials and voice-overs. The majority of performers, however, earn much smaller amounts of money, with the odd good year balanced by others where they may not make much more than £12,000 – and some, of course, would consider themselves lucky to get even that.

The other factor is that some careers can be relatively short – sportspeople and models, for instance, only have a top earnings life of 10–15 years. This, and the general unpredictability of incomes, make it highly advisable to pay well for experienced advice on tax planning and mitigation schemes. That, and sound investment counselling, is as important as having a good agent, though to judge by the frequency with which peformers succeed in losing their hard-earned savings, not many realise this.

Cameramen

Basic skills and aptitudes

The basic skills are either taught at film school or, in the case of a more senior generation of cameramen, learned on the job through a progression of duties. You gradually work up to assistant cameraman – a stage through which film-school graduates must also pass – to fully fledged lighting cameraman.

The benefit that the older generation of cameramen has is that in the course of doing all kinds of dogsbody duties they acquire a vast amount of basic technical knowledge about wiring, fixing up generators and what to do if the camera breaks down on a location which is miles away from the nearest technician. They will probably not be called on themselves to sort out the problem – in the highly unionised film industry that might indeed cause additional trouble – but at least they will be able to supervise the work and know when the technicians are trying to blind them with science. That can be as important on occasion as the creative side, which is to be the director's right-hand man on everything concerned with the visual aspect of film-making. In that role the cameraman works with designers, make-up people and the costume department. He or she has also, of course, to have an eye for composing shots and to be aware of the technical problems or opportunities that may be related to the choice of a location. Apart from a good eye you also need to have a fairly thick skin. Rejections and reverses are part of everyone's experience in the film business.

Equipment

Potentially the costs of equipment are huge, but very few cameramen equip themselves with anything more than light meters and perhaps a polaroid camera to record a particular location once it is selected. The reason for this is that everything you can possibly need can be hired. For instance, a company called Samuelson Film Service Ltd has all the equipment you would need to shoot an epic and since few epics are made it is far cheaper to hire than to buy. The same is true of more specialised bits and pieces like lighting equipment.

The market

Though it is very competitive – there are said to be 200 freelance cameramen in London alone – there is also a lot of work about. The usual areas apart from feature films – of which relatively few are made – are documentaries, TV dramas, commercials, industrial films and pop videos.

Finding work

Finding work largely depends on word of mouth recommendation. It used to be the case that the chief executive of the production company making the feature, documentary, commercial or what-ever chose the heads of departments who would then in turn assemble their own team; thus the cameraman would choose his own camera crew and technicians. Now these tend to be appointed by the production company, but quite often on the recommenda-tion of a department head. He picks the people he likes working with – a lot depends on getting on with people, especially when you are away on location for weeks at a time. It also means that you tend to be typecast in the sort of assignments you get – if you work in commercials you tend to be known by people who make them and less so by those who make documentaries, for instance.

Although to a certain extent work comes to you, especially if you are well known, you cannot rely on it entirely. Even experienced cameramen find they have to do the round of the production companies and for this purpose you need a showreel – a video of four to five minutes' duration showing your latest and best work. In the nature of things jobs go to those that are busiest. If you are over-frank about not having a lot of work on when you go to see a production company you are unlikely to get more. If you claim to be fully occupied but indicate that you might have a spare week or so it is much more likely that this will enhance interest in you.

Fees

Fees are usually paid on a daily basis. For a commercial the rate can be £400 upwards but it is much lower for making documentaries or working in other less affluent branches of film-making. To some extent what is available for the cameraman depends on the budget, which is always relatively higher in inverse proportion to the degree of social purpose entailed in the venture.

£400 a day plus sounds like a lot of money, especially when you consider that filming can take several days – or weeks in the case of a feature film – but it can involve a great deal of unpaid work, especially for those who are less established in their reputation. For instance, you may have to reconnoitre a location, put together lists of equipment and generally do a good deal of preparation which those on the staff do in the firm's time, but for which freelances have trouble getting paid. Indeed, one of the reasons why the film and TV industry uses freelances to such a large extent is that it saves them money, even when there is a lot of work about. When it is scarce, it also means that they have far fewer mouths to feed.

Expenses are a significant and sometimes controversial area of the fees picture. Generally, no expenses are paid when shooting in the London area where most of the production companies are based, even though the studios are generally some way out of town. On location some companies pay a location allowance of varying degrees of generosity. The more experienced freelances try to get expenses on the basis of actuality, which means producing supporting bills and invoices. What is allowed under this heading again generally depends on how big a budget the film has, but experienced hands in the business tend to have a fair idea of what you can get away with.

Administration

The basic personal administration – keeping records of expenses and invoicing production companies – is very simple. What can be very complicated is keeping one's diary of booked assignments and most freelances use a specialist agency for this. The system is that, because of the uncertainty of so many projects in the film and TV world, bookings are not confirmed until a fairly late stage. The first approach is the so-called 'pencil': you are pencilled in with a provisional booking and you may accumulate several pencils for the same or overlapping periods during the traditionally busy shooting months of May–September. If one of the later 'pencils' confirms the booking, the custom of the trade is to go back over all the earlier pencils for the same period and ask them if they now wish to confirm. It is only when they have indicated that they do not wish to do so that the confirmee is told you are available.

This is a complicated and sometimes embarrassing as well as time-consuming task which freelances are happy to leave to an agency – phoning in every day, though, to update their own personal diary. There are several agencies around and the best plan is to ask which is currently the best. Like restaurants, they depend in quality and reliability on the management at the time.

Occupational hazards

Some freelances cite the pencilling system as a problem area. It is more binding on them than the production company because you have very little redress when a confirmed pencil falls by the wayside, after you have turned down other prospective work. That is one of the disadvantages of working in a buyer's market with many hungry competitors.

The seasonality of work is another drawback and so is the very short warning you are apt to receive, especially on smaller assignments like shooting pop videos. The cameramen who are most in demand tend to get booked for the longest time ahead, but fame and fashion is not without its perils. Some say that getting a major award is by no means an unmixed blessing, because many producers think that you might be too expensive. There is also the danger, with those whose work is highly visible, that you might become 'flavour of the month'. Good, steady, unspectacular professionalism is thought by many to be the best way of securing a steady flow of work.

Professional organisations

There are no professional bodies as such, but it is absolutely vital to belong to a trade union – in the case of cameramen that is the Broadcasting, Entertainment, Cinematograph Technicians' Union (BECTU), 111 Wardour Street, London W1V 4AY; 071-437 8506. Indeed, one of the most prized results of having attended a film school is not so much the diploma as the fact that it virtually guarantees you the BECTU ticket, without which work in the film or TV business is virtually impossible to get.

Professional Singing

Basic skills and aptitudes

It goes without saying that you need a trained voice but that statement does not quite reflect the long and intensive training it takes to get to that state. Generally, it means a degree course or its equivalent and several years' post-graduate work. There are no grants available for the latter so musicians have to rely on prize money from competitions and/or part-time teaching to pay their way. Fortunately, there are now plenty of opportunities to take part in competitions, because as you progress the training becomes more expensive. Eventually, you have to have both a teacher and a coach: the former to teach you the techniques and the latter to help you learn the parts. Both are equally important because singing embraces a wide variety of work – operatic as well as solo and orchestral performances. That means you have to be able to act as well as sing – which in turn means you have to look good. Mountainous sopranos are no longer welcomed by audiences who now want their singing stars to look as glamorous as any other stage performer.

Actors and actresses, on the other hand, are not necessarily expected to be bright as well as beautiful. Singers are. You have to learn the music as well as the words and in many cases the latter are in Italian, German, French and even sometimes Russian. Though it is possible for someone with a good musical ear to pronounce a foreign language with near perfection while having no idea what the words mean, the international nature of the musical scene makes it difficult to get by without at least some degree of fluency in a language other than English. On top of all this you have to be absolutely reliable about turning up to engagements, even if you are not feeling like performing; and to swallow your pride about appearing as a stand-in for singers who are better known but less scrupulous in these matters.

Equipment and premises
You need a good piano, a very high-quality tape recorder and music-loving neighbours, if you work from home, though actual singing practice is restricted to an hour a day because of the danger of straining the vocal cords. A lot of rehearsal time is spent learning quietly. The biggest expense apart from travelling is in clothes. Men need evening dress and in venues such as Vienna, Salzburg or indeed any of the leading concert halls around the world, women must wear a black dress; those of the appropriate quality can cost over £400. Unfortunately, since the test case brought – and lost – by the barrister Anne Mallalieu for tax relief on clothes bought for professional purposes, the Inland Revenue have taken a hard line on dress allowances, even though it would be difficult to think of any place where a female singer would want to wear a dress bought for a concert performance other than when giving one.

Another item of expense which can run high are laryngologist's bills. Strains of various kinds in and around the throat are an inevitable and costly hazard of the singer's professional life.

The market
Not all work is at the glamour end of the market. There are a large number of local choral societies all over the country who bring in professional soloists for concert occasions and this is often the way to start being known. Singers in the early stages of their careers also

perform across a wide range of opportunities – musicals, operettas, opera and even, on occasion, in the chorus of one of the well-known choral societies. The next step up the ladder is being asked to appear as a stand-in for a better known performer who is unable for some reason to appear. You also have to be prepared to travel. Opportunities in Germany, where even medium-sized towns have their own opera house and often an orchestra, are much greater than in the UK.

Finding work

In the beginning finding work is a matter of coming to the notice of directors of local operatic and choral societies, conductors of part-time orchestras and similar sources through success in competitions. Generally, this results in being asked to go for an audition in the early stages of one's career, rather than an outright offer. Later on the aim is to get an agent, though it is not easy to find one to take you on until you are reasonably established. He or she will want to see and hear you first. It is only when you have built up a track record by doing many small and often unrewarding jobs that the work starts to flow in. When conductors start to ask for you, your career has begun to get under way, though you still need an agent. He or she takes 15 per cent of the fee and since this is often a gross sum out of which you have to pay travelling expenses and/or hotel bills, it represents a considerable chunk of your earnings. Equity membership, essential if you are performing on the stage, is also an expensive item.

Fees

Fees vary enormously and singers tend to be secretive about what they are getting because it is a matter of negotiation rather than of fixed rates. In general, however, fees on the Continent and in the United States are much higher than in this country.

Administration

Rendering invoices is done by the agent, if you have one. Until then you have to do it yourself, or have such matters dealt with by your accountant. The main thing is that you have to keep a note of everything you spend, and this can be quite complicated if you are doing a lot of travelling. Using a credit card is a good idea because you receive a summary of where you spent the money with your statement. The other vital area of administration is your engagement diary. Big opera companies book performers as much as five to six years ahead and even an artist who is not in the major league tends to be booked as much as 18 months ahead. But you also need to leave yourself enough space for study and practice – especially of modern music.

Occupational hazards

The voice is the most fragile of all instruments – you can only practise actual singing about an hour a day and a heavy cold or a strain can put you out of work for a couple of crucial weeks. Therein, however, lies the opportunity for lesser known performers to take over a major role. The big problem occurs when you are already booked up for something else – maybe something you want to do much less. It can be a question of how ruthless you are prepared to be to break an engagement – and what the benefits of that are to your career, as opposed to the damage or hurt you do by letting someone else down. You may also have to be ruthless about family commitments – it is very difficult to reconcile them with a musical career because of the amount of travelling that involves. At the same time, the travelling makes for a fairly lonely life. Although orchestras and operatic companies have a reputation for sociability, it is difficult for solo or guest performers to be part of it.

Professional organisations

The British Actors' Equity Association, 8 Harley Street, London W1N 2AB; 071-636 6367 takes into membership a wide variety of performers in what might broadly be termed the entertainment industry. It provides advice on business, legal and tax matters. There is an annual subscription, related to gross earnings.

The other professional body – useful for those who want to teach – is the Incorporated Society of Musicians, 10 Stratford Place, London W1N 9AE; 071-629 4413.

Modelling

Basic skills and aptitudes

Though there are courses in modelling given by private etablishments in several main cities, models tend to be born rather than made: and if made, it is a question of developing aptitudes and characteristics that are already there. For one thing you need to be photogenic, and to have the sort of looks that are currently fashionable. For instance, some years ago the trend was for models to be in most demand in their late twenties and those who were younger than that did their best to hide the fact. Today the reverse is true and top models of 28 or so do their best to look 18.

Age is obviously a factor in the modelling business. The preferred age for women is 16–25, though men can have a successful freelance modelling career up to about 50. In both cases, though, you have to stay fairly slim and women need to be slightly above average height: about 5'8" is the norm. Male models need to be at least 5'11".

Equipment and premises

Work is always on the client's premises, but models need to invest a fair amount of money in fashion accessories and they have to be convincingly well dressed when they go to appointments or modelling sessions. Other essentials such as photographs, hairdos and make-up are, in the case of top agencies, often supplied free by getting young photographers, hairdressers, etc to provide these services as publicity for themselves.

The market

The potential market for models is enormous, though the competition for it is fierce: magazines, packaging, catalogues, posters, showcards and advertisements are the major areas. So are TV commercials, for which acting ability is not required. Indeed models seldom make good actresses. The talents, though related, are actually dissimilar. Actors and actresses need to be unaware of the camera. For models the reverse is true.

Finding work

Though models are invariably freelances, even those at the very top work through agencies. The good agencies are very selective about who they take on. The top two or three agencies in London only have some 60 models each on their books.

The agencies make it their business to keep in touch with art directors in the various media. Knowing their individual preferences for types and faces is vital, as is a knowledge of their work schedules and casting projects. Models are sent round to editors with their portfolios – advertisements and features in which they have appeared – and with cards consisting of a photograph accompanied by some vital statistics. What gets work is a combination of personal chemistry, having the right looks for the job and a reputation for reliability.

The latter is extremely important. It extends not only to absolute punctuality, but also to turning up to appointments with precisely the clothes and accessories that have been specified by the art director. Indeed, failure to do so will generally lead to the whole session being cancelled and the model being billed with at least some of the cost.

Fees

Fees obviously vary widely, according to the fame of the model, but also to where the shot is used. Contrary to popular impression, having your photo on the front cover of a magazine or in an editorial photo is not particularly well paid. Newspapers and magazines, perhaps somewhat unfairly, regard that as good publicity by means of which a model can get entries into the much more rewarding world of advertising photos. Here they can earn around £400 a day.

That sounds like a lot of money but, as in the case of many other freelance occupations, a fair amount of unpaid running around is required to earn that. Even when a job is actually confirmed, attendance at such essential preliminaries as going to a fitting is paid for at a reduced fee – and sometimes not at all. Expenses are also often regarded as the model's own costs, except on overnight stays or when travelling abroad. Even then, only hotel bills and fares are paid. Working abroad for a foreign client is, however, much better paid than modelling in this country – nearly twice as much, in fact.

The agencies play a vital role in negotiating fees and terms as well as making client contacts. For this they charge 5 per cent of the fee. However, they often advance models some of the money they are due from clients, since payment periods can run as long as three months.

Administration

Theoretically it is up to the model to invoice his or her client and pay his or her 5 per cent to the agency, but knowing that paperwork is not the average model's strongest suit, most agencies take that aspect out of his or her hands. The models simply send them the details of the client they have been working for, and the agency then invoices that client and pays the money over when it is received. However, models are regarded as self employed – not employees of the agency – and pay Schedule D tax. Agencies (at least the good ones) do, however, regard it as part of their job to see that models are properly organised to handle their tax and financial affairs. They are expected to have an accountant and to have made arrangements to pay their National Insurance stamp.

The other aspect of administration involves keeping track of bookings. In the case of top models these are made a long way in advance, but in other cases they may be at short notice. However, keeping a diary is essential. Models are also expected to telephone in daily to check whether any assignments have turned up for them.

Occupational hazards

Some hazards are self inflicted, according to some people in the business. You have to be totally committed to modelling to make a success of it, unfailingly reliable, pleasant to all concerned and totally organised when you turn up to an assignment. Such is the competition for modelling jobs that if you fail in these respects, the agency is liable to drop you – sometimes after only a week or two, sometimes after as much as a year when you might have thought yourself reasonably established.

You also have to watch your weight and your general appearance. Clients buy your services on the strength of your card and your headsheet – the latter is a poster with details of all the models on it, which is circulated to art editors. If you drastically change your appearance or either lose or gain weight you may be much less bankable than you were. The obvious long-term hazard is age – only the very top female faces go on after the late twenties. Then there is the 'flavour of the month' syndrome. Faces can become over-exposed, or the taste for a certain kind of appearance may change.

Professional organisations

There are none, but the London College of Fashion, 20 John Prince's Street, London W1M 9HE, runs a one-year course leading to a Certificate in Fashion Modelling which is highly regarded by firms in the business.

17
Book Publishing

Introduction

Freelancing has become widespread in book publishing since permanent staffs were cut back in the recession which hit the industry in the early 1980s. Since then, there has been some recovery in profitability and the output of titles is higher than ever, but publishers are still nervous about increasing permanent staff. In fact, many of them have discovered that using freelances is extremely cost effective in many editorial, production and design jobs, though internal procedures need to be well organised when what used to be integrated publishing functions are handled outside. A production consultant, for instance, has to be briefed about the marketing dimension of the job he or she is looking after; an outside editor may need to consult with sales as well as editorial staff for the same reason, and to talk to the production department as well.

It follows from this that, as in so many other freelance fields, you need to have previous experience in it. Even reading manuscripts submitted for publication, a chore that does not appear to require any knowledge of actual publishing procedures, calls for commercial judgement and an understanding of the editorial policy of the house to whom the work is submitted; thus a sensitive first novel, however good, could not be published successfully by a firm whose strong suit was commercial fiction. When you come to more technical tasks, previous experience in publishing is essential. Many publishers receive letters from English graduates offering to do 'editorial work'. Few of them even get looked at. What publishers want from freelances is evidence that they can do a professional job, quickly and reliably. Thus, examples of previous work or recommendations from existing clients which point in that direction are invaluable.

Quite a number of freelances in publishing are now doing work for previous employers, among other clients, because of this familiarity factor. There does not, in fact, seem to be any shortage of work, though the rewards are not particularly exciting except in the more specialised skills of design and production. Few freelance editorial people make more than £12,000 a year. The Nationa

Union of Journalists (NUJ) has a book freelance branch which sets out recommended rates, but they are not widely adhered to, except in one or two firms where unions are strongly represented. The average rate is £8–£10 an hour, though this can sometimes go higher for difficult or rush jobs.

Flat fees per job are fairly unusual as a basis of remuneration, but it is quite common for the freelance to be asked to give an estimate of how long an assignment will take. Though estimates are not binding, the clients generally expect the final account to come close to it because they will have done their costing on such a sum. Therefore, it is important before giving a figure to size up the length and complexity of the task and to point out any problems that might add to cost. Commissioning editors are sometimes unaware of detail of this kind.

Though the market for publishing freelances is good, there are also enough of them around on the editorial side for the situation to be fairly competitive. This is less the case in more specialised parts of publishing, such as book production. Clients can lose or save large sums of money in making the right decisions here and, as in any other field where larger sums are at stake, the rewards reflect that. In fact, freelance packagers, creating a finished product in terms of editorial, design, printing and marketing concept, can make quite large incomes. On the other hand, they have to be able to raise at least five-figure sums and to take financial risks.

There are about 60,000 books published a year in the UK, but by no means all of these are produced by recognised publishers. Many firms and organisations produce literature which carries an international standard book number (ISBN): promotional books, manuals, reports, company histories, and so forth. Many of them have plenty of money, but not the remotest idea of how to put a publication together either editorially or in production terms. To give just one example, many types of professional practices – architects, accountants and lawyers – are now allowed to advertise and are tending to do so by putting out booklets which exhibit their expertise to potential clients. It is a field PR firms are moving into. It is one where publishing freelances could be very competitive, both in price and quality.

Editorial Work

Basic skills and aptitudes

Freelance editorial work for publishers involves various stages of dealing with textual matter, both before and after it is set up in type. Each of these stages calls for a different set of skills.

The first and most exacting one is structural editing and re-writing. This would involve taking an author's manuscript – generally, though not invariably, a non-fiction work such as a textbook or a professional reference book – and making order out of chaos: arranging the facts in logical sequence, tying together paragraphs and sentences that at first sight bear no relation to each other, re-writing passages to clarify their meaning and making lists of queries to take up with the author. This kind of work calls for a feeling for the general shape of the way information should be presented. It is often possessed by people who are themselves writers or journalists; certainly it requires some writing ability.

Copy editing is a slightly more mechanical task. Essentially it is a matter of preparing a manuscript for handing over to the publisher's production department. It means not only correcting spelling and punctuation but making sure that headings are clearly and consistently marked, that illustrations are correctly referred to, that paragraph beginnings are properly set out, and so forth.

The least creative stage is proof reading – looking out for 'literals' (mis-spellings), missing words or numbers, errors in pagination, to mention just a few of the things that can go wrong in the typesetting stage. At one time printers used to read their own proofs, but with the advent of computerised setting this has become rarer. At the same time standards of setting have gone down.

The general feeling among publishers' editors is that freelances who are good at structural editing are poor proof readers and often indifferent copy editors. They call for different abilities which are not usually found in the same person. What they all have in common, however, is that in each case freelances need to be able to work on a wide variety of books, on schedule and sometimes under pressure.

They also require an ability to solve the vast majority of the problems that arise without referring them back to the publisher's editor. If you come back at him or her with a long list of queries, they will have to read the text themselves, which negates the whole point of using a freelance.

Equipment and premises

Apart from an answerphone (desirable) and a typewriter (essential) or a word processor (preferable) you will need some basic reference books. You should have dictionaries or companions related to your specialisation if you have one. You will also find it useful to have an atlas and a really good dictionary of quotations. Apart from that there are a number of references that are used specifically by editors: *Hart's Rules for Compositors and Readers The Oxford Dictionary for Writers and Editors* and the Chicago University *Manual of Style.*

You should also have some printed letterheads of your own.

The market
Virtually all book publishers use freelance editors these days, though in general they stick to people they know and trust – which often means ex-employees. But invariably outsiders can break in if they have a specialist subject and are literate. Courses on copy editing are given by the London College of Printing in conjunction with the Book House Training Centre, 45 East Hill, London SW18 2QZ; 081-870 9055. Napier Polytechnic of Edinburgh, 219 Colinton Road, Edinburgh EH14 5DT; 031-444 2266, also runs publishing courses.

Finding work
If you do not know the publishing scene, the *Bookseller*, and especially the bumper Spring and Autumn export numbers, gives you a fair idea of the size of the various firms and the kind of books they do. Find out the name of the managing editor and write to him or her, outlining your experience and/or specialist knowledge. If they are interested, they may well give you some work as a test. It will probably be something rather boring, but if you do it well more interesting assignments will come your way.

Fees
Fees are usually paid on an hourly basis. The NUJ (Book Branch) quotes rates ranging from £10.50 for proof reading, £11.50 for copy editing and £12.50 for structural editing and re-writing, but as with their rates for journalists, these are honoured more in the breach than in the observance. Most publishers pay somewhere between £8 and £10 per hour; some rather less.

You can sometimes get a higher rate for undertaking a job in a hurry or on a highly specialised subject; and you should get extra for expenses, for instance, if you have to visit or telephone the author/illustrator to sort out queries.

Do not provide an estimate of hours on structural editing until you have studied the manuscript. Good typing is not necessarily an indication of literary quality.

Administration
Reliability of delivery is crucial to publishers because a book that misses its turn at the printers in the busy latter half of the year may be delayed fatally. Try and get an idea of the jobs that may be coming your way and book them into your diary so that you can plan ahead. The mere fact that you are doing so places the publisher under some moral obligation.

You will need only simple accounting records: a cash book showing receipts and expenditure. The important thing is to note both as soon as they happen. It also helps your accountant if you provide some simple analysis: stationery, travel, postage and so forth. Keep as many bills and invoices as you can to substantiate your claims. As far as accounting for small items of expenditure, most firms will accept your word on reasonable items like telephone calls.

You can buy pads of invoice forms at any good stationers. A firm called Rediform produces quite professional-looking numbered ones, each with a copy so that you can chase up late payers by quoting numbers and dates. You can also create professional-looking invoices on a word processor.

Occupational hazards

The one mentioned by most people is loneliness. Editing, perhaps more than any other kind of freelance work, is an occupation that can bring one into hardly any touch with other people. It is very much a case of sitting at your desk for hours on end, reading what are often extremely boring scripts – in-house editors tend to work on those that are fun to do, or that have glamorous authors.

Briefing by publishers on what exactly they require is often poor, especially if the in-house editor has not looked too closely at the material before handing it over. It is fairly common, for instance, for a manuscript to be sent out for copy editing when it requires drastic structural surgery. If the job is more extensive than you had been led to believe, you should report this back to the editor before proceeding with it.

Another hazard is slow payment – and, sometimes, bad debts. One recent recruit to the freelance scene did his first major job for a small packager who promptly went bankrupt. If the client is not an established firm you should insist on progress payment.

Professional organisations

The Society of Freelance Editors and Proof Readers publishes a monthly newsletter and a directory of members, classified by specialisations, available for work with publishers and authors. It also runs short training courses in such subjects as proof reading. There is a small membership fee. Details of the Society are available from the membership secretary, Michèle Clark, Rosemary Cottage, Fore Street, Weston, Hitchin, Herts SG4 7AS; 0462 79577.

Reading for Publishers

Basic skills and aptitudes

Reading and assessing manuscripts that are submitted to publishers sounds like an ideal freelance job and publishers get a fair number of approaches from those who want to undertake it. However, it requires more than a love of books or the ability to write well oneself, or even a track record as a book reviewer – useful though all these attributes are. Chiefly, you need a feeling for what works commercially and a knowledge of what fits into the publisher's list; an avant-garde novel, however meritorious, would not, for instance, be published successfully by a firm with a reputation for doing popular historical fiction.

You also have to be able to size up a work very quickly. Despite the well-publicised fact that it is very difficult for all but a tiny minority to make more than a pittance from writing, publishers are still deluged with scripts from individuals, from agents and from American publishers trying to get their titles published in the UK. Unless you have the ability to detect dross almost on sight – about 98 per cent of everything that comes in from private people and about 50 per cent of other offerings come under that heading – you will soon drown in paper.

Equipment and premises

A desk, a typewriter or word processor, a telephone, good light and strong coffee is about all you need. Some freelance readers, in fact, have a temporary desk in the publisher's office where they spend a day a week or a fortnight sorting out the obvious non-starters, writing brief reports on the possibles for in-house editors and taking home with them scripts or books on which the editors want a more detailed opinion. If you work any other way you will either need a very large suitcase or a lot of packing materials and string. The postage will be expensive, too.

The market

Apart from hardback publishers, books and manuscripts are submitted to paperback houses, book clubs, magazines and film companies.

Finding work

Unless you have an area of special expertise – in which case publishers might be very interested to hear from you if they do books which are relevant to it – you have to know someone reasonably influential to be considered. It helps enormously if, apart from possessing the attributes already referred to, you have worked in a bookshop, a library or, of course, in a publishing house. You have to have a feel, which can only be acquired through first-hand dealings with the public, for what people want to read – even if it isn't the sort of thing you enjoy yourself.

Fees

There are recommended NUJ rates for freelance work of this type, but in general it is a buyer's market in which publishers pay what they feel like. About £50–£65 for a day's work, which might involve ripping through a pile of typescripts and reporting briefly on the most promising ones, would be about average. More careful reading and reporting would be paid on an hourly basis which varies somewhere between £7 and £12, depending on the nature of the book and how specialised it was. Similar fees would be paid if you were asked to re-structure and re-write a work. Sometimes the author has produced something that is nearly publishable but is unable or unwilling to knock it into shape. This is particularly true with technical or scientific manuscripts.

Administration

Though fees are modest, the consolation is that administration is minimal. All you need is a cash book, a record of hours spent on a particular job and any extras like postage or photocopying. It may also be useful, if you have a larger traffic of work coming in and out, to keep a record of its movements. Publishers also like to be given time dates for when reports or other work can be completed.

Occupational hazards

Since work depends so much on knowing people, you are equally dependent on them keeping the influential jobs they hold and you have to stay in touch with them when they move. Keeping an ear open for trade gossip and an eye on the *Bookseller* and *Publishing News* (either or both are available from good reference libraries) announcements of people on the move is worthwhile; so is sending a tactful postcard to friends when they go to a new job.

The other great hazard is that of giving wrong advice and encouraging an editor to make a bad publishing decision. It is always, of course, easier to say no than yes, but it is not invariably the safest course. In the autobiographical early chapters of *Sophie's Choice*, William Styron tells of his years as a reader with an American publishing house. The final manuscript he read before he left that job was one on which he was able to report that it was at least passably literate and entertainingly written. Alas, he reported, who on earth would be interested in reading a book about a bunch of lunatics who had crossed the Pacific on a balsa raft to prove theory about where the Polynesians came from? The book he rejected was Thor Heyerdahl's *Kon-Tiki Expedition*, one of the biggest sellers of the post-war period.

Picture Research

Basic skills and aptitudes

The main attributes you have to have as a picture researcher are organising ability (there is a formidable amount of administration involved), a good visual sense and a detective-like nose for clues which lead to sources beyond the obvious ones. For this reason picture researchers often specialise in an area where they already know the subject matter. The only real skill you need is good typing ability. A lot of letter writing is involved in obtaining permissions and specifying exactly what rights are being sought. Some knowledge of print processes is also useful – you should at least know what the reproduction implications might be of using certain types of illustrations; eg half-tones where the originals are no longer available.

Equipment and premises

You don't need much in the way of equipment except an answerphone, a typewriter or word processor, a viewer for transparencies and a magnifying glass for examining the state of any illustrations you have borrowed. You do need to spend quite a lot of money on books in your area of specialisation, though there are now two principal sources which have taken the sweat out of tracking down such things as special collections. First, there is the *Picture Researcher's Handbook: An International Guide to Picture Sources and How to Use Them* by Hilary and Mary Evans (published by Van Nostrand Reinhold). It is a very thorough and well-arranged compilation which describes the principal collections, gives addresses, methods of access and opening hours, quantifies the number of pictures, and sets out the methods of charging. It is well indexed and classified in various ways to make reference easier. The other recommended source is *Picture Sources UK*, published by Macdonald.

You can work from home – nearly all picture researchers do – but you do need plenty of space, good surfaces, good lighting and clean, well-organised storage.

The market

The people who mainly use freelances are book publishers and packagers – design, writing and production units who deliver ready-made books to publishers who then market them under their own imprint. Other sources of work are advertising agencies, magazines, publishers of part-works and, increasingly, television companies. Though the latter pay very well (they use picture researchers to provide stills, for instance, in historical documentaries), they are a difficult market to break into because the Broadcasting, Entertainment, Cinematograph Technicians' Union (BECTU) operates a *de facto* closed shop and dominates this particular industry. Reportedly, though, it is sometimes possible to get past them if you have good contacts with TV companies or the production companies that put together programmes for them.

Finding work

The usual method is to start by already having contacts. Most freelance picture researchers previously worked full time for publishers in that capacity or became involved with doing research as part of an editorial job, though there are also some who have no such background at all.

Whether you have contacts and want to expand them or whether you are starting from scratch, the best way to proceed is simply to look in your bookshop or library for publishers who do a large number of illustrated books. The major ones will have a picture research manager; otherwise write to the managing editor and state your qualifications and areas of interest. There is no published source of packagers, but any experienced editor will be able to give you some names. Once you get started you should ensure that you are given credit as picture researcher in the publication concerned. This will bring your name to the notice of possible clients.

It is also worth joining the Society of Picture Researchers and Editors (SPREd). They have regular meetings in London (see page 210 under 'Professional organisations' for further information).

Fees

The minimum rate for book publishers is £10–£12 an hour at 1991 prices, plus expenses and travelling costs. Sometimes publishers ask for an estimate, but it is difficult to judge beforehand how hard it will be to get pictures. The best plan is to agree an upper limit and inform the client if you are likely to exceed it. It is fair to say that no great fortunes can be made as a freelance picture researcher: about £14,500 a year by current prices is a good average.

Administration

Record keeping is extensive and absolutely vital because there are so many people involved in handling pictures and other illustrative materials which may be fragile and often irreplaceable: the publisher, the printer or process maker and sometimes the author as well as yourself; and don't forget the postman or messenger service on top of that.

The library or agency that owns the picture will usually sign it out to you as if it were a library book. You will be responsible if it is lost or damaged, so the first essential is to note its state and inform the owner if it is in any way damaged at the time it was handed over to you.

Having got it in your custody you have to keep track of its movements. If the publisher loses it he or she may be unscrupulous enough to claim that he never got it. You cannot prove otherwise but you can at least keep records of when you sent it off. You can also show from these same records that the publisher never sent it back to you, because you should log incoming materials as well. To prevent argument many researchers either deliver packages in person or have them sent by recorded delivery; and insist that the publisher does likewise.

Ideally, who is responsible for what, and in which circumstances, is set out beforehand in some form of agreement or an exchange of letters. SPREd, in fact, have produced a very useful 'freelance engagement form' for this purpose. It covers such essential points as whose job it is to clear permissions and pay copyright fees, as well as the actual physical details of who is to return the material to the library or agency it came from. It also sets out at least an outline brief – how many images are wanted, by when, in what size, whether black and white or colour, and so forth. One curious omission from this otherwise admirable form is that it does not say anything about insurance. Certainly, the publisher ought to be responsible for insuring materials that are in his or her possession, but some researchers try to get the publisher to cover them as well, being, as it were, a temporary agent for this particular purpose. They are not too keen on doing so, so this can be an extra expense for the researcher and one that is difficult to assess exactly from the point of view of getting quotes for premiums. The problem is, of course, that you may have £10,000 worth of materials one week and almost nothing the next.

Apart from records relating to the material itself you should also keep a job book on which all costs – phone calls, travel, postage, and an amount for insurance – should be logged against the assignment that relates to them. These should in due course be related to the invoice you render to the client.

Occupational hazards

The chief one is the time some clients take to pay and the cash-flow problems that can arise out of that, especially if you are being required to pay copyright fees yourself. In that case, it is essential to get progress payments from the client – another reason why all costs should be logged. Delays in payment are also often due to the fact that the client has not briefed you properly, and that you therefore have not come up with exactly what he wants. Again, it is essential to establish the brief and confirm it in writing.

Professional organisations

The Society for Picture Researchers and Editors, SPREd, issues a code of practice, holds regular London meetings, publishes a quarterly journal and keeps a register of freelance members which is consulted by potential clients. To get on it, you have to be proposed and seconded for membership and to be able to show that you have been engaged in research for two years. It is currently run by Miranda Smith, 36 Bulwer Road, London E11 9BX; 081-539 6758.

Book Production

Basic skills and aptitudes

There are two main types of production freelances – those who work as an external production department for publishers who prefer to operate in this way, either for individual titles or for their whole list, and those who package individual books as a finished product, in essence handing over distribution to a publisher. Freelance production may also involve working for an organisation or a firm that creates its own literature for promotional or publicity purposes. But whatever the circumstances of the actual task freelance production calls for a considerable, internationally based knowledge of print and paper buying, and the ability to control a number of different jobs, at different stages and at various locations. Administrative ability as well as commercial know-how and negotiating skills are essential because the amounts of money involved can be relatively large. For this reason it is also extremely important to be able to formulate a clear brief about such matters as price, purpose and quality in relation to the market for which the product is intended.

Equipment and premises

Many freelances start out by working from home but this is one occupation where it is advisable to secure proper commercial accommodation of some kind as soon as possible. For one thing you need a space in which you can efficiently store records, manuscripts and illustrative material; for another, you need to be able to talk to clients and suppliers in a business-like atmosphere

You will also, in due course, need some space for equipment. It may not be essential to start with, but at some point you will need the basic tools which invariably now include a microcomputer for record-keeping and possibly creating copy for setting. It is, however, important to establish from the outset what services you will want your facility to offer to clients, so that you do not buy equipment you will hardly ever use – or find yourself short of cash with which to buy items you really need.

The market
In the main the market is among book publishers who are either facing an overload or a production task with which they are unfamiliar, or who are too small to have their own production department. However, many freelances who come from the book publishing world tend to overlook other outlets which can sometimes be much more remunerative: PR-related publications, one-off company histories, special reports produced in book form and many other kinds of printed materials produced by firms and organisations other than orthodox publishers.

Finding work
In the book publishing world, work comes mainly through contacts and by word of mouth. Outside it, it is worth keeping an eye on literature you see going through printers with whom you are in contact. Many organisations use PR agencies to produce their literature, often at an exorbitant cost because they either do not know or do not care about printing prices. A tactful approach to the client suggesting you can do a similar job for far less money can sometimes be productive. Advertising, however, is not thought to be effective and can pull in business from problem customers.

Fees
Packagers simply charge a cost-plus price agreed beforehand with their client. A production consultant proper works on an hourly rate or an annual charge, plus agreed expenses. In both cases it is very important to take into account the cost factors described in Chapter 5.

Administration
Very considerable administrative gifts are needed and those who do not feel their talents lie in this direction ought to think twice about taking on this type of freelance work. You need to keep constant checks on work in progress and to be able to give clients accurate reports on the state of play. During busy periods of the year, mainly late summer and autumn, you will have to have a good

picture of the flow of work in the printing industry generally to be able to make sure that deadlines can be met. In this respect, liaison with clients and a close watch on turnround times of work coming in for checking is essential. A high degree of skill in controlling costs is also required. This calls for close attention to detail, because a simple mistake can cost a great deal of money to rectify.

Occupational hazards

The main hazards are in fact financial. It is important to establish at the outset what expenses the client will be responsible for, and above all who pays the printer's bills. If you are operating as a consultant, this is the client's responsibility, but nevertheless it sours relations with the printer – with whom you may be placing work on behalf of other clients – if a client proves to be a reluctant payer. For this reason it may be advisable to insist that a client who is an unknown quantity should make progress payments to the printers. If you are packaging, the hazard is that you then carry the risk of paying printers – which means that you are liable if your customer fails to pay you on time or at all. Here again, it is worth trying to get progress payments and it is also one of the cases where setting up a limited company could be justified.

Apart from purely financial considerations, one reason why payment might be delayed or refused is because the product does not meet the client's specifications. It is absolutely essential, therefore, to establish a clear brief and to confirm anything that concerns it in writing. Clients tend to be vague about briefing freelances – particularly if they are not accustomed to using them. For this reason, one-off jobs can be dangerous.

18
Journalism and Writing

Introduction

The National Union of Journalists has defined a freelance as a journalist who works for more than one employer. It is a practice that is growing, partly because of the instability of the magazine and newspaper world and partly because some proprietors find it cost effective to run their publications on the 'flexible firm' basis described in the Introduction to this book (page 11): a small core staff supported by a larger number of outworkers who are not on the payroll. Some journalists at the top of the profession also choose to work as freelances. They find it more profitable to negotiate their own rates, trading that and the freedom to write on a wide range of topics for the security of employment.

The charm of journalism is the informal atmosphere of what is, after all, a literary pursuit, but this can have some disadvantages for freelances. The NUJ has tried to introduce some order into the situation by publishing 'minimum rates' based on circulation numbers and advertising revenue, but few editors observe them, nor do most of them have written terms when they commission a piece, as the NUJ suggests they should. Commissions are usually verbal and rates seem to be determined by a mixture of editorial policy and whether the contributor is a 'name' who can command a premium price. Whatever your situation, though, you should try to establish beforehand what the fee is going to be and whether it covers expenses.

It is, however, unwise to try to dot every 'i' and cross every 't'. Editors are wary of sea lawyers and do not have the time to engage in correspondence over individual contributions. To attempt to get them to commit themselves to paying a rejection fee – another NUJ suggestion – is at best a counsel of perfection and is more likely to be regarded as a sign of lack of confidence in your own abilities.

A more serious issue is that of subsidiary rights. Strictly speaking a commissioned piece carries with it publishing rights only for the publication or medium to which it is submitted unless further rights are specified, such as its use in other publications of the same company or even total copyright. In practice, such rights are something of a grey area and if you find a piece published by one paper appearing in another, you can claim a further fee, but there is virtually nothing you can do to enforce payment unless you have specifically reserved subsidiary rights. The extent to which you can do this depends partly on your position in the writing market and partly, again, on editorial policy. If you become too disputatious about your rights, however justified, you are likely to be advised to take your typewriter elsewhere, unless you are a star name.

Within these limitations, journalism is a good area for freelancing, particularly if you specialise in a technical subject that attracts a lot of advertising: electronics is, at the moment, a notable case in point. On the other hand, it is very difficult to break into more generalist fields or into art, music, sport and travel. These are apt to be covered by staffers.

Newspapers and magazines are not, however, the only outlets for freelance writers. It is difficult to make money out of books, or even to get one published, but writing PR and advertising copy can be very lucrative. However, such opportunities are hard to come by and seem to appear out of the blue or through personal contacts. Whatever branch of writing you decide to have a shot at, though, there is one universal principle. Reliability is all, and delivering even fairly pedestrian stuff on time is worth almost any amount of unpunctual genius.

Freelance Journalism

Basic skills and aptitudes

You need no formal qualifications or training to work as a freelance journalist, though there is one attribute which is essential: the ability to see a potential story in what those without an instinct for journalism would regard as a workaday and even uninteresting piece of information. The 'nose for news' that journalists are supposed to have is just that. Exclusive stories are usually made, not born.

Equipment and premises

You need very little in the way of equipment beyond a word processor, a telephone, an answering machine and some decently printed letterheads and cards. A small, inexpensive tape recorder is also useful though a lot of subjects get self-conscious when you have one out. It is less inhibiting if you make notes while conducting an interview. Shorthand, in that context, is useful but not essential. The ability to pick out the salient points in a statement is.

The market

It is difficult to break into at the glamour end – glossies, Sunday supplements, and so forth – which is dominated by a handful of highly paid freelance 'names'. Equally difficult to find is a market for general interest articles – travel, food and wine, politics, mainstream sport (some of the more esoteric ones that are now becoming popular are a better bet) and fashion. Staff writers keep these fun and sometimes perk-laden areas for themselves.

The secret is to specialise. The best fields are those in which there is a lot of advertising around – usually technical or semi-technical subjects in which the experts tend to be illiterate but with which the vast majority of journalists are unfamiliar. A case in point is information technology. Other promising fields are business and economics. If you can write intelligible stuff about pensions and insurance, editors will come to you with tears in their eyes.

The pickings can be even richer if your specialisation has an international dimension. That puts you in line for every freelance's dream: syndication in other papers, which means extra money for no extra work.

The great source of information on media of all kinds is *British Rate and Data* (otherwise known as BRAD). It is published monthly, but any reasonably up-to-date edition – which a good reference library should have – will do. It is meant for advertisers and lists the circulation and advertising rates for an amazing array of publications, from national dailies down to the *Irish Gardening News, Service Station* and *Petrol Pump Independent*. It also covers TV and local radio. Another reference source is the annual *Willings Press Guide*. Either of these books should point you in the direction of outlets for specialist freelance contributions.

It is worth bearing in mind also that national newspapers frequently publish supplements on special subjects (eg freight handling, new industries in the north-east, etc) if the ad manager thinks he or she can raise revenue from them. These features are planned and sometimes – though not invariably – announced well ahead of time.

Finding work

The first thing to do is to start looking at specialist publications and feature articles in your field. Study the length, level and subject matter of the articles they publish. You may find an obvious gap – or that some topic you want to suggest to them has lately been covered. The fact that this is true in the case of one publication should not put you off the idea of doing something on the same lines for another one if you know the subject – the fact that they have not done so might merely mean that they haven't been able to find anyone to write about it. But above all, study the level and length.

Peter Paterson, who was a successful freelance specialising in trade union and labour relations matters before becoming TV critic of the *Daily Mail*, used to act as an editorial adviser for some magazines. 'A lot of would-be contributors never seemed to have read the publications to which they submitted things,' he says. 'They would send a 5000-word piece to a magazine that never published anything more than 1500 words long. No matter how good it was, we wouldn't even look at it.'

Rather than send in articles out of the blue, it is generally better to make a specific proposal. Don't ask if they are interested in a piece on, say, bee-keeping. Say exactly what angle you would like to cover, how long your piece would be and what your credentials are. Once you get published, try and meet the editor or staffer who took your article. It is better, from a work-getting point of view, to be a face rather than a name on a letterhead.

Fees

Initially, don't get too worked up about fees. The first thing is to acquire some credibility by getting into print. Once you move from sending material on spec to getting commissions you can start to think more seriously about the money side.

The NUJ Freelance Branch publishes a recommended set of minimum fees based on rates per thousand words. The minimum rate at the moment is £105 per thousand though national newspapers pay at least double that amount. So do established magazines. Many editors will plead poverty, though most are open to some negotiation, particularly once you become a known name. Some idea of what they can afford to pay can be gleaned from their advertising rates, which are shown in *British Rate and Data*.

In practice, competent freelances currently gross around £600 a week and the more experienced ones say that you can haggle about fees to a certain extent. Naturally, rates for commissioned work should be agreed beforehand – so should expenses, where these arise. Most papers will accept reasonable claims for travel telephone and subsistence if the commission calls for them Commissions are generally given over the phone and such points should be settled at that time. In fact, the NUJ recommends that telephone commissions should be confirmed by the recipient in writing, but few freelances bother to do so and it's probably no really worthwhile unless there is a lot of money involved.

The NUJ also say that you should be paid in full if a commissioned piece is rejected once it's been turned in. In practice, one ha to say that you will be lucky to get any money at all, even if it ha been rejected for reasons outside your control – like a change of staff or policy.

Administration

Apart from keeping the books and records you need for tax purposes – and also to substantiate your claims for expenses – the main bit of paperwork you will have to do is invoicing. Get proper invoice blanks – you don't need expensive ones specially printed with your name. Invoice at the time you send in your piece, stating the subject matter, length, agreed rate and VAT particulars if applicable. You may think that some of these details are obvious, but the invoices will go to the accounts department who have to marry them up with marked editorial copies. The easier you make it for them, the quicker you will get paid, though payment is apt to be slow at the best of times. It can be as long as three months after publication and four to six weeks is not unusual, even with national newspapers. You can produce professionally laid-out invoices on a word processor.

Invoices should stipulate 'first British rights'. A publication only buys rights for its own use in that particular medium unless you have agreed otherwise, but making the matter crystal clear protects you further from reprint rights being sold without your permission (and hence a further fee to you).

Occupational hazards

Slow payment is one of them. Another is that work is irregular – either not enough or too much. Very few freelances can afford to turn work away, though the more successful ones do pick and choose – not always on purely financial grounds. They might take on a job because it is something they want to write about or involves visiting a place they want to get to or because it has potential spin-offs. (Spin-offs – being able to rework the same piece of research or information for a number of publications – are the lodestone of the freelance's course through working life.) The golden rule is never to let an editor down. If you can't do a piece, say so in time for him or her to find someone else. If possible, suggest a name.

The other great hazard is loneliness. Writing is a solitary business but journalists are a gregarious bunch by nature – and meeting people is an important part of the way they operate. Ideally, you should have one regular source of work and point of contact – maybe someone you work for one day a week, even at lower rates. But be careful that when such an arrangement is governed by contract, it is a contract *for* service not *of* service. The latter would make you liable to be taxed on a PAYE basis, which is much less advantageous than Schedule D (see Chapter 6). It can also inhibit you in other ways, for instance, in writing for competing journals.

Professional organisations

The NUJ Freelance Branch keeps a freelance register and issues a directory to editors (*Who's Who in Freelance Journalism*). Opinions differ about the value of NUJ membership which costs around £140 a year in current prices. For that, apart from listing in the directory and register, you get free advice on a wide variety of work-related topics and there is a free legal service. The NUJ's recommended fee scales, though they have no real clout, tend to be at least approximated to by editors of magazines and papers with a large NUJ membership. The most valuable aspect of being a member may be that you are issued with a Press card which can get you into places and occasions where the general public is not admitted. Not everyone is accepted for membership, though. You have to show that you are earning a living from journalism and you must be sponsored by two members. About 20 per cent of applicants are turned down. Some freelances maintain that you can get more benefits by joining the Society of Authors, 84 Drayton Gardens, London SWID 9SD; 071-373 6642.

19
Working with Foreign Visitors

Introduction

Travel is an aspect of the leisure industry – one of the few sectors of the economy which is confidently expected to go on growing. Indeed, in a sense it even benefits when other sectors of the UK market are weak, inasmuch as the decline in the value of the pound against other currencies – which generally accompanies that process – makes Britain a good buy for foreign tourists. However, tourism covers not only holiday makers, but also business travellers' leisure time and that of their accompanying dependants. Indeed, the borderline between business and recreational travel is often blurred because a holiday element is frequently built in to an overseas trip as an executive bonus. Educational travel for language or skill-learning purposes is another area where the distinctions between recreational and functional tourism overlap.

The UK is a favoured destination for visitors from a number of countries and for a variety of reasons. The largest number are from the USA and the Commonwealth, where Britain is still regarded as the mother country in a historical and cultural sense. For students from non-English speaking countries, it offers the opportunity to learn English at relatively low tuition and living costs. For businessmen and -women, the UK is still a large market in its own right, and also the gateway to the EC and to some extent to the old Commonwealth.

Minor industries grow round major ones and travel is no exception. There are, for instance, 160 interpreters working as freelances in Britain and several times that number of translators and tourist guides. No counts are available of teachers in English as a foreign language (TEFL) but it is thought to run well into four figures.

In working with foreign visitors, as in other branches of freelancing, specialist knowledge pays off. Those with commercially useful languages which not many people in the UK command (eg Chinese, Japanese and Russian, Balkan and Scandinavian languages) do best. A significant minority of interpreters are reported to earn over £20,000 a year as freelances. In TEFL the same principle applies. Those with a knowledge of special areas of English (scientific, medical, business, etc) can command premium rates in sterling terms which nevertheless look reasonable on the rate of exchange to foreign visitors, compared with their domestic rates.

Teaching English as a Foreign Language

Basic skills and aptitudes
Although there is no statutory requirement to possess any particular qualification to teach English as a foreign language (EFL), you are unlikely to be able to do so effectively without having taken the relevant course. This is the Royal Society of Arts Preparatory Certificate. That can be taken either as an intensive four-week programme, or in the evenings over a longer period of time. Places where such courses are offered are available in a list from the Royal Society of Arts, John Adam Street, London WC2N 6EZ. There is also a more advanced course – for those who already have some teaching experience – which spreads over eight intensive weeks, and some special courses which relate EFL to particular subject areas, like business English. Grants are not available for this form of training and for the preparatory course you have to allow for a cost of around £500. A great deal of learning has to be crammed into the available hours, so an ability to handle long hours of concentrated study of sometimes fairly dry material is essential.

Equipment and premises
You can work from home and/or on the premises of a language school. Very little equipment is needed, though a good tape recorder is a useful and inexpensive teaching tool.

The market
English is the world's leading international language, so the demand for instruction exists both abroad and from foreigners who come to the UK to study. The latter trend is generally related to the value of the pound and is therefore a fluctuating one, but the demand is always significant. Students come mainly from Italy, France, Spain, Latin America, the Middle East, Hong Kong and Japan, and that is also where the main overseas opportunities are. The work is to some extent seasonal in the UK and the summers are the busiest, though Latin American students come in their summer, which is our winter. There is also some year-round demand for crash courses for corporate employees, particularly in the special-purposes area indicated in the introductory section.

Finding work
ARELS-FELCO (Association of Recognised English Language

Schools-Federation of English Language Course Organisations), 2 Pontypool Place, Valentine Place, London SE1 8QF; 071-242 3136, publish a list of members who may be contacted by teachers seeking work. They also issue a monthly bulletin for members where teachers can advertise. It is obviously worth making yourself known to them and to other potential clients. These include further education colleges and even foreign firms operating in the UK who may send executives here. The leading private training school for EFL in the UK is International House, 106 Piccadilly, London W1V 9FL; 071-491 2598). They take both foreign students learning English and UK teachers going for the RSA Preparatory Certificate and seek to place many of their alumni, both within the UK and abroad. The other source of work overseas is through the various British Council offices.

Fees
In the UK these can be around £20 per hour for one-to-one teaching. Rates are much higher overseas, but one has to relate these to local costs of living. What seems like a very generous rate can shrink alarmingly when you take account of things like food, travel to work and accommodation.

Administration
In the UK you have to keep a proper programme of work done, together with a register and attendance records. Because of immigration restrictions, Home Office officials may check the attendance of non-EC nationals. They have to do 15 hours a week as a condition of temporary residence.

Occupational hazards
The main hazard is exploitation. In the UK it ought to be fairly easy to avoid this by confining work approaches to recognised schools, but the situation can be more difficult abroad. In whatever location, though, the basic conditions ought to be checked before you commit yourself: the number of guaranteed hours, if you are being paid an hourly rate, and what is actually defined as a working hour. For instance, do preparation times, marking students' work and attending staff meetings count? Twenty-five paid hours per week is about the average.

Professional organisations
In the UK many EFL teachers belong to a special branch of the General and Municipal Workers Union which embraces manage-rial, administrative and technical personnel, including language teachers. They have virtually no power to negotiate rates, but

regular meetings are a good place to exchange information about current practices and working conditions.

Translating and Interpreting

Basic skills and aptitudes

Fluency in a foreign language is the most obvious skill that is needed, but the total picture is a good deal more complicated than that. Translation work is nearly always from another language into the mother tongue or the one of the translator's common use. In most cases that would be English, so the ability to write well (as well as to type) is essential, particularly when it comes to translating novels or general books.

That field of translation is also the least well paid, certainly where the commoner European languages are concerned. Business and technical translation is much better rewarded. If you can combine knowledge in a special field, such as computers, with familiarity in a language not widely spoken by Anglo-Saxons but nevertheless with its own strong population base – Arabic and Japanese or Chinese are obvious examples – you can command quite substantial rates.

In spite of the importance of accuracy in many areas, no formal qualifications are needed to set up as an interpreter or translator. However, the translation agencies, through which translators get most if not all their work, generally use the index of the Institute of Translators and Interpreters as a prime source of names. Full or associate membership of the Institute is by examination and in the former case you also have to have had demonstrable experience as a translator. Interpreters at the highest level – for instance, simultaneous translation at conferences – would need to belong to the Association of International Conference Interpreters, which is based in Geneva but now has an office in London (AIIC, British Isles Region Contact Point, 46 Theobalds Road, London WC1X 0NW; 071-404 8847). Here again, membership is not actually mandatory, but an organisation setting up a conference would look to their list of members as a source.

Though many people do both translation and interpreting, the skills are not quite overlapping. Interpreting calls for the ability to think, very rapidly, on your feet. A translator has more time and can consult a dictionary if necessary.

Equipment and premises

No equipment is needed apart from a typewriter or word processor, though some translators say that they also find a tape recorder invaluable. They speak a rough translation into it and edit it. You do, however, need to spend money on really good dictionaries and these can be quite expensive, especially in the case of technical dictionaries and those relating to the less common languages. Until you are sure that you can make an adequate income from freelance translation, it might be a good idea to rely on a good reference or academic library. You cannot take out dictionaries, but you can do a rough translation and make lists of the words you need to look up.

The market

There are quite a number of translation agencies in the major cities. Their names can be found in the Yellow Pages. Since clients have to pay the agencies as well as you, it is likely, however, that agency work will be less remunerative than working for a client direct. Possible clients include business firms, manufacturers, organisers of exhibitions and conferences, magazine and book publishers and also, these days, local authorities and the police. The latter would come into your sphere if you spoke or wrote one of the languages of the ethnic minorities in the UK.

Finding work

Taking the examinations of the Institute of Linguists and going on their index is an obvious step for those who want to do technical translation. For books and other literary work the corresponding body is the Translators' Association which is linked to the Society of Authors. Both these sources are consulted by agencies, though you should also contact them direct. They will probably give you a test or at least want to see samples of your work.

If you have a special area of expertise, some translators advise advertising in the relevant specialist journals. Foreign ones may be a better bet in that regard because there will be few people around whose mother tongue is English. Rates are also very much better.

Alternatively, you could try writing on spec to companies in your neighbourhood that conduct export or import trade with countries where you are familiar with the language. That is important, not only in itself, but because such an initiative demonstrates that you take an intelligent interest in their activities. The same is true with on-spec letters sent to book publishers. It is worth keeping an eye on those which regularly publish translations. By no means all of them do. Book publishers, incidentally, also publish translated technical books and in those cases will usually pay higher rates than the modest ones they allow for general books.

Never translate a book on spec and then offer the results to the publisher. Except when the text is out of copyright – that is, when the author has been dead for more than 50 years – the publishing rights belong to the firm that published the book in its original language. If they refuse to allow a translation, or have already sold the rights to someone else, all your work will be in vain. You can, however, approach a publisher with an offer to translate a book and if you can show it has some special merit or saleability he or she will be at least interested in your proposal. If you get the go-ahead you should have a proper translation agreement which will usually be on a flat fee basis.

Working as an interpreter requires skills of a very high order if it involves something like simultaneous translation of a speech. Below that level, though, it may only call for the ability to translate standard dialogues between businesspeople at trade fairs and exhibitions. If this kind of event is held in your locality, it is worth offering your services to the organisers who are usually a standing exhibition company, not the actual body under whose name the exhibition is mounted.

Fees

On technical translation from the principal European languages into English you can expect to earn around £35 per thousand words at current rates and about £45 per thousand for the less common ones. The rate goes up by as much as 80–90 per cent for Arabic and oriental languages. Higher rates are also paid for translating into a foreign language from English: add an extra £5–£8 per thousand. In both cases they are lower if you work through an agency.

Translating fiction or general interest books for publishers is much less well paid. The Translators' Association who look after 'literary' as compared to technical or commercial translation recommend a rate of £30 a thousand for common European languages. The problem book publishers have is that in addition to paying the translator, they also have to pay a royalty to the author of the work in its original language. The combined costs make translations very marginal economically – for all concerned.

The best paid work is conference translation. The rates for that are about £240–£270 a day plus expenses, but the number of high-level conferences is not large. There are probably about 40–50 such occasions a year in Europe. However, even *ad hoc* interpreting at exhibitions and business meetings is quite well paid at around £110–£150 a day, depending on the difficulty of the language. In both cases it is exhausting work which requires intense concentration.

Administration

Very little administration is required beyond keeping the usual books. On longer jobs it is advisable to ask the publisher to provide a word count. It is tedious to count 10,000 words yourself, though at 3p or 4p a word, it may be worth doing! Some word-processing programs, though, include a word count.

Occupational hazards

Since it is not obligatory to belong to any professional, standard-setting body to get work as a translator, there is a fair amount of cut-price competition to contend with, especially in the commoner languages. You are less likely to suffer from this if you work through an agency who will also shield you to some extent from the bane of freelance life: clients who are unable or unwilling to pay at all. The hazards, particularly from competition, are reduced if you can offer special expertise in a particular field.

Professional organisations

There are two major ones. The Institute of Translators and Interpreters, 318a Finchley Road, London NW3 5HT; 071-794 9931, is open to members of the Institute of Linguists (24a Highbury Grove, London N5 2EA; 071-359 7445) and looks after the interests of mainly commercial and technical translators. It issues an index of names on its register, together with their specialities in language and subject matter which goes out to translation agencies and other possible markets for members' work. Quite a lot of potential clients apparently approach them in the first instance, so being on their index is an important basic step in getting work. They have about 900 members who receive a regular newsletter (three times a year) and a bi-monthly bulletin which update them on new developments in matters relating to translation.

The Translators' Association, 84 Drayton Gardens, London SW10 9SD; 071-373 6642 is much smaller, with about 200 members. It is affiliated to the Society of Authors and also maintains a register of people interested in doing literary work. Publishers get in touch with them, particularly for people to translate the rarer languages. The Association provides advice for translators on matters like rates and publishers' contracts.

Tourist Guides

Basic skills and aptitudes

As with so many occupations, freelancing as a tourist guide is a lot more complicated than it looks. The basic qualifications are obvious, though in themselves far-reaching: you need a working knowledge of history, art and architecture generally and specific information about the key tourist attractions in your locality. If you are conducting small, semi-private groups, good contacts are a help since they may want to see the places that are not offered in a standard package: country houses that are not open to the public, but where a phone call from the right person can open closed doors.

Since tourism is an international business, knowledge to interpreter standard of at least one foreign language is a great asset. Indeed, even in English you have to have a skilled lecturer's fluency with the spoken word, coupled with the ability to linger just long enough on any subject to give the necessary information on it within a limited time span. In fact, a good deal of administrative ability is required to shepherd a group of tourists around, as well as tact. Inevitably there are always people who lose interest and go off on their own, or who are so interested in one item on the tour that they linger on after you have taken the group to the next one on the agenda. Counting them all out and counting them all in is as essential as it was to the BBC reporter in the Falklands, who made himself famous with that one phrase.

Apart from duties that are specifically connected with sights or objectives (these, by the way, are not always historical or cultural, because you may, for instance, find yourself taking a party of Japanese golf fans to look at famous seaside courses in the southeast), you are expected to be well versed in British etiquette as well as that of the party you are taking round, and to understand such common problems as how much to tip and what 50p is worth in Luxembourg francs.

In view of all this, it is not surprising that freelancing as a tourist guide is an occupation where special training is required. It is not actually mandatory but in London and in several other tourist centres – a complete list of these is available from any tourist information centre – you cannot gain admission into the principal tourist attractions unless you carry the badge of a qualified guide. The requirements for the necessary examinations are quite tough, both academically and financially. The course lasts a year (though it can be taken in two separate six-month periods), costs £1000 plus VAT, and concludes with a three-hour written exam and an all-day practical in which candidates are taken round key places by coach and examined verbally. Unfortunately, since the course is not a recognised qualification in the academic sense, it does not qualify for a grant.

Equipment and premises

The only major requirement is a car. Even that is not absolutely essential unless you want to conduct private tours for one or two people, though this is a lucrative aspect of the trade that some guides prefer as a matter of individual temperament. In that case you would need a vehicle that was clean, comfortable and reliable. A clean driving licence would be an essential prerequisite to anyone entrusting their lives to you. A fairly comprehensive selection of relevant books on art and architecture would be useful, as would a subscription to *Country Life* and *World of Interiors* which contain authoritative and interesting articles on important houses and other places of cultural significance.

The market
The main market is obviously tour operators. There are also guides attached to or on the books of the regional tourist boards. Below this level and operating on a more casual basis are guides connected to individual buildings that are significant enough to be on the tourist trail but not sufficiently important or well endowed to afford a curator to take visitors round.

Finding work
The London Tourist Board – and it must be said that a major part of working with tourists centres on London and the south-east – produce a regular list of qualified guides and this practice is followed by several other tourist authorities. It is sent to tour operators, travel agents, hotels and information centres where tourists go. For each guide it lists name, address, age group, special qualifications in relation to taking people round certain places and any foreign languages spoken.

There is also a section of information on clients, giving contact names and specialities. It is worth getting this document even if you do not live in the London area because it might stimulate you to think of the less obvious ways of finding work. Putting your name about with local hotels if you live in a place where orthodox work-getting channels are not so effective is one such.

Fees
Assignments are usually paid by the day or half-day. The Office of Fair Trading has ruled against set rates, but guides are reportedly earning around £80 for a full day and around £50 for a half-day.

Administration
Being a tour guide requires little in the way of personal administration since the requirements are largely laid down by the tour operator. You do, however, have to keep your wits about you over such matters as issuing vouchers for meals or for overnight stay in hotels. In the latter case, looking after baggage and making sure that it all gets on the coach will be among your duties, as will taking

care that everyone in the party fully understands the instructions about such things as departure times.

When taking small parties on private tours, you will obviously have to keep a check of all expenses and to sort out beforehand who pays for meals and hotel bills. You should never pay out of your own pocket unless that is agreed with the operator or whoever commissioned you.

Occupational hazards

'Keeping the party happy' is said by one experienced guide to be the most important part of his job. The chief occupational hazard – apart from people wandering off on their own and keeping everyone waiting – is that of encountering malcontents and fusspots. The other danger, often connected with those two unlovely attributes, is that of finding someone who knows or thinks he or she knows more about a subject than you do and noisily corrects you on matters of fact. The advice is not to get involved in argument, but to say that different sources hold different opinions about a date or a fact. In matters historical the exact truth is seldom unequivocal.

Professional organisations

Most guides belong to the Guild of Guide Lecturers (2 Bridge Street, London SW1A 2JR; 071-839 7438). They issue a monthly newsletter about places of interest and generally provide a focus of news and developments for their 1000 or so UK members. There is an annual fee of £77. The Guild publishes a nationwide list of members.

20
Further Reading

Books from Kogan Page on topics related to this book:

Part 1
The Cash Collection Action Kit, Philip Gegan and Jane Harrison, 1990

The Entrepreneur's Complete Self-Assessment Guide, Douglas A Gray, 1987

Getting Started: How to Set Up Your Own Business, Robson Rhodes, 2nd edition, 1990

Law for the Small Business: The Daily Telegraph Guide, Patricia Clayton, 7th edition, 1991

PAYE, Carol Anderson, 2nd edition, 1990

Working for Yourself: The Daily Telegraph Guide to Self-Employment, Godfrey Golzen, 12th edition, 1991

Part 2
How to Write Articles for Profit and PR, Mel Lewis, 1989

101 Ways to Succeed as an Independent Consultant, Timothy R V Foster, 1991

Start and Run a Profitable Consulting Business, Douglas A Gray, 1989

Running Your Own ... a series, including: Antiques Business, Boarding Kennels, Building Business, Catering Business, Estate Agency, Hairdressing Salon, Mail Order Business, Photographic Business, Playgroup or Nursery, Private Residential or Nursing Home, Pub, Restaurant, Shop, Small Hotel, Smallholding, Word Processing Service, Working for Yourself in the Arts and Crafts

A full list of Kogan Page titles, including many on running businesses, is available from: 120 Pentonville Road, London N1 9JN

A number of other publishers also produce books on the above topics. Since titles in print change frequently, the best plan is to ask them to send a catalogue. Publishers are usually happy to do this.

A & C Black, PO Box 10, Huntingdon, Cambridgeshire PE19 3SP (Crafts, DIY, Publishing, Writing)

Argus Books, Argus House, Boundary Way, Hemel Hempstead, Herts HP2 7ST (Crafts, Small Business)

B T Batsford, 4 Fitzhardinge Street, London W1H 0AH (Building, Crafts, Design)

Croner Publications Ltd, Croner House, London Road, Kingston upon Thames, Surrey KT2 6SR (loose-leaf manuals for small business)

David & Charles, Newton Abbot, Devon TQ12 4PU (Crafts, Picture research)

Dorling Kindersley, 9 Henrietta Street, Covent Garden, London WC2E 8PS (Crafts, DIY)

Ebury Press, Random Century House, 20 Vauxhall Bridge Road, London SW1V 2SA (Cookery, Photography)

Haynes Publishing Group, Sparkford, Nr Yeovil, Somerset BA22 7JJ (Cars and Motorcycle manuals)

Heinemann Professional Publishing, Halley Court, Jordan Hill, Oxford OX2 8EJ (Catering, Travel and Tourism, Hotel and Guest House Management, Journalism)

Longman Group, Longman House, Burnt Mill, Harlow, Essex CM20 2JE (Teaching English as a Foreign Language)

Piatkus, 5 Windmill Street, London W1P 1HF (Crafts, Business, Writing, Homeworking)

Pitman Publishing, 128 Long Acre, London WC2E 9AN (Business, Building)

Reader's Digest, c/o Hodder & Stoughton, 47 Bedford Square, London WC1B 3DP (Home and Furniture Repair and Maintenance, Gardening and Garden Maintenance)

There are also some specialist bookshops in and around London which carry a comprehensive range of titles in their field and are also prepared to do business by mail order:

Roy Arnold, 77 High Street, Needham Market, Suffolk IP6 8AN

Business Bookshop, 72 Park Road, London NW1 4SH

Books For Cooks, 4 Blenheim Crescent, London W11

Building Bookshop, 26 Store Street, London WC1E 7BT

Motor Books, 33 St Martin's Court, London WC2N 4AL

Photographer Gallery Bookshop, 8 Great Newport Street, London WC2H 7HY

Parks Bookshop, 244 High Holborn, London WC1V 7DZ (anything on business)

A Zwemmer Ltd, 24 Litchfield Street, London WC2H 9NJ (anything on art and design)

Index